Troubleshooting and Repairing

TVRO SYSTEMS

STAN PRENTISS

TAB TAB BOOKS Inc.

Blue Ridge Summit, PA

FIRST EDITION
FIRST PRINTING

Copyright © 1988 by TAB BOOKS Inc.
Printed in the United States of America

Library of Congress Cataloging in Publication Data

Prentiss, Stan.
Troubleshooting and repairing TVRO systems / by Stan Prentiss.
p. cm.
Includes index.

ISBN 0-8306-0592-4   ISBN 0-8306-2992-0 (pbk.)
1. Earth stations (Satellite telecommunication)—Amateurs'
manuals.   2. Earth stations (Satellite telecommunication)-
-Maintenance and repair—Amateurs' manuals.   I. Title.
TK9962.P74   1988
621.388'5—dc19   88-2213
                              CIP

Questions regarding the content of this book
should be addressed to:

Reader Inquiry Branch
TAB BOOKS Inc.
Blue Ridge Summit, PA 17294-0214

Contents

Introduction   v

Acknowledgments   vi

1 Analyzing TVRO Reflectors and Mounts   1

Tolerance Factors—The $Y^2 = 4PX$ rms Curvature—Mounting—North/South Pointing—Tutorials—Demonstrator Mounting—Changing Mounts—Far-Field Reflector Analysis—The Range—Sidelobes—TVRO Site Surveys—Interference Must Enter the Feed—Model 5111—Antenna Construction—Perforated Reflectors—Mesh Reflectors—Fiberglass Reflectors—An Offset Feed—Typical Installation—Small Reflector Setup Problems—Hints and Suggestions

2 Feeds and Cabling for C and Ku Bands   22

Typical and Special Feeds—Chaparral Communications—The John Seavey Contribution—Something New and Interesting by N.A.D.L.—Boman Introduces Cost Effective Feeds with Heaters—F/D Ratios Up or Down?—Cable Facts (No Fiction)—Cabling Considerations—Cable Measurements—Cable Facts (*and* Fiction)—The Final Word

3 The Signals to the Receiver   38

Mathematical Parameters—Slant Range—Space Attenuation—System Noise Temperature—G/T, the Figure of Merit—Carrier-to-Noise and Signal-to-Noise—Audio Transmissions—Actual Measurements—Propagation at C and Ku Bands—Direct Satellite Signals—Popular Satellite Spectrum Displays—The Best and the Worst—Comments—VSAT Is Blooming—Equatorial Earth Stations Number in the Thousands—Equipment—Code Division Multiplexing

4 Satellite Receiver Systems and Circuit Analysis   **57**

Tuning Systems—Local Oscillators and PLL—FM Video Detection—Detection Process—FM Audio Selection and Detection — Audio Demodulation — Dynamic Noise Reduction — The T6 Receiver/Positioner—Theory of Operation—Block Diagram—The Front End—I-f, AGC, and Detection—Audio Detection Process—Power Supplies—ZA-4000 Receiver/Positioner—PLL Tuner Unit—Antenna Positioner

5 Testing Basics for Downconverters and Receivers   **79**

Characteristics Are Important—Local Testing—Deluxe Testing—Testing Receivers—Direct Testing—Conclusions—Equipment Checkout—Single and Dual Conversions

6 The Ku-Band Picture   **93**

Ku-Band Reasoning—The RCA Ku Story—The GSTARS—The SPACENETS—Satellite Business Systems (SBS)—Ku Installations—Azimuth and Elevation at K Band—Low Side Injection—Ku Troubleshooting—Late Developments—A New Spectrum Analyzer—A New Low-Cost Oscilloscope—A PSN B-MAC Receiver—Boman's Confocal Feed

7 Satellite and Cable TV Scrambling   **119**

VideoCipher®—VideoCiphers® I and II—Multiplexed Analog Component (MAC) Signals—Oak's Orion—Oak's Cable System—Zenith's Z-TAC®—Z-VIEW—Troubleshooting Descramblers—The M/A-COM VCIIC Descrambler—VideoCipher® II Descrambler Checks

8 Test Equipment and Applications   **135**

An Electrical Introduction—Power Supplies—AC Power—DC Power—Oscilloscopes—Controls and Displays—Adjustments—Circuit Design—Waveform Examples—Spectrum Analyzers—Analyzer Controls — Live Examples — Digital Voltmeters — Conversions — Fluke's Model 77 DMM — DMM Applications—Troubleshooting with Oscilloscopes—Pulses—Linear Displays—Troubleshooting with Spectrum Analyzers—Good/Poor Spectral Signals

9 Troubleshooting Problems and Solutions   **170**

Troubleshooting Procedures—Tech Tips—ESR-24—ESR-224—ESR-240—ESR-324—ESR-424—APS-424—Satellite Technology Services—LSR Receivers—MBS-AA Receivers—SR Block—MBS-SR Block—M/A-COM T-1

10 Terrestrial EMI/RFI Interference and Solutions   **192**

In-Band and Out-of-Band Interference—In Band Solutions—Out-of-Band Solutions—Microwave Filters for TVRO—Typical Filters—Microwave Filters—Phantom Engineering—An Inexpensive Spectrum Display—In Summary—T.I. Symptoms Review

Index   **216**

Introduction

This is a C- and Ku-band troubleshooting book directed towards the TVRO consumer-products-satellite-earth-station community. The contents are considerably broader than mere troubleshooting and encompass many different segments of the space industry and the latest technologies available. All this was accomplished with the aid of satellite operators, managers, manufacturers, engineers, tradesmen, service specialists, TVRO equipment designers, distributors, test equipment people, and companies such as Tektronix, Wiltron, Fluke, B & K Precision, Microwave Filter Co., and Phantom Engineering. Special thanks, too, is due to M/A-COM in Hickory, N.C. (now owned by General Instrument Corp.), Zenith Electronics Corp., Chaparral Communications, Boman Industries, Seavey Engineering, R.L. Drake, National A.D.L. Enterprises, GTE Spacenet Corp., RCA Americom, Hughes Aircraft Communications, Satellite Business Systems, MCI, IBM, STS, and many others for both large and small contributions.

You will find special chapters on C, Ku, and C/Ku feeds, mounts and reflectors, in addition to an in-depth discussion of the characteristics and effectiveness of mesh, perforated, and fiberglass reflectors. New and *complete* satellite receiver systems are also described in detail with audio/video detection carefully analyzed. You will also find instrumented testing basics for downconverters and receivers, EMI/RFI interference indications and corrective actions, a VSAT system/description, and one complete chapter on VideoCipher® I and II, Orion, Z-Tac, line shuffling, and other methods of video/audio scrambling.

There is a great deal more awaiting the reader/student as the table of contents reveals. I firmly believe you can't accomplish worthwhile troubleshooting without knowing the big picture: here it is!

Acknowledgments

To all those who have given of their time, technical aid, equipment, and free flow of information, I gratefully respond with many thanks and merited recognition. They include: Bruce Loyer and Paul Fisher, M/A-COM; Rich Renken, Neil LeSaint, and Michael Brubaker, R.L. Drake Co.; Jerry Von Behren and Hal Sorenson, Winegard Co.; Jim Berry, AJAK Industries; Michael Capin, International Engineering Mfg.; Russell E. Hollis, Venture Mfg.; Mark Sheldon and Tom Verna, Chaparral Comm.; Dr. Michael Olson, Equatorial; Ralph Woodward, Mark Riley, and Bob Mahood, Boman Industries; Gerry Blachley, National A.D.L. Enterprises; Bill Benedict, Terry Burcham, and Len Garrett, Tektronix; Al Hart, Wiltron; Robert Dalton, Phantom; Al Smith, SBS; W.P. Kinsella GTE Spacenet; Roger Herbstritt, Charlie Magin, and Joe Harcarufka, FCC; Ron Schmidt, Elect. Marketing Associates; Jacob Aronovich, Hameg, Inc.; Bill Rowse, Private Satellite Network; Wendell Bailey, National Cable TV Assn.; Gus Rose, B & K-Precision; John Nevius, John Fluke Mfg.; Dave Patterson, Toshiba America; John Seavey, Seavey Engineering; Jim Cooke, Scientific-Atlanta; Steve Fox, Wegener Communications; Paul Miller; Belden Electronic Wire and Cable; Reed Burkhart, Hughes Communications Galaxy; Dr. Mark F. Medress (Linkabit®) M/A-COM; Jim Byrnes, AT & T Communications; John Williamson, RCA Americom; Jay LaBarge, Bill Johnson, and Glyn Bostick, Microwave Filter Co.; Jim White, Dick Wilson, Ted Cash, Chuck Sindalar, and John Taylor, Zenith Electronics; Dave Waddington, Channel Master; and especially Jerry Thorne of Microdyne Corp., without whose mathematical guidance we might have strayed from fact into fancy when computing downlinks.

Note: M/A-COM's Consumer Product Division has been purchased by General Instrument Corp.

Chapter 1

Analyzing TVRO Reflectors and Mounts

BY FAR THE MOST DIFFICULT OF ALL TVRO ANAL-yses is the reflector examination, especially if it is defective. This is why it's essential to have all cabling, feeds, amplifiers and even satellite receivers thoroughly checked before starting on the receive radiator. If this reflector is assembled on uneven ground, specific instructions are not followed, the wrong feed or amplifier is used, all sorts of problems can result. This is why we always recommend working with a single manufacturer's product rather than attempting to combine several *unless* you have an engineering evaluation first that would favor alien components.

You would also like to have the reflector adequately illuminated—actually feedhorn and radiator matched—so that more than a 10-14 dB dropoff in signal handling doesn't occur toward its perimeter. If there is unusual spillover or the feed is picking up abnormal interference or noise, efficiency drops, gain decreases, and good signal-to-noise ratios rapidly fall apart. In television, the tolerable threshold is just above 35 dB, but in satellite receivers,

the closer to 50 dB S/N becomes, the better video detail appears in your nominally full-bandwidth picture. Carrier-to-noise (C/N), carrier-to-interference (C/I), and signal-to-noise (S/N) are all inviolate measurements that must not be ignored from preamplification on through to the moment pictures and sound are fully reproduced.

TOLERANCE FACTORS

All of these factors may even become more pronounced as we enter the Ku-band area. Reflector and pointing tolerances are tighter, and the LNA/B/C combinations will have *higher* noise factors. Polar mounts for Ku are in their infancy, especially when combined with C band, and eventually DBS (the direct-to-home-broadcast service) so often erroneously associated with Ku which, remains with C band, part of the Fixed Satellite Service. Transponder output for C band rarely exceed 9 W; Ku, 20, 40, and 60 W; while DBS (12/17 GHz) ranges between 100 and 230 W per transponder, when and if it ever flies. Obviously there is a differ-

1

ence. Conversely, 10 to 20 times the power of C band, although tripled in frequency, will make a difference in reception over much of CONUS and possibly Hawaii, Alaska, and Puerto Rico with spot beam usage. So be prepared for both the best (faster installations, better hardware) and the worst (much sharper tuning and the rainfall problem) all rolled into one, even though reflector/mount/amplifier servicing may be less because of physical size and increased reliability.

THE Y^2 = 4PX RMS CURVATURE

Many of the small Ku band reflectors may even measure as little as 0.6 meter (1.968 ft.) and as much as 1.8 meters (5.91 ft.) and can be installed anywhere there's a reasonable perch—and that includes office buildings, homes, motels, industrial parks, or other similar locations. And reading the multiple announcements of various corporations going to Ku communications of all descriptions, installations of these little radiators (and some, indeed, will also become uplinks), should evolve into a profitable undertaking. Many or most should be simple AZ/EL mounts aimed at a single satellite and therefore considerably easier to position. They will, however, require extreme accuracy and undergo specific testing before any payoff. The first thing, therefore, is to be absolutely sure the reflector's shape is virtually perfect.

Without a fancy curve-measuring theodolite that's not conveniently possible, you can draw two taut strings across the parabola more or less at right angles to one another to make sure that any or all panels in these reflectors are properly aligned. As you probably already know, if the two strings connect solidly in the center, the reflector is at least assembled properly. We make a habit of doing this with every C band 8- or 10-footer and almost inevitably find one panel that isn't quite on the beam. A hand massage of panel joints will often tip you off to some small anomaly that can easily be corrected.

Even if the reflector is mounted and already sighted in, a small adjustment is entirely possible by slightly loosening the panel connecting bolts between feed holder and rim and smartly tapping the offending panel with a rubber hammer. Usually it falls into

place immediately, and the crossing strings make prompt contact. Retighten the nut/bolts and your reflector is once again secure and correctly aligned. It's that simple! And to hold the string in place, ordinary wood clamps do the job nicely. Most any old string or cord will do, as long as it's taut and extends from rim to rim of the reflector, crossing with another line in the center. Naturally, more than one panel may be checked by this method if there is more than one misalignment in question. Just move the clamps and string directions around to your heart's content, but keep the two crossing in the center. The more panels there are, the more closely you must check. Even at Ku, signal improvements of 4 dB can be realized by careful panel adjustment with segmented radiators.

How about the solid reflectors? You'll have extreme difficulty popping them back into shape. Crossed cords are once again a convenient means of establishing the rms or $Y^2 = 4PX$ factor with considerable confidence. This does not, however, guarantee that the reflector is designed correctly, it simply illustrates edge and panel continuity. If in doubt, try a few calculations, or at least measure some of the angle curvatures to see if they are reasonable and relatively uniform. Otherwise, you're ready to follow the manufacturer's instructions for mounting. Adequate curvature, by the way, can be determined by sidelobe analysis and, to some extent, by reflector illumination. Otherwise, lasers and computers are needed to establish a complete radiator's rms tolerance.

MOUNTING

Let's assume you are following the manufacturer's instructions precisely and have the ironwork and reflector securely fastened. Let's also assume that the mast has been firmly set in reinforced concrete that's completely cured: usually 5-7 days under normal, non-freezing weather conditions (Fig. 1-1).

Now, you're ready to connect mount and reflector to their "king-post" and do a little *gross* positioning that should require only touch-up adjustments for final channel-satellite acquisition. Obviously you have to know your own *latitude* for the pointing an-

Fig. 1-1. Any worthwhile TVRO installation requires a suitable hole and concrete foundation with reinforcing bars extending below the local frost line.

gle and the amount of declination needed to make your polar mount track throughout its range (Fig. 1-2). This means a call to the nearest airport, Naval installation, or the Coast and Geodedic Survey to plot *both your longitude* and *latitude,* since they are *absolutely necessary* for adequate geosynchronous tracking. The term ''declination'' (usually undefined by most) is actually the angular distance from the earth's equatorial plane intersecting the earth, with *you* positioned at some particular point. North declinations are positive (+) and south declinations are negative (−). Consequently, as your position moves relative to the equatorial plane extension, more or less declination is required to maintain your relationship with the equator. Our own declination in Maryland, for instance, is 6.2°, and *must* be *added* to the latitude position for an accurate fix.

NORTH/SOUTH POINTING

Compass variation is also extremely important since the magnetic and geographic poles differ considerably around the globe. Variations in the earth's magnetism not only vary from region to region but also change in those same locales with time. Therefore, use the most recent magnetic information available when adjusting your compass headings for true north readings. An easterly reading from magnetic north is always added (+) and a westerly reading subtracted (−). In our situation, the variation correction is 9° east, and therefore positive. Consequently, true north is really +9°, or 369°, if you'd like to consider that type of reasoning. Actually, 369° is not very useful since in our setup we will use a due south heading rather than true north. But if you do a little compass ''boxing'' and draw a 369° true

Fig. 1-2. Always set your mount/reflector latitude and declination precisely with the antenna pointing due south.

north/south intersection, you'll find true south at 189° rather than 180° magnetic.

The reason for the true south heading involves both satellite positioning and reflector pointing angles. In our eastern location, the latitude is 39.8°, placing the reflector at virtually its maximum elevation. It's therefore easy to set your pointing angle of approximately 40° first, then precisely adjust for declination, adding the two which, in this instance, amounts to 46° (39.8 plus 6.2). See Fig. 1-3.

So with declination variation, true *south*, and pointing angles all nicely entered into the mounting system, all that remains are a few minor compensating turns on the latitude fine tuning adjustment for maximum satellite acquisitions, which can amount

to as many as 15 individual C band "birds" often with 24 transponders, each, *if* you have erected at least a 10-foot reflector. Any radiator less than 9.1 feet is always subject to C/I problems even at C band, and probably presents additional difficulties for Ku, even though 50- to 78-thousandth's-inch reflector holes may handle 3.7 to 4.2 GHz frequencies adequately.

Note that we have said nothing about deviation. This is little more than an additional magnetic field exerted by the antenna/mount steel and should have no effect on your readings if you will just back off a few feet from the mount and mast when sighting north and south—just the same way you'd adjust your auto's compass—externally, and far enough

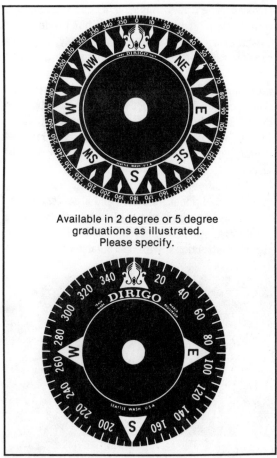

Available in 2 degree or 5 degree
graduations as illustrated.
Please specify.

Fig. 1-3. Be exact in your north/south mount adjustment. Use a good compass and don't neglect the local variation (courtesy of DIRIGO marine compasses).

away from any local fences and the auto itself to avoid any extra magnetic pickup. Here, just a little avoidance goes a very long way.

TUTORIALS

The foregoing may sound much like a *tutorial* on reflector and mount installations—and that's exactly what it is—but you have to know what's required in order to rectify many assorted and sundry problems. Occasionally you'll find a mount that won't track correctly or a warped reflector; that would be par for the course. Once in a while these things will

happen despite even rigid quality controls. Consequently, you'll have to be prepared for almost any eventuality laying between negligence and sabotage, with what's left over caused by the elements. True, there were a number of problems arising from poor fiberglass construction in the early days of TVRO, but metal reflector faults will probably far outweigh those found among "glass." As for the later fiberglass thermal compression units, we suspect they'll be around long after most of the see-through "holey" variety have long since been replaced at least once. Rust, corrosion, and warpage are hard to overcome. Good fiberglass, as the boating fraternity have discovered, is hard to beat when not hampered by local ordinances. Unfortunately, it looks better in the water than the back yard.

In summary, check for physical damage to mounts, reflectors, insufficient rotary joint *graphite* lubrication, damaged or defunct actuator arms and gears, improper cabling to the probe for skew, actuator, or signal feeds, a blown fuse supplying dc to the LNA/B/C, and the usual shorts and opens that will always occur from poorly attached F and N connectors that permit shielding to come in contact with the center conductor or open up completely.

To these ends, we highly recommend separate sets of positioners, receivers, LNA/B/C amplifier-converters, and suitable leads, all of which are in top serviceable condition for positive checkouts. Later when there are comprehensive and reasonably-priced test equipments available we'll happily recommend these over all else since with them the job can be done more quickly and with considerable confidence in numbers such as voltage, gain in dB or dBm, current, modulation and carrier displays, interference positions, etc. Meanwhile, simply lug along an extra set of receiving and positioning gear for positive assurance.

DEMONSTRATOR MOUNTING

For those who are planning either mobile or demo reflector transport, you'll have to add another several precautions unless your rig is especially designed to be carried on an RV or similar vehicle. Even then, road jostling and rut bounce can loosen many a nut, screw, and mounting bolt, causing all sorts of difficulties including reflectors falling by the wayside. Once your reflector is mounted and checked, another turn or two on the securing hardware isn't a bad idea every time you hit the road. Loose nuts are always a multiple hazard!

As for the demonstrator jobbies, a $199 trailer will give you nothing but horrendous problems. Our single axle, designed to carry an 8-foot reflector comfortably, came from Cox Trailers in North Carolina and cost over $1,000. Designed by Channel Master, this two-wheeler has a rear center of gravity, good fenders, tires, and adequate springing. The body is of all reinforced steel (Fig. 1-4) with underneath ribbing to firmly support excellent, heavy hardware supplied by M/A-COM specifically for that

purpose. The trailer tongue is of sufficient length to remain clear of its towing truck but produces no "fishtailing" at higher speeds. Actually, it's quite comfortable bouncing along at 55 mph on the interstates and seems to handle truck passings with no problems. This is because the *back* of the reflector and its convex surface sheds the truck blow-bys easily and does the same with the usual highway winds. In gale force winds, however, I'd be inclined to seek protective shelter and depart open roads with alacrity.

In addition, the reflector is mounted at a 15° angle for additional windshed and little drag behind the truck since the lead vehicle acts as a substantial windbreak. All this generally follows the manufacturer's instructions, with one notable exception: in-

Fig. 1-4. A well built single axle trailer with balanced mounting can easily accomodate an 8-foot reflector and heavy mount. Be sure you keep adequate grease in the axle bearings (courtesy of Cox Trailers).

stead of allowing the reflector to hang supported only by its mount, we added an old tire and tube to the rig to support both mount and reflector. This may cause some extra jiggling, but at the moment, it seems considerably easier on the reflector and its supports rather than using nothing at all. Other people have used 2 × 4 beams covered with strips of thick rug to break the bouncing, but we think a tire is best of all.

We also discovered that a plumb bobbin suspended from the fixed portion of the mount would serve just as well as a spirit level. Finally, when all the mounting was completed, a pair of crossed, good quality cords, secured by four C clamps will easily confirm your accurate or inaccurate reflector assembly. Ours was out by a few centimeters on one panel,

but quickly rectified by loosening only one set of securing nuts and bolts and smartly tapping the panel into place with a rubber tire hammer. With the same bolts and nuts retightened, both X-crossed strings touched at the center, and we were sure the reflector was properly assembled (Fig. 1-5).

The X-string procedure is especially important in servicing older systems that have the usual parabolic-shaped reflectors. After several years of operation, some of this earlier equipment is bound to have faults you may advantageously rectify without too many problems. If one or more panels of a *metal* reflector are either bent or warped, an entire new reflector may be required. If so, use a relatively deep "dish" with a beamwidth of less than 2 degrees for best results, provided the azimuth aiming polar

Fig. 1-5. Crossed cords can ensure antenna alignment/symmetry. Measure reflector depth at the center intersection (courtesy of M/A-COM).

mechanism can produce equivalent accuracy. If not, replace with an equivalent reflector and hope for the best.

CHANGING MOUNTS

Mounts, of course, and programmable positioners are due to change rapidly almost with the seasons until we probably will have an AZ/EL arrangement on some sort of King post that will already have all satellite positions preprogrammed, and all you'll need to input are your own longitude and latitude. This is possible now, but the rig is somewhat complex and clumsy, and the price (for consumers) is prohibitive. Time, however, brings about many changes, and this is one we're sure to see as major improvements continue. Reflectors are due for changes also but not necessarily radically, even though one would-be manufacturer is making big noises about a small rectangular planar array with tuned elements. As of late 1986, however, we haven't seen a single production model, just talk. Key developers, we understand, are Matsushita and Comsat.

In the meantime, you'll want to look carefully at all outdoor components presently reaching the market for both design and durability. Before the industry once more settles down on a steady course, many "bargains" with dubious antecedents are bound to appear at ridiculous prices. As one of our most noted sages of times past once remarked, "that which is cheap is often dear." Fortunately, good reputations have never been built on shoddy products. Word-of-mouth advertising is forever cheapest and best!

This is why we always like to add a few supporting words to those who have the ability and industry to bring forth new and worthwhile products when the TVRO industry has been struck such a grievous blow by program scrambling/enciphering. Fortunately, recovery—at least partial—is on the way, and we see signs of considerable improvement in both merchandising and new products already.

FAR-FIELD REFLECTOR ANALYSIS

In one way, analyzing reflectors for simple gain isn't at all difficult as long as you obey the tried and true *far field* dictums and find some means of absorbing (or preventing) terrestrial reflections from distorting the transmitted image. Conversely, rotating your reflector for meaningful sidelobes is considerably more difficult, and does require very good equipment and somewhat extraordinary skills.

THE RANGE

First, let's take a somewhat typical (or atypical) situation such as the one we have and offer a straightforward calculation to illustrate the point (Fig. 1-6). What we have in front of the dwelling is a 10 acre marsh with a narrow road leading down to the water's edge. Above this marsh, our house stands on high ground approximately 50 feet above the beach. We have a clear view of the water and the marsh actually absorbs any and *all* reflections that would ordinarily appear from smooth, hard ground. Consequently, you may regard the ensuring analysis as a good, practical field check of all reflector parameters with minimal (but initially expensive) equipment, which we hope, in time, will be supplanted with much less expensive and just as effective test gear having the relatively few basic requisites.

As you may remember from high school trigonometry, one angle and a side will supply all the information you need for a tangent equality, and the remainder of the triangle can be calculated from that. And once you have the base line of any triangle, the hypotenuse is easy. Here's how it's done.

Angle A, representing the transmitting declination, measures 4° from the perpendicular altitude *(b)*, then the Tan of A equals 86° (Fig. 1-7).

Reducing A to numbers amounts to 14.3, and this multiplied by the 50-foot height of b results in side a measuring 715 feet. The hypotenuse, then, simply becomes the sum of the squares of the other two sides.

$$a = 14.3 \times 50 = 715'$$
$$c^2 = a^2 + b^2 = 716.75'$$

Therefore the three sides now become:

$$a = 715' \quad b = 50' \quad \text{and } c = 716.75'$$

Fig. 1-6. Marshy ground is very useful for nonreflective far field antenna range.

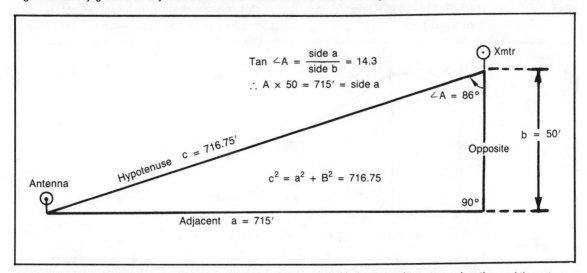

Fig. 1-7. Home antenna ranges may be set up over absorbent areas with the transmitter at one elevation and the antenna at another. Simple trigonometry provides the dimensions.

and you have all distances for a working right angle triangle which, of course is the antenna range of 715 feet, and a slant range of 716.75 feet. We'll talk more of slant ranges—between you and the selected satellite—as our general information progresses.

To use our range, of course, you must know the lambda (wavelength and frequency factors) as well as the reflector's diameter, in addition to the correct focal length, center reflector depth. Lambda (λ) is established first since this is vital to all range measurements when establishing either far field or near field requirements.

$$\text{Far Field} = D^2/\text{lambda}$$
$$\text{Near Field} = D^2/\text{lambda}$$

Lambda is for a frequency of 3.95 GHz and the speed of light in terms of ft./sec., since the radiator diameter is in terms of feet also, and you cannot mix feet with inches or miles and not include conversion dividers or multipliers. In other words, all terms in *any* equation must be directly related. Therefore:

Lambda (λ) = 984 (light speed)/freq. in MHz 3.95 $\times$ 10^3 (since this is in terms of GHz) = 0.2491.

And so the far field range for a 10′ reflector becomes:

Far Field = 2 $\times$ 100/0.2491 = 802.9 feet; for an 8 footer, 513.85′.

Our range, of course, measures 715 feet, but is suitable for even a 10-footer *provided* the first sidelobe (if that's what you intend to measure in addition to normal gain) can be brought down to baseline. In this instance, as you will shortly see, this was entirely possible, though slightly difficult and a little rough on our particular analyzer.

The next step is to use one of the parabolic curvature measuring strings stretched across the reflector's perimeter to measure center depth, since from this the ultimate focal length is quickly determined. This measures out to 15¾″, or 15.75 which becomes 1.31 ft. So, focal length F = $D^2/16c$ (center depth) = 64/16 $\times$ 1.31 (now all in feet) = 3.05 $\times$ 12″/ft. = 36.6 inches (Fig. 1-8). The design feed ratio may now be calculated as f/D = 3.05/10 = 0.305, followed by the beamwidth θ = 70 $\times$ 0.2491/8 = 2.18°. That is just outside our arbitrary 1.9° limit for 2° spacing which should be met since the distance between satellites at this juncture is only 918 statute miles—a large distance here on earth but very short when viewed from 22.3 kilomiles up in the sky. Therefore, 2.18: X = 2:918, or X = 1000 miles. Nothing more or less than simple ratio and proportion, but in this instance, an 8-foot reflector is decidedly subject to C/I (carrier to interference) whereas a 10-foot reflector with a beamwidth of 1.732° is not.

That pretty well sums up the analysis of this particular 8-foot reflector, and teaches a good lesson

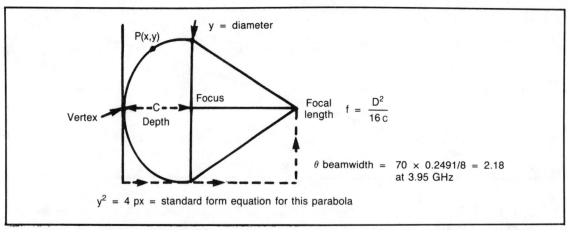

Fig. 1-8. Classic illustration of parabolic reflector (this one an 8-footer) with standard Y^2 = 4 px equation. Focus and focal lengths are dissimilar because f = diameter ^{2}/16 $\times$ depth of reflector.

in why you should have a 9.1-foot array at C band to avoid the inevitable problems the smaller reflectors are certain to cause.

But just to make this complete, we will continue with a sidelobe analysis using the same two major test instruments and my own Tektronix 7L12 spectrum analyzer—a departure which may be of considerable interest since a spectrum analyzer with a frequency range up to 1.8 GHz, costs thousands of dollars less than one that goes all the way to 20+ GHz. They're simpler to make, that's all, and for my money, a darned sight easier to use in projects such as these.

SIDELOBES

Only on multi-thousand dollar test ranges are you usually required to test for further antenna characteristics and then specialized equipment does all this with automated readouts...Your only responsibility being to pay the hundreds or thousands of dollars required to raise tall towers and operate the highly accurate test gear someone else designed and installed for you.

In our "field-type" category, however, a signal generator and spectrum analyzer will do a pretty good job and at least offer a good indication that undesirable frequencies from stray signal sources will or won't enter your reflector and its feed within reasonable tolerances (Fig. 1-9).

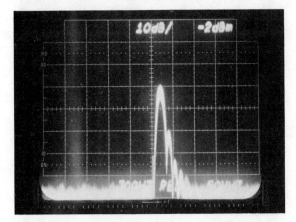

Fig. 1-9. An example (but not perfect) of antenna main lobe and sidelobes that must meet 29-25 log θ specifications to qualify for best reception. The first sidelobe should bottom out on the baseline.

To make such measurements, however, your spectrum analyzer must be able to reduce its own measuring parameters to a few hertz resolution while permitting as much as 50 MHz/div to remain as the frequency range apparent. You will also need a strong incoming signal from the transmitter or the various sidelobes won't show. And despite some mis-registry of the dBm signal at the top due to 100° F plus heat and a dirty contact, the other numbers of 300 Hz resolution and 50 MHz/div are plain at the bottom and easily recognizable. Such sidelobes are usually separated by about only 2-3 degrees, and normally are not seen beyond 10° in normal measurements. They should show exactly the same on the left side of the main carrier as on the right. Would these fit the 29-25 log θ curve? Let's see. Given the 1st sidelobe at 3° to the right,

$$29\text{-}25 \log 3 = 29\text{-}11.93 = 17.07 \text{ dB versus the } 20°$$
apparent.

The other sidelobes fall even much lower in relation to the main lobe, and so the answer, in this instance, would be "yes."

TVRO SITE SURVEYS

If these are simply 6-12 ft consumer types that could find troubled waters, then the task is simple. Monstrous arrays, on the other hand do require special precautions and investigations and need considerably more preparations involving area microwave beam charts and local signals of all types that might have strong enough harmonics to interfere. There is, however, one element that's common to all, the interfering signal, and whether direct or bounce (reflected) must enter the receiving reflector's feed horn and be amplified down to the receiver. Otherwise, you have nothing to fear "but fear itself," as Franklin Roosevelt once said during the 1932-1937 great depression.

On the other hand, the very large radiators differ, usually on both transmit and receive, and the Federal Communications Commission does take a dim view of those whose microwave intrusions make bad neighbors out of good. Unfortunately this happens from time to time and, therefore, both large

Fig. 1-10. A good 8-foot reflector with prime focus feed will do well in all site surveys for C and Ku bands.

panion color TV receiver, and how can this be coordinated with your main instrument, a spectrum analyzer?

All this, of course, largely depends on analyzer quality, your familiarity with the instrument, and any amplifiers that may be supplying source "pictures" for video and sound. Recall, too, that FM video modulation may be positive on one side of the carrier and negative on the other, along with some extraneous modulation that could affect the negative portion, even cancelling it. This is why some reflector sidelobes on the lower frequency side are largely invisible.

INTERFERENCE MUST ENTER THE FEED

Fortunately, however, much of the site survey endeavor becomes fairly straightforward in the majority of instances and isn't a real problem. Recalling that interference *must* enter the feed to be effective, you simply have to elevate your test feed to the same height of the proposed installation and sweep the horizontal and vertical planes involved (Fig. 1-11). We would definitely recommend, nonetheless, that a suitable reflector and 50 dB + block downconverter be used to simulate as closely as possible actual receive conditions prevalent in the area. Sometimes only a few feet make a consider-

receivers and transmitters in critical areas must apply to the FCC for guaranteed "private" space in which to conduct their operations. Usually this should remove any interfering factors.

You might think that ordinary TVRO consumer units might be (Fig. 1-10) in considerably more trouble because of their often undersized reflectors, poorly designed or "general purpose" feeds, slightly offset focal points, and reflector irregularities. Fortunately this is not necessarily so. Regardless of the other factors, EMI/RFI has to enter the feedhorn from one source or other, and if absent, that's all there is. You then proceed to find true north and south, set your latitude and declination, and touch up for a few degrees one way or the other. Wide beamwidths, however, do invite stray RFI anytime.

The most difficult job of all, however, is waveform interpretation. Is that excessive modulation you're observing or is it in-band interference? Do the blips in between various transponder outputs really signify problems? What about straight spikes of apparent voltage that seem to thrive in some of the better channel modulations? Do you have to see all the channels operating at the same time, or can you expand selected transponder outputs and view such signals in considerable detail? How about a com-

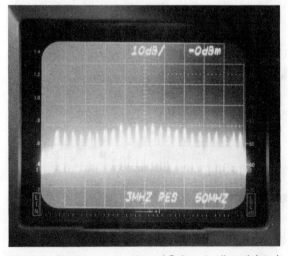

Fig. 1-11. The 24 transponders of Galaxy 1, all modulated and many scrambled. But a number of scramblers are moving to Telstar 303.

able difference. Naturally, commercial installations with their huge radiators are exceptions, but there, again, complementary or equivalent situations can always save a lot of eventual grief. We feel that using simply a standard-gain feed horn and some weak amplifier without benefit of a spectrum analyzer is decidedly not good enough.

You *always* need maximum signal strength for careful evaluation and, above all, good instrumentation in the final assessment. Our usual procedure is to take Polaroid photos of the analyzer display in both all-transponder and half-transponder numbers to accurately assess overall satellite and individual channel response. In this way, you should know exactly what you're doing and why—no guessing, since that can involve a great deal of money and frustration when the time comes for final earth station erection. We would further suggest at least a cursory check *outside* the band(s) of immediate interest to be positive there's no real threat that could develop at some inopportune time. In commercial installations, of course, an FCC permit would be in order if you're near Ma Bell or other microwave transmitters likely to interfere now or in the foreseeable future.

We would also recommend that you know your *true* azimuth and elevation angles *before* attempting the survey for one or more satellites, and then check the specific site for both look angles and position with an inclinometer and compass *before* setting up for the final analysis (just another step in the process to avoid extra grief).

We recently did a site survey in Washington, D.C. near the U.S. Capitol, expecting to find all sorts of interference. Instead, there were buildings all around blocking our line of sight to Galaxy 1, except for one particular location. Finding this spot first, saved a great deal of time and energy. Thereafter it was a simple matter to push the reflector trailer around, aim carefully and find our "bird." Fortunately, except for a few channels, there was very little interference involved and our report was well received by those requesting the survey (Fig. 1-12).

If signals are scrambled, however, you do have additional considerations, and these particular transponders should be monitored on both satellite and

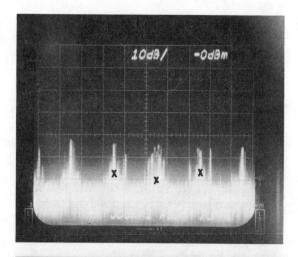

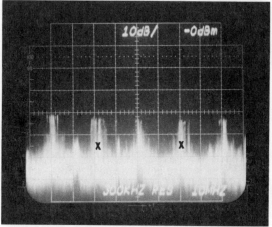

Fig. 1-12. The same 24 transponders spread out as we change the analyzer's readout from 50 MHz9/div to 20 MHz/div. Now note both in-band and out-of-band interference indicated by the Xs.

TV receivers just to make sure. Unfortunately, very clean broadband reception is required for satisfactory descrambling and your spectrum analyzer resolution may not pinpoint everything that can show up in the final picture. A little herringbone or chopsticks here and there can be very disturbing to critical viewers. Should such an unfortunate circumstance arise, you're either going to filter or move to another, more suitable location. Halfway measures won't suffice, and sometimes in-band filtering will interfere with the descrambling operation as well. All these factors are the reasons for site surveys becoming highly important. You never know, especially in the big cities or industrialized neighborhoods.

MODEL 5111

When time came for the actual descrambling performance, there was considerable need for specific filtering, especially on channel 5, Showtime East. With i-fs set at 140 MHz, in-band microwave was readily apparent. Initially notched out by variable Microwave (Fig. 1-13) Filter Model 5111, then permanently replaced with Model 3217 M1, channel 5 came in with fair resolution and definition, but what seemed to be a little loss of relatively saturated colors. As we will repeat in the EMI/RFI chapter, don't filter unless necessary, and then only filter to minimum requirements. By filtering at 130 and 150 MHz, you now have only a 20 MHz band to work with on Channel 5, with the incoming signal approximating 36 MHz. So there is an obvious loss, even though mid-picture detail is reasonable, at least in this instance.

You should understand that due to heterodyning actions of each individual receiver, *your* filters must be specifically designed for a *particular* receiver's i-f, and not just any number that appears handy. Also, you're going to find that $300-$500 for a good filter isn't necessarily Tripoli pirating. The good ones do, indeed, cost real money. This discussion is continued and considerably enlarged upon in the specific portion of the book set aside for combatting interference. Some scrambling relief may come, however, when RCA and Home Box Office begin operating their K-3 satellite under the name

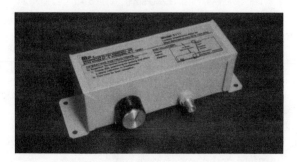

Fig. 1-13. A very valuable tunable trap (Model 5111) that will find in-band interference; (courtesy of Microwave Filter Co.).

Crimson Satellite Associates, scheduled for launch sometime in 1989. All 16 transponders will serve cable systems and home subscribers—whenever and wherever. This is also a Ku band "bird," like K-1 and K-2, transpondering the downlinks at 11.7 to 12.2 GHz delivering 45 W output/channel at 54 MHz bandwidths. With this one and its kissing cousins, you probably won't have the C band filter problems we've just enumerated for two prime reasons: Ma Bell operates in the 4-6 GHz band and signal output from these satellites are at least five times stronger than maximum 9-10 W/transponders at C band. Obviously, a frequency change and considerably elevated power (even at Ku) definitely makes a significant difference, especially because of both C/I and C/N factors, which both gain in this instance.

We also understand that K-3 will deliver 60 W/transponder instead of the 45 of its two sisters—taking the power level up to a maximum calculated point of greatest efficiency versus raw power. In other words, at Ku that is all the coverage possible without losing efficiency after 60-W maximum.

Now with scrambled channels from Galaxy I moving to Telstar T303, and HBO, Cinemax, etc., shifting to K-3, several particular satellites may absorb all the scrambling and leave the rest for you, me, and the advertisers (bless them).

ANTENNA CONSTRUCTION

For now, there are three prime types of TVRO antennas available in the market from 1.2 meters (4-footers) up to 12-footers, with an occasional 15 ft. reflector sandwiched between for especially difficult conditions where narrow beamwidths and high gains are absolutely needed for acceptable signals. Otherwise, almost anything from 6 feet up for C band and 4-footers for Ku are the usual offerings, many of which are *not* necessarily close tolerance and others just plain flimsy. Most all, however, use prime focus feeds—a subject we'll thoroughly investigate in another section—with more and more designed to accommodate both C and Ku bands together as special in-line feeds are developed for this particular purpose.

The cheapest (in all respects) is the mesh reflector (Fig. 1-14), usually with many panels, diamond-

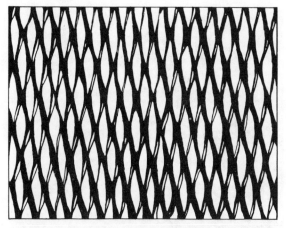

Fig. 1-14. Diamond-shaped mesh used in less expensive C-band reflectors is normally not suitable for Ku.

shaped holes, and dubious antecedents often like the hand-layup fiberglass reflectors of the early 1980s. Everyone claims computer design, but paper claims and production excellence are two entirely different goals. In the beginning, panels were known to blow off, others rippled, inadequate bracing permitted "wind" waving, and non-conductive oxidization was commonplace. Today, however, *major* manufacturers have overcome many of these difficulties with larger, stronger panels, and the mesh antenna does enjoy a certain acceptance among dealers who work with the less expensive systems. Its price, however, has increased proportionately and the better meshes now almost rival the good perforateds in cost. Cheap products, nonetheless, still appear from the backyard operators, and installers who don't know or don't care and are erecting them by the dozens. We suspect their replacement rate will become a subject of many articles by the TVRO press as complaints flood in after a year or two combatting the elements.

Our main attention, therefore, will be devoted to perforated and fiberglass reflectors, which are still the prime receptors in a temporarily slack market. Top manufacturers, here, are designing for a number of years *good* service that should see many of these units operating for as many as 10 years or longer. This is especially true for fiberglass reflectors, where hail storms or some rowdy individual

hasn't put a dent in the superstructure. In all sincerity, even though some mistakenly think cosmetic appearances outweigh performance, good, compression molded fiberglass will be around and hold its shape for a long, long time if it's made correctly. Meanwhile, there will be fewer and fewer consumer reflector manufacturers left to struggle, and we'll probably reach considerably better uniformity in the process of TVRO antenna making, probably by the beginning of 1989.

In the meantime, there is a great deal of activity in the commercial world as Ku band proponents try and place a 1.2 or 1.8-meter antenna on every business rooftop. All these, of course, are probably solid reflectors with most tuned to a single satellite for largely data and voice traffic. Teleconferencing should play a great part in these business transmissions just as soon as corporations discover it's considerably cheaper to link their peripherals by satellite than tying up a few dozen phone lines for expensive minutes or hours. Even in 1988 there has been a great deal of activity in this respect, from which we have already received some very valuable information. Even now, large service organizations are forming for Ku-band installations and repair.

PERFORATED REFLECTORS

In the best of manufacturing circles, perforated reflectors are first laid out in sheets of 0.040 gage aluminum, cut to general shape, perforated by a large punching dye, formed and stretched by a pneumatic device over the mold, and then trimmed for the final product. As compared to mesh, there is little flex, the panels are considerably stiffer, not diamond-shaped, and don't dent as easily. Winegard, especially, has been granted a patent on ribs and panels being manufactured in the same parabolic plane.

The Burlington, Iowa Co. is also now producing compatible C- and Ku-band antennas with perforations of 5/64 inch instead of the maximum Ku-band hole size of 1/10 inch, in addition to an rms surface tolerance of ± 0.030 (Fig. 1-15). They are also using a hard, corrosive resistive, and abrasion resistive powder coating for their antennas that is actually dry paint applied by an electrostatic spray which is

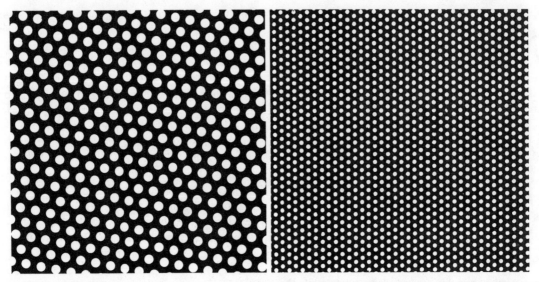

Fig. 1-15. Actual C- and Ku-band perforated hole sizes in newest aluminum reflectors. $\frac{1}{10}$ wavelength is the magic number (courtesy of Winegard).

nonconductive and firmly adheres to the reflector's metal surfaces in curing ovens.

Original C band perforates by this company had $\frac{5}{32}$-inch diameter holes on $\frac{1}{4}$-inch centers. The new C/Ku reflectors are also on $\frac{1}{4}$-inch centers with patterns staggered and 36-percent open spaces. Winegard's new 4-foot Ku perforated reflector will have an rms tolerance of ± 0.015.

MESH REFLECTORS

From at least one top manufacturer (Prodelin), a 10-foot reflector mesh with stretch-formed ribs and especially rolled panels is coming on the market with both a monopod feed and horizon-to-horizon geared drive. The dual, worm-geared drive is permanently lubricated and sealed against the elements, and is said to track all satellites "quickly and accurately," and can be driven by "most" antenna positioners. The monopod aluminum support tube does away with guy wires, allowing single or dual feeds to remain firmly in place and always at the correct focal point. Designed for quick assembly, holes are pre-drilled, and the inner rim holds ribs in place for any required panel replacement. Gain for this antenna is fixed at 39.1 dB, with an f/d ratio of 0.40.

FIBERGLASS REFLECTORS

Most fiberglass radiators are built with easily assembled panels, just like the usual perforateds and mesh assemblies. Probably the most representative of all the fiberglass units are, once again, manufactured by M/A-COM (now the Prodelin Mfg. Co.) in its new factories near Newton and Hickory, North Carolina. Personal experience with the 10-, 8-, and 4-foot systems have thoroughly demonstrated the durability and signal-handling abilities of compression molded fiberglass (Fig. 1-16). Yes it's heavy, and there is certainly more wind resistance *below* 40 mph than the metal reflectors with holes, but these antennas don't rust or corrode and they deliver constant microwave signals whether summer or winter. Even in a hurricane we've noticed not a bit of "flutter" usually prevalent with strong wind gusts exceeding 45 to 55 mph. So if an antenna is structurally sound and mounted correctly, it should survive and operate in winds very close to 80 mph without permanent effects.

This particular unit is a M/A-COM/Prodelin product, pressed by precision steel dies at 5×10^6 lbs. with considerable parabolic accuracy. Fiberglass panels have molded inside ribbing for additional

16

Fig. 1-16. Typical well-designed compression-molded fiberglass antenna with heavy mount, intermediate bracing, and linear actuator (courtesy of Prodelin).

strength and are both rust and corrosion proof. Mounts are formed from heavy, precision-stamped parts and welded together for extra strength and tracking accuracy, while drive assemblies are tested and approved for 1500 pounds of load. A texturized surface scatters IR radiation while it maintains maximum reflected signals for the feed and preamplifier. Gain midpoint between 3.7 and 4.2 GHz measures 39.5 dB, with monopod feed and an f/D ratio of 0.30.

AN OFFSET FEED

Also manufactured by Prodelin, principally in 1.2- and 1.8-meter sizes, these little antennas with their offset feeds are specifically built for Ku band and thousands of them have already been installed around the country (Fig. 1-17). Investigated with both prime-focus offset and Gregorian bisected systems, characteristics were very similar and, because of mechanical (and possibly cost) factors, the prime focus feed in an offset configuration was chosen. We therefore will concentrate on the prime focus offset configuration and not enter into details on the Gregorian, which is much like a Cassegrain, but with an inverted reflector.

The center phase of this feed is placed at offset in order for the peak of any received primary pattern to focus directly on it. By offsetting, the horn and its supports are removed from the main incoming signal path, with both gain and sidelobe pattern improvements. Further, horn and reflector mismatch is reduced, in addition to offering more effi-

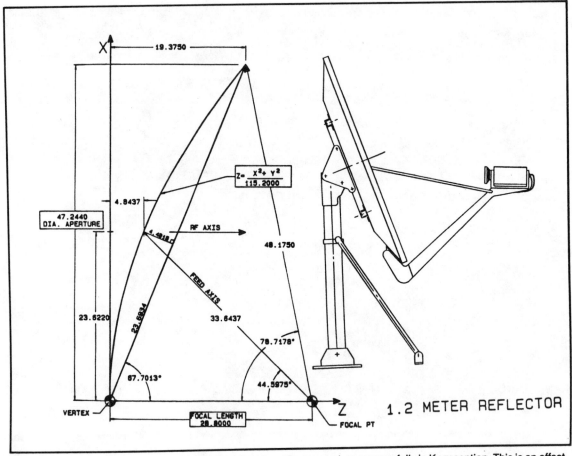

Fig. 1-17. Specifications and outline drawing for 1.2-meter reflector used so successfully in Ku reception. This is an offset-AZ/EL rig.

cient rain, snow, and icing condition removal. A circular aperture was chosen for best electrical and mechanical performance. In any non-circular aperture, reflector efficiency and gain must be compromised to a certain extent because of feed design required for proper reflector illumination. Here, a basic corrugated conical feed horn is quite adequate for low cross polarization, beam symmetry, and broadbanded operation.

Production surface accuracy was then set for 0.025 inches rms and, had the Gregorian system been selected, the subreflector accuracy would have been 0.015 inch rms. Total feed loss, including VSWR then amounted to only 0.16 dB. Gain is 41.43

dB in receive and 42.96 dB in transmit for the 1.2-meter unit and 44.96 receive and 46.48 in transmit for the 1.8-meter reflectors, while respective noise temperatures at 10° and 40° elevations amounted to 49.3° K and 31.1° K for the 1.2-meter reflector and 46.7° K and 29.1° K for the 1.8-meter unit. Efficiencies for the two were listed at 0.616 and 0.615, respectively, including diffraction spillover.

Briefly, but succinctly, that's the antenna story. It should be just enough to let you become familiar with the better units available in the late 1980s on the market and good comparisons to make with those to come. As we are steadily discovering in this "land" of microwaves, quality must be foremost or vexatious troubles soon follow, despite the growing pains of a new industry which are usually felt by everyone at some stage or another.

Let us not, however, leave this discussion without a bona fide installation (our own) to back up all this "happy talk" theory which is great for the who, why, what, and when, but does seem to neglect the *how*. So here's what is *also* firmly rooted, county-inspected, and passed in our own back yard (Fig. 1-18) just awaiting an 8-foot reflector and dual C- and Ku-band feed for an AJAK horizon-to-horizon mount we hope will access *everything*!

Our particular installation may not be practical for everyone in the U.S. because it's especially designed for 8- and 10-foot reflectors and their mounts, but you won't "suffer" using it in reasonable soils and ordinary wind velocity areas. Where hurricane and earthquakes persist, you'd better research the problem carefully before being caught between the proverbial rock and some other hard place. Preparation "X" won't mitigate a lawsuit or alleviate property damage liability.

TYPICAL INSTALLATION

A typical single pole (Kingpost) installation

Fig. 1-18. One of my installations showing 10′, 40 formulation steel mast, 48″ deep hole, with 6-bag reinforced concrete foundation.

would involve the usual 18-inch diameter, 48-inch deep excavation, a 4-inch outside diameter 40-formulation steel pipe, ½-inch reinforcing bars cut to lengths of approximately 16 inches, and the usual six-bag concrete. The pole should have two sets of butterfly wings welded to its lower extremity and about 12 inches above the end. Height above the concrete mixture will be determined by reflector diameter, allowing approximately 6 feet for a 10-foot antenna, and 5 feet for an 8-footer. Just be sure you take into account any increase or decrease occasioned by the mount.

To calculate the concrete quantity, simply use the equation for the volume of any cylinder:

$$V = \pi r^2 h \text{ or } \pi d^2 h/4$$

where $\pi = 3.1416$, $d = 18$, and $h = 48$, all measured in *inches*.

$$V = 3.1416 \times 18^2 \times 48/4 = 3.1416 \times 324 \times 12$$
$$= 12214.54 \text{ in.}^3$$

But, you need this measure in terms of cubic yards, and so: $12214.54/46656 = 0.2618$ yd.^{3}, or just a little over ¼ cubic yard. But you haven't allowed for the volume of the 4-inch steel pole and its butterfly wings, and so a quarter yard at approximately $50 is more than sufficient. In fact, you will have enough left over to build a substantial holding rectangle *above* ground framed with four pieces of spare lumber that easily measures $36 \times 36 \times 2.5$ inches, guaranteeing your mast support will go nowhere even in the roughest weather. Knock off the loose concrete and re-use the frame for something else. Be sure, however, your concrete platform has enough slant to allow rapid water runoff.

The pole, by the way, was first scoured with metallized sandpaper to remove loose rust and then painted silver with a rust-preventive paint available at any paint or hardware store. Your local building inspector should heartily approve!

SMALL REFLECTOR SETUP PROBLEMS

Try an ordinary 8-foot reflector for 15 satellites on the east coast, for instance, and you won't do it! Even if you hook up a power divider and connect both receiver and a spectrum analyzer to the block downconverter, very carefully watching each satellite as it's tuned, including all the transponders on it, you're still going to lose a bunch. The prime problem is that even though you may have reasonable illumination, a decent reflector and receiver, etc., there simply isn't enough signal capture area to deliver requisite gain from any but the most powerful transponders.

What we're suggesting, we do in all our installations just to see the benefits and problems arising in each and also to evaluate LNB output signals [50 dB + (-90 to 100)] dB wherever they are. It turns out that -40 dBm into most receivers having a -20 to -50 dB range produces a reasonable picture. Anything much less than that is pretty bad.

With small reflectors, however, *every single dB* becomes critical. After carefully setting your north-south polar mount axis with the reflector pointed due south, and compensated for both magnetic variation and equator arc deviation, you will still have to compromise at either arc extreme, with subsequent loss of gain and some picture fidelity. This is regardless of the quality of the receiver. Of course, a 65° K LNB may help, but not that much. And you may also find that just a little W/E shift of the antenna on its kingpost may make several dBs of difference, and possibly enough to bring in another few channels that weren't worthy of the name before.

All this, of course, is taking time, not to mention the programming of East and West electrical azimuth stops, and then the various satellites. True, a few transponders will respond agreeably to both fine tuning the channel as well as manually shifting the reflector's position. Once again, however, all this, along with polarity (skew) settings takes time; and pretty soon you've tied up a whole day diddling with a 6- or 8-foot reflector in some geographical location it had no business being in the first place.

HINTS AND SUGGESTIONS

Your easiest C band installation? Find two good LNBs, a decent feed, pop them into place with either a single-pole or buttonhook feed support and go about your business after, naturally, installing them on at least a 10-foot fiberglass reflector. The "struggle factor" is probably less than 50 percent considering all the programming and lame explanations you won't be required to make.

But if you're still in the 8-foot category back East, don't attempt to use any receiver that doesn't offer *both* manual reflector positioning and channel fine tuning, as well as our old friend skew—the customer will need all the various aids available. Also, if you can, find a dual positioning mount (both azimuth *and* elevation) and sell him one of these, too. Then, perhaps, he'll have a fighting chance to at least know there are a fair number of satellites in geosynchronous orbit, even though he or she can't see too many. Of course, the bill could well exceed $3,000 for all this special small-reflector attention.

Our final thought—and this may be strictly parochial—allow one day for installation and mounting, and another for programming and instructions—if you are an individual, and 1.5 days if you're twins. The above is based on LNB experience with fairly sophisticated programming and various shapes and sizes of reflectors. Do beware, however, if you're doing TVRO with anything but a parabolic, you could run into miserable sidelobes and possibly additional C/I under the right (wrong) circumstance. Our momentary inclination for Ku being, dig up a high pulse count *separate* positioner and down-geared linear actuator, connect signal lines (and dc for the LNBs) through a low or no loss switch, and operate one *individual* reflector with *orthogonal* downconversion for C band, and a skew-controlled feed and 1.2 to 1.8-meter reflector for Ku. This arrangement may *not* cost as much as you might think considering that you're using the same receiver for both bands. A new horizon-to-horizon mount we're testing may well have resolutions within 0.15°, which is well within the 0.25° tolerance for Ku.

You might like to know that Venture Manufacturing in Dayton has a Von Weiss linear actuator that will actually move at 64 counts to the inch rather than its normal C band 32. Sort of "rhymes" with the Winegard hole ratio between their C and Ku band perforated reflectors, doesn't it?

One question we can answer, however, is that at least one other perforated reflector manufacturer is not using 0.064-inch holes for Ku but something a bit larger. Seems when protective paint began to flow over the smaller perfs it also covered the holes. The solution? Make 'em larger, by all means; apparently a few dB doesn't really matter. Or does it? The 20-W Ku transponders during rainstorms could change some of this thinking as continued application unfolds. We also doubt seriously that anything less than a 6-footer will develop enough gain to rescue the few 20-watters still operating during inclement weather. The 40-60 watt group should be able to illuminate a 1.2-meter reflector sufficiently to avoid problems from the elements provided curvature and reflector laws are strictly obeyed.

So you can see that with new challenges, the resolution of old problems, and onward-racing technology, there is still a great deal to be done before we even begin to approach a generally satisfactory television receive-only earth station that will access both C and Ku bands, not to mention the forthcoming DBS satcasting.

Chapter 2

Feeds and Cabling for C and Ku Bands

WRITING ON THE SUBJECT OF TVRO FEEDS PRE-sents a distinct dilemma—but no relation to the dictionary definition of some conditional choice between "equally undesirable alternatives." Basically, there is a choice between two paramount types of feeds, prime focus and Cassegrain and their derivatives; but there's nothing bad, simply a Cinderella-type situation where one fits the foot and the other doesn't.

The two main feeds used in both data/voice and video transmissions are either primary or secondarily illuminated types designed for specific purposes and applicable to certain reflector illumination with somewhat different results. Usually both types are circular when designed for standard parabolic reflectors, while a few units are rectangular to accommodate these types of reflectors. But all have one common objective: maximum receive or transmit illumination from or to the reflector with the least amount of edge spillover and lowest sidelobes.

Spillover, for your information, is nothing more than lost reflector energy; while sidelobes, if large enough, will permit interfering signals to enter system electronics and intrude into (usually) the picture because they cover a very broad band of frequencies, nominally between 30-60 Hz and 4.2 MHz NTSC (Natl. TV Systems Cmte.). RF audio, as always, is 4.5 MHz *above* the video carrier and has a maximum bandwidth of only 50 kilohertz, even with multichannel sound, and only 25 kHz with monaural.

TYPICAL AND SPECIAL FEEDS

The typical corrugated (shaped in parallel curved ridges and hollows) prime focus feed at the 3 dB down points exhibits a beamwidth approaching 80°, which (Fig. 2-1) is shaped much like a broad-beamed all-metropolitan television antenna, but without the usually attendant backlobes that permit ingressive signals from alien sources. However, the less filled spaces between 90° and 270° have to do with feedhorn efficiency, and all detected energy *below* 90° and 270° denote spillover. So there are two prime considerations in evaluating feeds, in addition to any blockage resulting from poor design or massive sup-

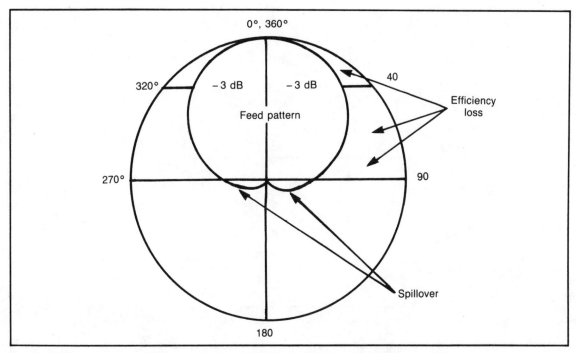

Fig. 2-1. Typical prime focus feed may cover ±40° at −3dB with corrugated horn mounting.

port struts, which could radiate or deflect energy and, therefore, increase sidelobes (Fig. 2-2). This is why the Federal Communications Commission imposes a strict standard on *transmit* radiators they must meet for approved licensing, namely, 29 - 25 log τ with theta being the horizontal distance in degrees from the carrier for each sidelobe.

Cassegrain and Gregorian feeds—basically reversed concave/convex subreflectors—actually replace receive prime focus feeds with an (Fig. 2-3) additional reflector that refocuses all electromagnetic energy into a feedhorn at the center of the radiator, which also has a secondary focus. In transmit, the process is reversed.

Although Cassegrain types deliver uniform phase between the reflector, subreflector, and feed, subreflector diffraction (scattering) tends to limit their use to large antennas, usually above 40 lambda, and are not normally used on 3-4 meter reflectors, especially in consumer products where inexpensive prime focus feeds are prevalent. Further, precise positioning of Cassegrain and Gregorian subreflectors and exact focusing make their uses rather im-

practical except for commercial uses. These feeds, however, do produce somewhat reduced sidelobes, and the Gregorian is said to offer even greater reduction here than its predecessor, the Cassegrain.

In designing feedhorns, the larger the f/D (focal length to diameter) ratio the flatter your reflector and the greater its beamwidth. But, because of 2° mandated spacing for *both* C and Ku bands, numbers now should be small, around 0.3+, so you'll have a reflector beamwidth that is *less than* 2°, which, of course, also produces a deeper reflector inviting less interference and usually higher gains but requiring additional pointing accuracy. Tradeoffs apparently are everything, at least in this portion of microwave technology at the present. For Ku we would want 0.375 f/D for better results.

As for corrugated horns, these are usually used in both transmit and receive because, they deliver a constant beamwidth over multiple frequencies. There is also a multimode feed for earth stations quite similar to the corrugated, but its radiation is considerably more frequency sensitive.

Now, since this isn't a design book, we'll dis-

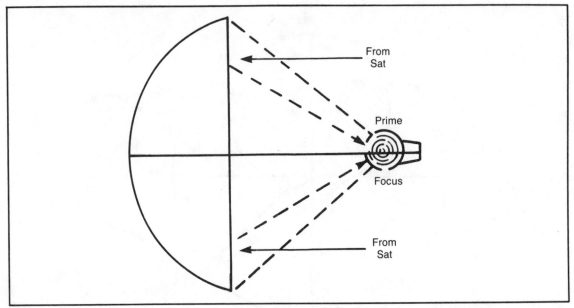

Fig. 2-2. Prime focus corrugated feed—often used with many types of equipment, but primarily TVRO.

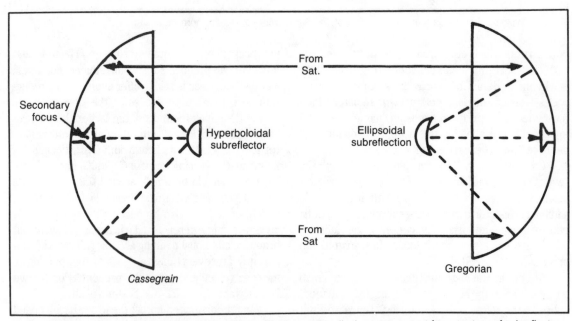

Fig. 2-3. Cassegrain (left) and Gregorian (right) reflector feeds are virtually the same except for curvature of subreflector.

pense with further ''gory'' details and deal directly with the newer feeds now appearing on the market, most being the prime focus variety of which several are adaptable to both C and Ku reception on modest-sized 8- and 10-foot reflectors. Prime focus feeds have better gains than the dual reflector variety, although they are not as adequate for sidelobes, but are easy to install, focus, and respond to phase-angle skew control.

CHAPARRAL COMMUNICATIONS

A major manufacturer of prime focus feeds for the entire TVRO industry, Chaparral continues to manufacture its Polarotor® I and II for conventional C band receptors. The difference is in the skewing probe motorizing to move it inside the feed for accurate receive phase (Fig. 2-4). As you are probably aware, the Westars and SATCOMS differ in signal phase, in addition to atmospheric diffractions that can and will occur as microwaves enter the earth's fields and atmosphere. Each, however, has f/D ratio limits on reflectors it will accommodate, so check your reflector's dimensions carefully if you're matching one of these with a "strange" radiator. Polarotor I uses a servo motor for probe change positions with flip switch and control knob for precise skew correction, in addition to automatic operation when connected to most receiver switches for odd and even transponders. Polarotor II offers the same performance but has a dc motor instead of the servo, with polarization peaked visually.

Being switchable, the Polarotor I may, occasionally, have slight servo motor oscillation which vibrates the probe. First move the probe from one extreme stop to another, and then center it at ± 45 degrees. At this point the control pulse is 1.5 msec in duration and may be measured with an oscilloscope for accuracy. Then check all wiring, especially noting that the control cable is both shielded and has three conductors, especially where the reflector is more than 300 feet from the receiver. The recommended control interface also has a 100-ohm resistor in series with the white pulse wire at the receiver. You may also discover a random motor oscillation with no control applied, noticeable as TV screen black bars. One remedy is a 1,000 μF capacitor of 10 Vdc or larger shunted with its positive electrode to the $+5$ V terminal and black wire connection (ground). For 200 foot runs, 18 AWG wire is recommended to carry activating signals.

Chaparral has also recently introduced its new solid state TWISTER™ that has no moving parts and can be attached to the Polarotor I controls. Having *no* moving parts, it permits virtually instantaneous polarity switching during all weather conditions, total skew adjustment, and lowest feed loss. Avail-

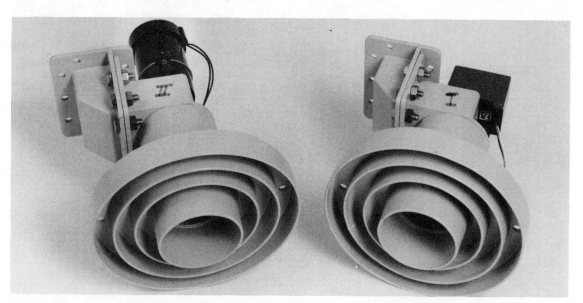

Fig. 2-4. Conventional Polarotor® I and II feeds for standard C-band reflectors (courtesy of Chaparral Communications).

able in three models, it may connect to any Polarotor I controls, stand-alone controller with rocker switch and thumbwheel skew adjust, or it may be had with no controls at all but does need a variable dc power supply of ± 15 V and some 100 mA. When installing, however, be careful of the WR 229 flange because the ferrite-holding adhesive may be ruptured and result in loss of performance and even cut wires connecting the terminal strip.

The second feed type from Chaparral is called the Sidewinder™, and is dual orthomode equipped with a Twister I interface and its ferrite (no moving parts) technology. The unit in two positions appears as shown in the illustration (Fig. 2-5) and requires two LNB/C amplifier-converters for horizontal-vertical transponder reception. Here, skew may or may not be required, depending on TVRO location and special considerations. In our own orthogonal C band system we do *not* use skew on the east coast and still receive some 15 satellites, most of them reasonably well; but some could be cleaner using skew.

The third current offering by Chaparral is a 4-12 GHz Polarotor® called a dual-band feed with optional golden ring for off-size (Fig. 2-6) reflectors, designed for 0.33 to 0.45 f/D ratios in regular antennas and 0.28 to 0.33 f/D for the narrower ones. With 35 dB 4 GHz isolation and 25 dB 12 GHz isolation, standard ports are designed for the usual WR 229 and WR 75 waveguides, respectively, with servo-positioned probes in each feedhorn for H/V transponders. Servo motors may be independently or parallel controlled by receivers delivering standard T²L logic and +5 Vdc operating voltage.

Two notes of warning: old reflectors with fifty-thousandths tolerance and "chicken wire" reflector facings will not operate at 12 GHz Ku, and actuators that can't track at ¼° aiming accuracy or better won't work either. And even if you do have a reflector tolerance of at least 0.25 inch for Ku, you probably should have *both* positioner and Rf fine tuning for anything like accurate azimuth and transponder tracking. Also, with the C band input offset, there is a slight loss in 4 GHz gain, and any marginal in-

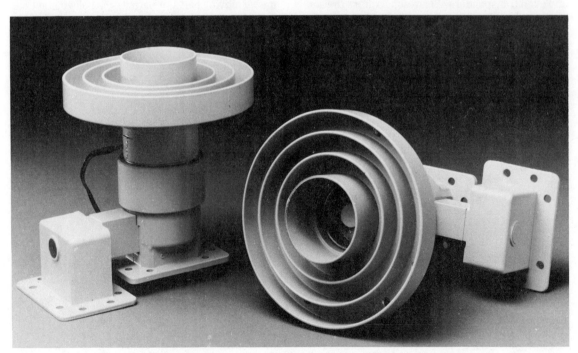

Fig. 2-5. Sidewinder™ orthogonal C-band dual feed, complete with skew control (courtesy of Chaparral Communications).

Fig. 2-6. Chaparral C/Ku band feed should work with selected reflectors (courtesy of Chaparral Communications).

stallation will certainly suffer. So think about the conversion carefully before attempting the change. But then again, you might "just get lucky."

THE JOHN SEAVEY CONTRIBUTION

Excellent commercial and military feed designer John Seavey, President of Seavey Engineering Associates, Inc., is the first that we know of to offer single and double polarization for C and Ku, with the second being orthogonal for both.

The significant point about each is that they are in-line and not piggybacked to or on one another. Figures 2-7 and 2-8 show what we mean. Here polarization isolation is 35 dB minimum, phase centers (inputs) are coincident, and a three-wire servo adjusts polarization of the two-port model over 180°. The dual orthogonal (Fig. 2-7) is manually adjustable at the feed. The f/D ratios may be had for these feeds from 0.25 to 0.55, and there are also available options for 12.25-12.75 GHz, as well as

10.95 to 11.7 GHz, along with waveguide elbow kits and circular polarizers.

President Seavey tells us that C-band signals propagate between coaxial inner and outer conduc-

Fig. 2-7. A Seavey coaxial conductor feed (Model ESR-124H) for both C- and Ku-band signals (courtesy of Seavey Engineering Associates).

tors, and a patented microwave resolver conducts this energy to a circular CPR-229F waveguide connected to the polarizing rotator and its three-wire servo for skew control. It also mechanically rotates both C and Ku polarizers simultaneously.

The inner conductor, being hollow, passes Ku band signals to its own WR 75G waveguide. This description applies directly to the Model ESR-124H with single ports for C and Ku. The ESA-124D is completely orthogonal for both horizontal and vertical feeds in the two 4-12 GHz bands and so requires no servo motor. Here, two orthomode transducers are mounted to accommodate the four LNB/Cs for simultaneous access to *all* dual band satellite transponders (Fig. 2-8).

We should see a good deal more of these dual-band, coaxial-feed systems soon on the market as quickly as patent rights (Seavey already has them) and final designs are systematically sorted out. In early 1987 a number of manufacturers are still working on special products that will deliver the Ku/C band goods, and you'd better study published parameters carefully. Among other things, circular waveguide inputs and rectangular waveguide outputs do have some losses and a little SWR. Check these out because standard gain feedhorns are all delivered rectangularly. You just might save a dB or two of insertion loss, a little added noise, and lots of Ku band grief. Microwave plumbing doesn't take kindly to quick-changing kinks of any kind.

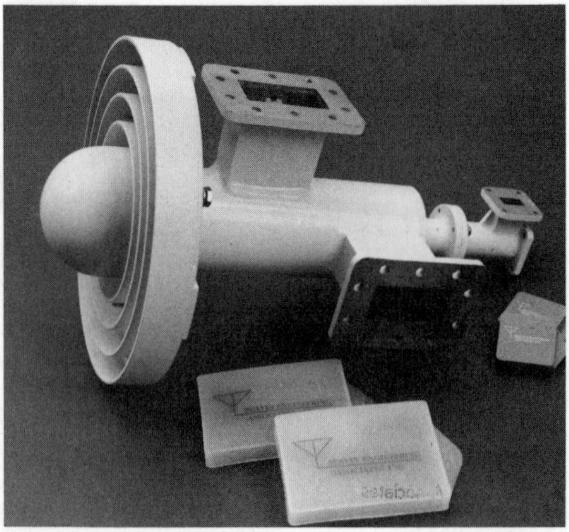

With strong input signals, however, from spacecraft such as K-2, a round/rectangular mismatch won't be a problem, especially with a high-gain, low-noise LNB. We found a 2.2 Northsat LNB conversion from the original Panasonic 2.5 NF used in the original USCI ANIK C2 system, a very good match even with the added feed and rectangular LNB input window. Power consumption is 1.9 W, i-f output 950-1450 MHz, gain 52 dB, and operating voltage requirements of 14.4 to 19.8 Vdc. Used with a Zenith ZS-4000 combination C/Ku positioner receiver, this LNB supplied excellent performance on all K-2 transponders and, we believe, other Ku band satellites as well. The reflector was a 1.2-meter M/A-COM used during the test. A 2.0 NF Microwave Systems Engineering (NSE) did even better.

With those words of tempered wisdom, you should be ready to get on with the rest of the initial electronics as electrons flow into gallium arsenide amplifiers, commonly known as pre-amps where, unfortunately, thermal noise in poorly engineered high-gain amplifiers can be crowned king.

SOMETHING NEW AND INTERESTING BY N.A.D.L.

Considering that illumination for any parabolic reflector combines the qualities and quantities of beamwidth, sidelobe levels, crosspole performance, feed design, and matching antenna characteristics, it's obvious that careful feed engineering is extremely important. Further, any part of the reflected signal outside the cone formed by the reflector's edge and its focal point contributes to spillover resulting in additional antenna noise temperature and terrestrial interference intrusion (Fig. 2-9).

Most of you must be familiar with parabolic reflector scalar feeds marketed by Omni-Rotor™ and Polarotor™, owned by M/A-COM and Chaparral, respectively. Essentially, these differ only in degree and not necessarily a great deal in performance. And as long as you match the magic f/D ratios with their ringed signal collectors, they operate quite

Fig. 2-8. A second Seavey coaxial feed (Model ESA-124D) contains orthogonal ports for dual C- and Ku-band preamplifiers and converters (courtesy of Seavey Engineering Associates).

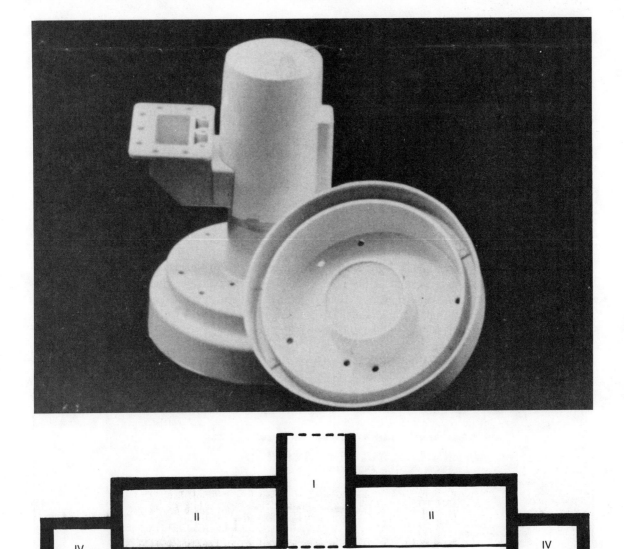

Fig. 2-9. External photograph and internal drawing of the new hybrid feedhorn featuring linear polarization and sharp skirts for T.I. rejection (courtesy of National A.D.L. Enterprises).

satisfactorily if mounted correctly and their probes are situated so that skew angles are easily compensated. This, of course, is primarily for C band because Ku feeds from the better manufacturers mate with rectangular openings rather than circular. The scalar portion of the feed, however, remains circular in external appearance. If they are orthogonal (feeds accomodating two LNBs), skew doesn't apply.

Hybrid-type feeds, however, are becoming increasingly popular since, theoretically, they would more nearly contain all the reflector cone energy and have little or no spillover accompanied by maximum gain. They would also handle equal vertical or horizontal polarizations, including almost constant phase. A dual-mode, coaxial feed is quite adaptable to prime focus requirements. It consists of a circular waveguide (I), two larger coaxially-loaded waveguides (II, III) and additional "regions" identified as IV and V. All these "regions" therefore combine in both the circular waveguide *and* coaxial modes, producing what approximates the ideal prime focus feed. Circular waveguide sections and depth of the shorted coax sections are then adjusted for maximum results, forming an almost linearly polarized electric field which, developer National A.D.L. Enterprises says, is really a device consisting of three circular waveguides.

In addition, A.D.L. explains that electromagnetic energy must access the feed aperture in-phase, limiting bandwidth, since each waveguide mode has phase velocities that vary with frequency. This results in very steep skirts contributing substantially to terrestrial interference rejection. In short, here is a new TVRO engineering development that contributes both to excellent signal-receiving characteristics as well as sharp interference rejection.

Results should be outstanding if feeds will operate optimally on *both* deep and shallow f/D reflectors.

BOMAN INTRODUCES COST EFFECTIVE FEEDS WITH HEATERS

Boman Industries of Downey, California also has some interesting developments involving both C- and Ku-band feeds. The EFH-75 has a peaking microwave tuning adjustment, a no-loss feed aperture cover, a gold extender ring to match special f/D ratios, precision-molded die-cast adjustable scalar rings, a heavy duty casting, and a special 24-karat gold plated probe previously patented by Sperry Rand, and quick-mount wire screw terminals (Fig. 2-10). There's also better filtering, a thermo-guard heater to prevent sluggish cold weather operation, a built-in surge protector, and a special voltage regulator that guards against receivers supplying overvoltage skew potential. In 1986 the price was only $29.50 *complete*. Yes, the decimal point is exactly where it should be!

The Boman unit is simply an improved open-throat waveguide with better skew control, good

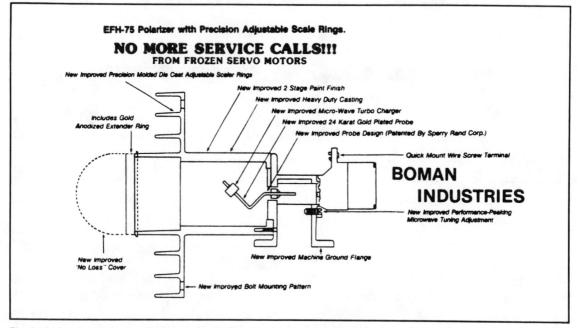

Fig. 2-10. A very new and useful Boman feed with probe heater and adjustable scalar ring for f/Ds from 2.8 up (courtesy of Boman Industries).

scalar rings, a microwave peaking adjust, and a well-designed probe operating at an approximately 55° angle from a horizontal line drawn below its elbow. Some of these specifications are seemingly miniscule, but they all contribute to better signal processing at C band (Fig. 2-11).

In the feeds discussion, we are concerned primarily with prime focus varieties because they constitute the major portion of all such units sold in the industry. There are, however, the offset variety designed to illuminate the reflector at some angle, usually from bottom to top. But as to the feed itself, the two types are very similar and their differences are basically in mounting. We will not discuss these further because the reflector is the prime difference in the way it handles signals rather than the way such a feed operates. We might add that offset feeds are usually round rather than rectangular, entirely different from point-to-point microwave reflectors and their semi-square waveguide feeds that are capable of absorbing only a *single* polarity. Could you use one of these to access satellite transmissions? It's possible, but unless there was some means of rotating the waveguide you'd only see a single polarity. In addition, the 2° spacing could come back to haunt you since your microwave antenna probably couldn't handle the requirement.

Said succinctly, use what has been designed for TVRO receive/transmissions and nothing else, then there'll be fewer headaches. The Boman Ku feed

Fig. 2-12. Special Boman Ku feed with 60-80 mA heater for freezing weather.

is interesting, too, since it has both a skew(ing) probe as well as a 60-80 milliampere heater to keep it moving even in the coldest weather (Fig. 2-12). You northern folks might just make real good use of this one!

F/D RATIOS UP OR DOWN?

When dealing with C and Ku frequencies you'll find a conflict in f/D measurements. Read along with us and we'll try and explain.

Keep f/D Ratios Down

The best information says that C band reflectors with f/D ratios above 0.3 are in trouble with sidelobes—and check both the E and H plane patterns. We might also add that beamwidths of 1.8° or less are also desirable to meet 2° spacing requirements. Gains are of not less than 39 dB with first sidelobes down at least 18 to 20 dB to meet the FCC's 29-25 log θ noninterference (transmit) standards. Receive reflectors don't positively require such measurements, but carrier-to-noise (C/N) and carrier-to-interference (C/I) factors pretty well demand that such specifications be met. One last note is that fiberglass reflectors have a 5 dB front-to-back gain measurement over wire mesh, and we *still* think that any of the ''holey'' metal reflectors with prime focus feeds should always absorb more earth noise than their fiberglass competitors. After all, the *feed is pointed* directly *at* the *ground* with little intervening surface blockage, especially for C-band antennas with their larger holes.

Fig. 2-11. The new, low cost scalar-adjustable Boman C-band feed.

Ku reflectors, so far, are mostly either fiberglass or solid aluminum and this problem isn't obviously apparent. In addition, smaller reflectors nominally have offset feeds and this reduces both pointing angles and ground clutter, not to mention snow and rapid water discharge. As the f/D measurement implies, a small ratio indicates a deeper reflector, while a large ratio, such as 0.4 means a flatter and more shallow unit with a considerably longer focal length. Which permits entry of the most interference? Think about it for a minute in terms of your dinner plate. Do peas slide off a plate quicker then they do in a bowl? It is the same difference with T.I. Narrower reflector apertures (openings) and shorter focal lengths are always more desirable where interference is probable, even though they're more difficult to aim and maintain under adverse weather conditions.

The circular waveguide opening determines the reflector's efficient wavelength transmissions, and the scalar rings outside help collect the various frequencies that are then processed through to the initial amplifier, whether it be LNA, LNB or whatever. Misadjustments, including improper focal distance, skew, or waveguide constrictions will always cause problems. Recall that Satcom F3 is 20 degrees off-axis compared to other geosynchronous satellites.

Keep the f/D Ratios Up

Sounds like heresy following the C-band reflector and feed analysis; but, fortunately or otherwise, it's all true. You need a considerably flatter reflector for Ku operations, beginning, probably, at an f/D reflector ratio of 0.375. Now, since a 0.3 f/D for C band is preferable, we have an obvious conflict, and it all boils down to the compatibility of attempting to work with both spectra on the same antenna. True, you will have feeds capable of receiving both frequencies, but accuracies and efficiencies may deteriorate. At C band, of course, flat reflectors absolutely invite undesirable C/I (carrier to noise), while at Ku, the flatter reflectors with considerably tighter tolerances are necessities.

It's no wonder, therefore, that some manufacturers are already designing dual positioners that are capable of working two reflectors, possibly at the same time. At Ku, however, you should have your feed bored for 0.75 instead of 0.62, as is customary, since dual polarities require the larger orifice.

Although a number of us still advocate C and Ku combined systems on the basis of *economics,* it may be a while before a truly effective dual-band arrangement comes to market. As yet, we haven't seen one; therefore, the interim period will probably become one for testing and hard evaluation in an attempt to determine various advantages, disadvantages, and probabilities.

Top feed people such as National A.D.L. Enterprises, however, are saying that "good" f/D ratios should begin at 0.375 and go to 0.4, at least for Ku. And the combination, momentarily, probably should be about the same. I, nonetheless, maintain my "druthers" about wide angles and expanded beamwidths for C band because of the carrier-to-interference factor that is always present in an already crowded lower frequency spectrum. The entire matter eventually may be solved by more efficient and effective feeds that can properly illuminate *deep* reflectors without excessive spillover and undesirable sidelobes. Watch the specification sheets! At the moment, we're just as much in the dark as everyone else. But we will comment that offset Ku band feeds have a slight advantage over prime focus types because there is less physical interference with illumination plus somewhat better sidelobe performance.

Meanwhile, half a dB loss in some feed isn't going to kill any reasonable signal, but 3-6 dB loss in the LNB-to-receiver link can and will drive your 500 MHz channel spread right into sparklies for a first class lousy picture. We're speaking of coaxial cable, of course, and this topic, while not purely scientific, merits serious consideration all the way from its outer jacket to internal shielding and the all-important center conductor. Therefore, our next subject will naturally be TVRO cabling, including the newest and best products available—at least those we know of and consider relatively cost effective and suitable for consumer/commercial TVRO. We are primarily concerned with frequencies from dc to 1.5 GHz, which include those emanating from the block downconverter in most systems.

CABLE FACTS (NO FICTION)

One of our all-time favorite topics has to do with cabling. For no matter how excellent your LNA/LNB/C checks out, and regardless of the superb characteristics of your receiver, poor quality coaxial cable (thank goodness it isn't twin lead) in between positively destroys the value of each. And not only do you require worthwhile cable, but connectors have to be both secure and waterproofed. If because of price, competition, or availability some portion of your TVRO installation must suffer mediocrity, don't let it be the connecting cables. The other parts can easily be substituted according to necessity and demand, but once your cable is strung, especially underground, it's total murder to dig it up and replace without considerable loss in time and money. It's even good practice to check the cable *before* installation so that you know your electron carrier is properly handling the load. And it even makes more sense to use webbed cable for the combined actuator, feed probe (skew), and *double* signal lines, forseeing the eventual probability of combined K- and C-band feeds or at least orthogonal (dual block down) amplifier-converters for one of the bands. Eventually, when cost becomes less, you may even want to install orthogonal LNB/Cs for *both* C and Ku to avoid the nuisance of adjusting skew. At the moment, however, only one designer has such a dual orthogonal feed, and his price is considerable because of quality, engineering, and patent rights. Later, several other feed vendors and manufacturers such as Chaparral, Boman, and National A.D.L. will probably have these also. For the moment, however, Seavey Engineering is King.

CABLING CONSIDERATIONS

Logically, you should always conceal all control cabling to avoid the usual prank problems and sometimes outright sabotage. PVC (polyvinyl chloride) 1.5-inch pipe is an excellent candidate and will contain the webbed variety comfortably. A stout cord and fishing line sinker can be used to pull the cable through individual sections (10 or 20 feet) as each is joined and glued to a connector, while someone on the other end feeds the cable and pushes a bit (Fig. 2-13). In relatively soft earth you only need a good spade, not a trench digger. There may be times and places where you'll have to go below the frost line for your trench, but in moderate climates this is probably not necessary. But do try and slant the pipe at some downward angle, allowing for breathing openings at either end via 90-degree goose necks and a pair of small drain holes at the bottom— all of which disperses any accumulated moisture. If costs or pipe availability prohibit this type of installation, check out the possibility of high density polyethylene jackets for longer wear, otherwise use good quality PVC jackets and hope for the best. But there are risks in using ordinary cable as *cable facts (and fiction)* will point out later on. A PVC pipe affords a very considerable amount of protection for both cable and earth station owner, and products seldom become any cheaper than they are right now. On the other hand, if you're only interested in a 10-year installation, stuff whatever there is in the ground and go about other business—but do give the earth station owner all the facts first. Such information is often profitable for everyone and does, indeed, promote better system performance.

CABLE MEASUREMENT

Just expounding the virtues of good cable, though, isn't really justification for that extra cost and the author's ardent recommendations. Facts must speak for themselves, and the following are those to look for.

Attenuation/hundred feet. This is the loss in decibels that every cable suffers at some specified frequency. Keeping in mind that the half-power point is −3 dB and half voltage point is −6 dB, let's look at some of the better cable losses:

	Frequency	dB Loss
59/U 22 AWG conductor with solid polyethylene core	at 450 MHz	7.5
59/U 20 AWG conductor with polyethylene foam core	450 MHz	5.8
6/U 18 AWG conductor polyethylene/polypropylene foam	450 MHz	4.6
11/U 14 AWG conductor polyethylene foam	450 MHz	3.4

Fig. 2-13. One lead sinker and a stout cord will pull webbed cabling through PCV protective pipe for ground installation.

Statistics supplied by Belden, these are obviously CATV nominal attenuation figures that only extend to 450 MHz. What we're interested in, of course, are frequencies to at least 1 GHz. Naturally, attenuation becomes considerably greater here, and much more care needs to be given to specific cable selections. Here, we're going to name specific cables and give available figures (Fig. 2-14).

Belden's 9213 and 9214 are similar except for "leg" No. 3 which, in the 9213, is a Beldfoil shielded triplet of 20 AWG stranded bare copper and PVC insulated conductors with 22 AWG drain wire. Otherwise, leg No. 1 has two 14 AWG stranded bare copper motor-drive PVC insulated conductors and a Beldfoil shielded triplet of 22 AWG stranded bare copper, and PVC insulated conductors with 22 AWG tinned copper drain wire. Both cables second legs are Duobond II shielded, with 61% covered aluminum braid, and RG/6 coaxial cables. The fourth legs

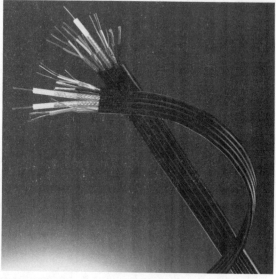

Fig. 2-14. Belden's new multi-leg cable manufactured especially for TVRO (courtesy of Belden Co.).

34

for both are a Duofoil shielded twisted pair of 18 AWG stranded bare copper with PVC insulated conductors and a 20 AWG stranded and tinned copper drain wire. The first drain was for motor arm sensors, the second for the downconverter, and the last for polarization. The two cables are sweep tested between 950 and 1450 MHz, having only a minimum of 17 dB structural return loss. Signal characteristics are as follows for 9213/9214 satellite LNB/C swept tested cable.

AWG	Insulation	O.D.	Shielding
18	cellular polyethylene	0.280	Duobond II® + 61% Al braid and 100% shield cov.

Impedance	Cap./ft.	Attn./ft.
75 ohms	17.3 pF	at 1.3 GHz, 8.9 dB

Note: on the 9214, RG6/U occupies *both* legs 2 and 3.

The cable we have been using for over a year was supplied by M/A-COM's Cable Home Group, now part of General Instrument Corp. in a buyout during August 1986. Signal cables have center conductors of 18 AWG copper-coated steel, formed polyethylene dielectric, in addition to bonded aluminum tape and aluminum braid (60% coverage). Cable 3 leg has three 20 AWG conductors, copper drain and shielded with aluminum polyester tape (Fig. 2-15). Cable 4 also has three 22 AWG conductors and tinned copper drain also shielded with aluminum polyester tape. There is also a pair of 14 AWG copper conductors for the actuator. Characteristics are as follows:

AWG	Insulation	O.D.(all cables)
18	Polyvinylchloride	1.464"

Shielding	Imped.	Cap.	Attn.
Al tape	75 ohms	16.2 pF	7.2 dB at 1.2 GHz.
60% braid			

Propagation velocity for Belden amounts to 78% and for Network Cable 82%. Although we haven't

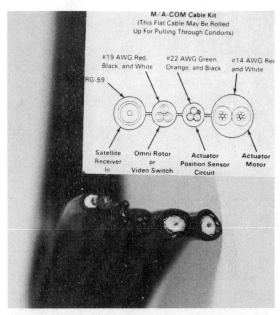

Fig. 2-15. An excellent TVRO multi-cable that has already stood the initial test of good electrical conduction and time (courtesy of Network Cable Division, General Instrument Corp.).

used Belden (small sample), the two manufacturer's products should evaluate well, with M/A-COM possibly having the edge in both attenuation and propagation. Otherwise, we see no real differences. Each manufacturer is top rated, and your particular supplier may have either one or the other—be glad that he has.

There may be other equally reliable brands here and there we haven't examined, but these two are first quality and are now available to everyone engaged in the TVRO endeavor. My preference has always been to stay with the top boys and stay out of trouble. One costly callback can ruin profits of a dozen succeeding installations.

CABLE FACTS (*AND* FICTION)

RG59U is just as good as RG6. Baloney! Yes it's cheaper, the inner-outer diameter is often less, but simple braid shielding and 22 AWG center conductors bring nothing but undesirable stray rf entry and signal loss. At higher frequencies such as 950 to 1450 MHz, signals tend to traverse the center conductor skin rather than its core. Therefore, a fat center conductor such as 18 AWG is always recommended for LNB (and LNA) electron passage. Aluminum wrap around the center conductor dielectric is also most desirable for both shielding and moisture rejection.

Foamed cable sponges moisture. Yes, *joined* individual foam cells in *series* do attract moisture and act as a long thin sponge. But the better cable dielectrics such as those by M/A-COM and Belden have individual cells that are actually isolated from one another and reject the elements as you would expect. For TVRO, their center conductors are all 18 AWG, too.

Steel With Copper-Flashed Center Conductors. At 1-2 GHz, copper flashing over strong steel center conductors are much more preferable than copper and have the same propagation velocity and impedance. Pure copper in any lengths will stretch and break fairly easily when flexed. For LNA/downconverter couplers in their usual short lengths, we would even recommend AWG 10 center conductors for the lowest possible loss. At 12 GHz we hope there are never anything but compact block downconverters available by anyone.

F Connectors. Buy the cheapest and expect rapid callbacks. Sure, two-piece F connectors cost less, but they also invite leakage and poor outer conductor connections. For a few cents more the single piece connectors are available and are insurance against the dissatisfied customer. However, you'll have to seal their block LNB contacts with some secure sticky moisture proofing such as Coax-Seal by Universal Electronics. It stays flexible for years and keeps out weather leaks. We also understand there are some gasketed connectors available that don't need any protective coating—but the cost differential could be rough. Check it out.

Deep six all burial cable. Another baloney! Although we prefer to enclose *all* reflector-to-receiver lead-in with 1 ½-inch PVC pipe and a couple of moisture drain holes, polyvinylchloride can be used with reasonable installation care. Special high density polyethylene jackets, however, are available that will last longer than the 10 to 15 years predicted for PVC. Ground shifting, rocks, and freeze-thaw conditions, nonetheless, are always hazards and the thicker your protective wall the better chance for long survival. Naturally, the customer has to be willing to pay the price. If not, sharp rocks and accumulating moisture can cause both leakage and cable jacket penetration resulting in signal loss and even catastrophic short circuits.

Swept cable isn't necessary. Deep six this one, too. If you want to be *sure* of transmission loss, impedance, and reflection coefficients your cable must be swept. Used are wideband sweep frequency generators, variable attenuators, bridging detectors, baluns, rf amplifiers, detectors, oscilloscopes, and even spectrum analyzers. At high frequencies, one big glitch can wreck all downconverted signals. For the extra per-foot difference, taking a chance isn't worth it? Simply pass the cost on—it's good insurance for both you and the customer.

Impedances change with cable types. Here 9914 50-ohm characteristic impedance cable using N-connectors is no match for 9116 Duobond II Belden at 75 ohms. To match the two, results in an attenuation of 5.72 dB. Just remember that half voltage points occur at 6 dB and half power points at 3 dB. There's no mix and match in this one. And remember that most higher frequency spectrum analyzers are 50 ohms input Z also. What a difference a few ohms make!

Cable lengths are immaterial. Better check manufacturers' cable specifications if you're involved in runs exceeding 100-200 feet. There are all sorts of cables, you know, and current flow, signal passage, and cable support all have to be taken into consideration. For extreme lengths you may have to use amplification, but remember that many amplifiers also increase both noise and signal at the same time. So try and stick within 100 feet of any dwelling or office. This can save you lots of grief and lost installation time.

Webbed cable over singles. Webbed cables have been checked for capacitance, impedance, current handling, and signal-carrying abilities. Randomly installed independent cables may not have been afforded this luxury. For LNA/LNB, actuator, feed rotor, and any other TVRO combinations, we strongly recommend webbed conductors all the way.

At least most of these are swept tested on the signal lines and are generally reliable otherwise. Singles often deceive, may be poorly shielded and loaded with undesirable capacitance.

Rooftop cables. Best not to let these cables even touch the roof, but support them with standoffs. A cable resting in water or moisture of any variety can deteriorate rapidly with alternate hot sun and liquid baths. And if the cable is lightly shielded, roof reflections may even seep through generating secondary images. In short, keep lines taut and clear, even as is done on shipboard.

Grounding. Cables grounded at *both* ends sometimes cause ground loops and signal interference. One end is often sufficient. Cable connections between receivers and amplifier-converters always, however, must have a hot (signal) lead and return—the latter being through the common or shield second conductor. Here, fittings must be secure and making good contact, otherwise you're asking for intermittents, opens, and possibly shorts. The overall subject of grounding we will not discuss in writing on the premise that any point with a direct ground strap is a lightning attraction—the ''point'' being some piece of metal tilted skyward. The sharper it is the more chance of taking a static charge. Ever notice how many people are killed sitting under trees in lightning storms? A wet tree may also become a conductor. Fortunately, most houses don't have wooden roots; just masonry, which *is* an insulator. But they do have power lines, and their surges are dc supply killers.

Home cable entrances. Rather than bore one or more large holes in some one's sidewall, why not find a vacuum cleaner plastic discharge pipe (with end flaps) and cut your hole to size for the plastic? Makes a clean entrance, and cable can be entered and removed at everyone's convenience without a scratch. It also takes care of ribbon cable very nicely as well as baseband or rf feed to the neighbors, if they're nice. There's not much winter hot air leakage either and, of course, it can be plugged with insulation or Mortite. Electrical distributors have plenty.

TV/Satellite mixes. For uniform system common connections, try and use similar cable for your TV installation as for earth station electronics. Once again, if you insist on several ''grounds'' you're likely to upset the ''humors'' and produce lousy pictures, including possible secondary TV images called ghosting. In this instance, one spook is too many. And if you decide to run a nice grounding lead from your TV mast down the side of your clapboard house and to ground, one of these days you'll probably replace the side of the house, or at least scrape and repaint it. Lightning isn't choosy.

Those are about the prime tips on cable usage that have been personally experienced over the years. We always find that good cable and tight connectors go a long way toward guaranteeing better signals. Conversely, poor cable is no insurance against anything. Just 5 to 10¢ a foot can make all the difference in the world.

THE FINAL WORD

Larger cables—that is their conductors and generally outside diameters—have less attenuation and better power handing abilities. Cable costs, too, appreciate by approximately the square of their diameters, and their temperature ranges are a factor also. You should be aware that cables that measure under 0.16 inch often have ''pull strengths'' of 35 pounds or less and won't stand excessing stretching. This is why copper clad *steel* center conductors are preferable, along with stout casings to withstand stresses often prevalent in the TVRO industry.

We may have ''attacked'' the cable discussion rather strongly, but past and ongoing results speak for themselves. In very few TVRO installations, even some over 200 feet, do you see extra amplifiers unless there are decidedly extenuating circumstances.

In order to maximize the use of good cable, you'll have to have sizeable reflectors, matching feeds, good block downconverters and adequate receivers. ''Going cheap'' is a highly risky procedure that may double your costs in the end—meaning the installation of an entirely new system having quality components. In TVRO, a ''real bargain'' is often nothing more than bad news, *especially* in discontinued LNA amplifiers.

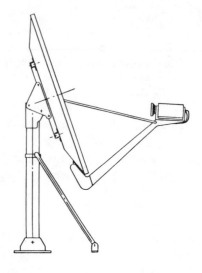

Chapter 3

The Signals to the Receiver

THE BIGGEST PROBLEM WITH THIS TOPIC IS THAT it involves working with isotropic radiators that transmit or receive satellite energy equally in all directions. This is great for the theoreticians, but a little difficult for us realists who have to gingerly match mathematical models and figures with hard-nosed electronics and come up with passable video and audio signals for everyone else.

MATHEMATICAL PARAMETERS

Of course you can always fire up a spectrum analyzer, calibrate it, make a measurement, then include LNA/B/C gain, add in the gain of the reflector, and tag the actual received signal precisely. But suppose one of these super analyzers isn't available, or you just don't know how to work one. In this chapter you'll suddenly discover why antenna (radiator) efficiencies are so very important. Compared to 100% efficiency of the perfect isotropic radiator, which always radiates the same energy it receives, any actual antenna that uses 70% of the received energy is pretty good. Often it's just 55-60% if you *don't* want excessive sidelobes.

SLANT RANGE

To really know what you're doing, the first item to be tackled is the slant range—the miles or meters between you and some selected satellite. Naturally, a computer program would be handy for those with a multi-thousand dollar, air-conditioned, and carefully shielded computer. But we don't have one, and most of you don't either. Most of us, however, do have a reasonable calculator of the hand-held variety, and that's all it really takes. If we let the computer do the heavy work, such as the distance from earth's center to some satellite, then insert a known constant, all that's left are a couple of cosine values to look up and then a simple square root to execute. In statute miles, therefore, the slant range of any satellite with respect to *your* position amounts to (Fig. 3-1):

$$\text{Slant Range} = 14{,}414 \sqrt{3.389 - \cos \text{lat. angle} \times \cos \text{lon. difference between your site and that of the satellite}}$$

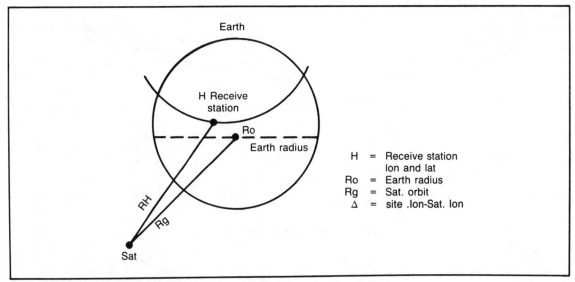

Fig. 3-1. Slant ranges from satellite to earth are possible with simple calculations.

A more explicit equation using a satellite's geostationary orbit in equatorial plane of R_g = 6.611 R_o, with R_o being earth's radius of 3959 statute miles.

Now, if you let delta (Δ)L be the difference between your longitude and that of the satellite, and H your latitude: The equation becomes:

Slant Range =

$$R_O\sqrt{6.611^2 + 1 - 2(6.611)\cos H \times \cos \Delta L}$$

Having said all that (with help from Microdyne and Scientific Atlanta), let's plug in a few numbers and see what really happens.

$$R_s =$$
$$14,414\sqrt{3.389 - \cos 38.9\ N \times \cos 84 - 76.6\ WL}$$

$$RS =$$
$$14,414\sqrt{3.389 - .778 \times .9917} = 14,414 \times 1.618$$
$$= 23318\ \text{sat. mi.}$$

Try a couple for yourself, especially your own location, for kicks and see if these figures don't come out nicely—rounded off, of course, without a dozen decimals. When all the profundities are extracted from many of the designed-to-confound mathematical equations, the results (but not necessarily the derivations) are often rather simple. Here, we took our own laboratory and SATCOM IV locations as examples.

SPACE ATTENUATION

Usually known as path loss attenuation between you and the satellite, has also been a humdinger of an equation if you took all the factors and broke your back defining them. We thought another of these pretty accurate simplifications might just work to perfection if we could just plug in numbers and come up with an appropriate result, which wouldn't snow the countryside. So let's see how you handle this one:

$$L_p = \frac{20\log(\text{range in miles}) \times 4\pi \times \text{frequency}}{\text{divided by the speed of light}}$$

So, here,

$$L_p = 20\log\left[\frac{23318 \times 4 \times 3.1416 \times 4 \times 10^9}{186,282}\right]$$

L_p = 195.98 db *for C band* at 4 GHz

L_p *for Ku* = 205.52 dB at 12 GHz, which is
(10 dB *above* C band)

39

You will find *both* of these path loss equations are pretty *constant throughout the geosynchronous range.* That wasn't hard, was it?

SYSTEM NOISE TEMPERATURE

Let's say our antenna noise temperature amounts to 32° Kelvin;

LNB/C noise temperature 80°K:

Receiver noise temperature 2500°K

G_{feed} VSWR loss 0.99

$G_{LNB/C} = 50$ dB or $10^5 = 100,000$

Therefore, temperature of the entire system amounts to:

$$T_{system} = T_{ant.} + \frac{T_{LNB/C}}{G_{feed}} + \frac{T \text{ receiver}}{G_{feed} \times G_{LNB/C}}$$

System Noise Temp. $= 30 + 80/0.99 + 2500/99,000 = 110.83°K$

As you can readily see, the noise temperature of the LNB/C is really the determining factor of the system, even though your antenna does enter into the equation to some extent, especially if it has an arbitrarily high T°K of its own, or there is reverse "leakthrough" from the 290°K ground that could occur with some of the perforated and mesh reflectors and their specific pointing angles. See Table 3-1. As you must or should know, the higher the pointing angle, the less *frontal* terrestrial noise pickup. And do note that the final T receiver and G feed X G LNB/C part of the equation adds very little to the overall figure. Remember, however, that Ku-band block downconverters have much higher temperatures than do C band (approaching 200° K) so the system noise temperature here will be about double that of a reasonable C band figure. All this, of course, has to be accounted for in the final figures, and the 40-60 watts/transponder of the newest Ku-band systems must still overcome severe weather outages whether sleet, snow, or heavy rainfall and, at the same time, adequately serve reflectors that are less than half the size normally used in C band.

So far, we haven't seen any problems with *our* 1.2 meter M/A-COM reflector and old Panasonic LNB/C (until it recently crapped out), and we hope nothing further happens; but there's always a pos-

Table 3-1. Noise Figures in dB Compared with Temperature in Degrees Kelvin. For C Band an NF of 1 Is Good. For Ku, an NF of 2 Or Less Becomes *Most* Desirable.

T °K	NF dB	T °K	NF dB		NF dB
10	.148	175	2.056	340	3.378
15	.220	180	2.103	345	3.412
20	.291	185	2.149	350	3.446
25	.360	190	2.194	355	3.480
30	.429	195	2.239	360	3.513
35	.496	200	2.284	365	3.547
40	.563	205	2.328	370	3.580
45	.628	210	2.372	375	3.613
50	.693	215	2.415	380	3.645
55	.757	220	2.458	385	3.678
60	.819	225	2.501	390	3.710
65	.881	230	2.543	395	3.742
70	.942	235	2.584	400	3.773
75	1.002	240	2.626	405	3.805
80	1.061	245	2.666	410	3.836
85	1.120	250	2.707	415	3.867
90	1.177	255	2.747	420	3.897
95	1.234	260	2.787	425	3.928
100	1.291	265	2.826	430	3.958
105	1.346	270	2.865	435	3.988
110	1.401	275	2.904	440	4.018
115	1.455	280	2.942	445	4.048
120	1.508	285	2.980	450	4.077
125	1.561	290	3.018	455	4.107
130	1.613	295	3.055	460	4.136
135	1.665	300	3.092	465	4.165
140	1.716	305	3.129	470	4.193
145	1.766	310	3.165	475	4.222
150	1.816	315	3.201	480	4.250
155	1.865	320	3.237	485	4.278
160	1.913	325	3.273	490	4.306
165	1.962	330	3.308	495	4.334
170	2.009	335	3.343	500	4.362

sibility of considerable attenuation as frequencies rise. All this is *not* true for the 20 W/transponder satellites, at least in the east. A heavy rainfall will wipe them out completely when beamed to a 1.2-meter system and 225° K LNB/C. A *new* 170° LNB does help.

G/T, THE FIGURE OF MERIT

G/T, as most of you already know, stands for gain over temperature, is usually expressed in dB/°Kelvin and is expressed as:

$$G/T = G_{ant.} - 10 \log \text{System temperature}$$

Antenna gain (with reference to an all-sector isotropic radiator) amounts to a specified number of decibels whether metal, ''glass,'' perforated or mesh in terms of diameter, and range from some 25 dB to 47 dB, depending on size and received frequency.

Here, we'll use a 9.6 ft. reflector with a *measured* and *calculated* gain of 39 dB and an efficiency of 55% developed over our own 716 ft. range at a frequency of approximately 4 GHz.

Therefore:

$$G/T = 39 - 20.45 = 18.55 \text{ dB}°K$$

CARRIER-TO-NOISE AND SIGNAL-TO-NOISE (FIG. 3-2)

C/N involves space loss, G/T, Boltzman's constant (-228.6 dB), and B, the effective noise bandwidth, and is written:

$$C/N = EIRP - L_s + G/T - 10 \log K \text{ (Boltzman's)} - 10 \log B + L_p$$

We will also use a figure of 39 dB for our EIRP, which is the ''footprint'' contoured power of our satellite downlink in the Baltimore/Washington area. See Fig. 3-2. (The $-10 \log B$ is the receiver's effective bandwidth in MHz).

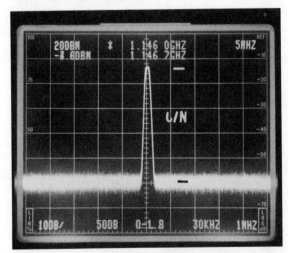

Fig. 3-2. An unmodulated signal riding many dB above noise. This one is from a signal generator. Resolution is 30 kHz, frequency per division 1 MHz, and the center is 1.46 GHz (all at 3.608 dB down).

$$C/N_o = 39 \text{ dB} - 195.98 + 18.55 - (-228.6) - 10 \log (28 \times 10^6)$$

$C/N_o = 15.67$ (Carrier/Noise Power Density Ratio = C/N_o)

Now you may also calculate the S/N (signal-to-noise) response of your system receiver. So, using standard video (FM) terms:

$$S/N = C/N + 37.5 \text{ dB (some use 35 dB)}$$
or $\quad S/N = 15.67 + 37.5 = 53.17 \text{ dB}$

Considering that 54 dB produces studio quality pictures, this is a pretty good TVRO to be working with, and also shows what good gains and low noise block downconverters can do. But we would perefer a 30 MHz bandwidth.

By the way, this same 39 dB antenna at C band would have a gain of 48.5 dB at Ku, if all else were equal, but due to space loss increase, LNB/C temperature rise, rain margin, and other factors, your signals won't be at all the same. However, a perforated C band antenna with .078 holes of this dimension would probably work fairly well at Ku with an agreeable prime focus feed. But a smaller Ku band reflector, will require 0.050 diameter or less holes to be effective. The old argument that gain of a given antenna increases as the square of its frequency (in this instance 16/13, or 1.23) *carrier-to-interference* really doesn't hold water.

C/I is taken mainly from two FCC documents and a terrestrial frequency coodination, and includes internal interference and adjacent satellite interference, adding up to a total of about 20 dB. C/I internal becomes 26 dB and C/I adjacent sat equals 21.9 dB—both FCC data. C/I terrestrial is then the earth frequency coordination given in one publication as 25 dB. The total then becomes 19.17 dB; therefore, a ''safe'' figure to use here and there is 20 dB, unless there are extenuating circumstances such as different figures for separate locations around CONUS.

Considering that uplink carrier-to-noise often amounts to as much as 30 dB, downlink (calculated) is 15.67 dB, and C/I total about 20 dB, the usual 7 to 8 dB of TVRO receiver threshold had better be watched for adequate margin. Fortunately, S/N is excellent, and therefore effective C/N should not be any problem at all.

By the way, mesh measurements have shown an additional 3-5° K increase in noise temperature due to reverse (backside) thermal pickup because of feedthrough from the earth's 290° K characteristc temperature. We presume that perforateds would check out the same since a hole is a hole.

If you wish to convert noise figures to temperature (T°K), just use the following equations, along with Table 3-1 that can do most of the common calculations for you:

$$F(dB) = 10 \log (1 + T/290)$$
$$T = 290 (10^{FdB} 10 - 1)$$

The above is actually designed for low noise amplifiers, but is useful in any noise-temperature applications where characteristics are critical.

AUDIO TRANSMISSIONS

Normally, not a great deal of attention is paid to audio transmissions other than to say they are usually pegged at either 6.2 or 6.8 MHz, or some combination that can produce excellent stereo. Many receivers have tunable monophonic abilities somewhere between 5 and 8.5 MHz, but this is seldom used since most carriers are already preset. This does not mean, however, that there won't be additional carriers added as the state-of-the-art progresses. At the moment, these two are frequency offset (see Fig. 3-3) some 3 MHz away from the video carrier and cause no interference. If additional carriers are added, however, and the offset becomes narrower, these could interfere and become a real picture liability.

What you're seeing in Fig. 3-3 are not actual carriers, but dual tones from a Hughes G-3 test pattern. This is the *composite* video-audio output of a T-1 M/A-COM receiver. Note that this signal, as opposed to the video carefully filtered and clamped output, is over 6 MHz wide, and certainly will permit additional narrow band tones/carriers should such a decision be made. Perhaps, in time, even broader-band video might be permitted also, produc-

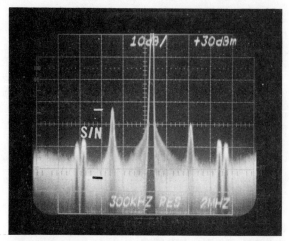

Fig. 3-3. Audio tones at 6.2 and 6.8 MHz, respectively, some 3 MHz removed from the chroma subcarriers on either side of the reference.

ing especially good color and luminance resolution/definition. It isn't bad now, but it could be improved—with FCC approval, of course. Video C/N ratio, by the way, is about 30 dB on the left of center tuning, which is correct, while the right side was subject to momentary analyzer sweep depression during picture taking. On an oscilloscope, this same video-audio response would appear quite indistinct and only the video and blanking intervals would be recognized. So in using oscilloscopes for waveform investigations and measurements, do use the video/audio baseband outputs rather than the composite since the non-modulation diversity sweep at very low frequencies is also a disturbing factor.

The audio subcarrier as received has a well-defined equation that, when simplified, may be written as:

$$C/N \text{ audio} = C/N_o + 10 \log \text{ i-f bandwidth} + 10 \log \frac{\text{delta peak deviation}}{\text{subcarrier frequency}}$$

And this deviation is the *peak* deviation of the main carrier by the subcarrier.

The remainder should be self explanatory because effects of the subcarrier filter noise bandwidth are in the hundredths of a dB and aren't normally of value. Don't, however, overlook the spectrum analyzer's filter and its 2.5 dB video detector factor which you may wish to use if appropriate.

As to the various modes of audio subcarrier and their applications, we'll talk about these *four* entities later in the discussion on receivers because all must be explained in baseband terms to be understood.

ACTUAL MEASUREMENTS

Since we've really been talking about SATCOM F-4 all along, let's go to the spectrum analyzer and make a measurement following the orthogonal (dual) block downconverters and a two-receiver, dual-channel electronic switch. Let's say the LNB/Cs have the usual 50 dB gain, the antenna 39 dB, and losses through cable and switch about 6 dB, since measurements are made from the switch's second (receiver) output rather than at the reflector feed and LNB/C assembly.

As you can see, the spectrum analyzer shows an *average* transponder value of approximately − 64 dBm. Now if you combine the two gains, you must add − 89 dB to − 64 dBm and then subtract 10 dB for cable/ switch losses. You then accumulate a received signal of − 143 dB as the actual received signal from the satellite (Fig. 3-4):

− 64 dBm measured from LNB/C output
+ 50 LNB/C gain / (but actually these numbers *combine* with − 64 dBm)

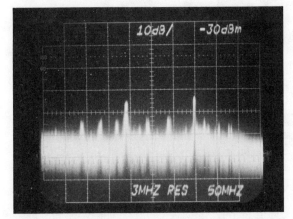

Fig. 3-4. A 3 o'clock F4 signal showing only two vertically polarized channels operating with maximum signal at − 64 dBm.

− 39 dB ant gain /
− 10 dB switch and cable losses (And this one subtracts from the total)

So − 143 dB = actual received satellite signal at the antenna. A quick glance at the EIRP footprint shows either 30 or 32 dBW for the Baltimore/Washington, D.C. area. How, then does all this correlate? We already know that space loss amounts to − 196 dB, and we also know that to convert dBW to dBm,

$$dBm = 30 \ dBW + 30, \ or \ 60 \ dBm$$

Therefore, + 60 dBm − 196 = − 136 dB. And a calculated − 143 dB versus a measured − 136 dB leaves only a 7 dB difference, and that's not too bad for rough arithmetic. Naturally, if you don't average all the transponders and just take the two largest, you cut this error another 2 dB; so, in reality, the calculated and measured decibels (signal strengths) are only 5 dB apart, and that's not at all bad considering several assumptions that could easily provide this error, *including* 50-ohm input spectrum analyzer attenuation, which is actually 5.72 dB when coupled to 75 ohms.

By now, you must realize there is a decided correlation between the given footprint for any satellite and its measured value. And you can also see why powerful and very high-gain LNAs and block downconverters are needed to preamplify and convert the signals to usable frequencies by the receivers.

Let's do a simple calculation for receiver threshold which you may find useful now or in the future:

C/N threshold =
$$5 + 5 \log \frac{27MHz/2}{4.2} = 7.54 \ MHz$$

Below 7 dB you'll probably see sparklies.

We're assuming you have a 27 MHz receiver and a video bandwidth of 4.2 MHz. Therefore, you take half the bandwidth of the receiver divided by maximum video, take the log, multiply by 5 and add the first 5 for your result. You'll find these numbers quite accurate for general calculations and certainly within 1 or 2 dB of the final answer.

By now you should be readily observing that a little practical mathematics here and there really do add up to working conclusions that are indispensable to the entire satellite industry. And when these relatively simple exercises are coordinated with reflector considerations, a complete system is very much in the making.

In addition, when there is obvious low signal strength or sparklie interference, you can use the foregoing calculations quite easily to ascertain what portion of your system is lacking. Obviously if the receiver's signals are on or about threshold, your trouble lies with the feed, LNB, or antenna. But with adequate signal into the receiver, either repair or substitution of the defective unit is an immediate requirement.

PROPOGATION AT C AND KU BANDS

Antenna propogation for both R_x and T_x is difficult enough to understand in any single medium, but when one begins to double and triple frequencies and play hanky panky with wavelengths, then the subject really becomes sticky.

In transmission, most power applied to an antenna is transmitted regardless of dimensions and frequency and is quite efficient. But the receiving antenna often extracts energy approaching a quarter wavelength from its feed conductor, and this effective receiving area varies directly with the square of the wavelength. So at higher frequencies, the antenna has less energy to work with, but remains at a similar gain. Therefore, even though efficiency decreases, large antennas with their considerable gains can overcome this microwave energy loss. And do remember that each time antenna diameter *or* frequency doubles or divides in half, gain changes by a full 6 dB.

So in going from 4 GHz to 12 GHz in our C- and Ku-band considerations, you have changed frequency 3 times, and therefore 39 dB + 9.5 = 48.5 dB, thus proving our point: 10 log $(12/4)^2$ = 9.5 dB.

Now, wavelength reaching a 10-foot reflector at 4 GHz becomes:

$$\lambda \text{ ft.} = \frac{984}{F \text{ (MHz)}} = \frac{984}{4 \times 10^3}$$

$$= 0.246 \text{ (a quarter wavelength)}$$

Wavelength reaching a 10-foot reflector at 12 GHz is:

$$\lambda \text{ ft.} = \frac{984}{f \text{ (MHz)}} = \frac{984}{12 \times 10^3} = 0.082$$

Or 33 1/% difference.

Therefore, reflector size, efficiency, hole size, and all the rest should have made their points: even in electronics there's never something for nothing. Large meshes or perforations just don't accept higher frequencies without complaining, and small reflectors don't illuminate lower frequencies without unacceptable spillover and loss of gain.

Therefore, surface tolerances greater than ±0.030 rms and ¼-inch on center-hole diameters no larger than 5/32 in. are going to have a difficult time handling Ku and C bands together. So far, it's fairly well established that solid reflectors such as spun aluminum, stainless steel, or close tolerance fiberglass are more suitable for straight Ku than the holey varieties because of size and ruggedness. We note that the better fiberglass reflectors are designed for 10 years service and not something less.

Winegard has a perforated Ku-band reflector with ± 0.015 in. rms tolerance. It's a 1.2-meter reflector with 0.050 diameter holes. Among metal reflector competitors, Winegard is certainly among the very top leaders and has already established an outstanding reputation for quality products and exacting designs.

As for solid reflectors, Andersen manufacturing of Idaho Falls, Idaho is bragging about a 6-foot reflector developed in a "hydro-form" process (they won't be more definitive) that meets the FCC's 29-25 log θ specifications and is certified for 2° spacing. It's an aluminum reflector with metal etching enamel finish and rim-mounted feed supports. Claims are no flat spots or humps, no ripples, a true parabola with 0.005-inch tolerances and both C- and Ku-band capabilities. Reflector size is 2.4 m or 8 feet. Unfortunately, they've never supplied one of these for tests, and so we have no means of verifying such claims.

DIRECT SATELLITE SIGNALS

This is probably as good a place as any to begin to explore actual satellite signals from the major "birds" and discover what they look like and what to expect in the way of reception. As many or most of you know, not all 24-transponder satellites are fully active all the time. In prime times after 5 p.m. Eastern Standard or Eastern Daylight Time, most transponders blossom forth on the more popular and stronger satellites, but several have few video signals at all. And while we won't dwell on the subject at any length, you can count their numbers at around 8 p.m. in the evening and decide the real amount of video/audio fare apparent. T301, T302, GSTAR 3, and SATCOM F1-R are not always too active. Therefore, when Galaxy 1 and SATCOM F3-R scramble a few channels, this doesn't leave a great deal in the way of prime programming on C band. Fortunately, however, many of these so-called scrambled channels aren't fouled up continually, and a bit of this "sky darkening" should abate once HBO and some of its cohorts move to K-3. By then more transponders should be operational at both C and Ku bands and fully active for even better viewing than we now have.

For the moment, let's quickly go through the various satellite transponder "shots" and make some general assumptions of what we're seeing, then we'll work with narrower passbands and specific interference problems so that you'll have a genuine "feel" for both overall and particular circumstances that positively will arise as you analyze the TVRO spectrum. These photos are with *orthogonal* (vertical/horizontal) block downconverters and no skew. So they aren't as clean as they might be.

As we work through C band, remember that most of these satellites are allocated 24 transponders, 12 of which are horizontally polarized and 12 vertically polarized. This is done to prevent adjacent channel interference while working as many of the 24 channels as possible to make the satellite cost effective. All this is done through "linear-orthogonal" and not circular polarization at a nominal transponder bandwidth of 36 MHz, along with low frequency energy dispersal for unmodulated video carriers at a 30-120 Hz rate to prevent terrestrial interference. Exceptions to the 24-channel group are the old Western Union Westars through Westar III, and the new hybrids consisting primarily of the Spacenets and ASC-1, as well as the pure Ku banders now represented by the Gstars and Ku-l through Ku-3.

Remember, too, that both C- and Ku-band satellites are still part of the Fixed Satellite Service and are absolutely not called DBS. Direct Broadcast Satellites are designed for space-to-home service, and are considerably higher powered.

A minimum 30 dB cross-polarization isolation level has been recommended by the FCC's 2° spacing advisory committee and should be adopted by the FCC without too much argument, and will include both antenna transmit and receive performance with the same separation figures.

We would also expect a redifinition of antenna performance parameters when characterizing reflectors with shaped rather than the usual circular/elliptical beams normally in use. And since patterns are "typically asymmetric", peak gains may not appear on beam axis at the traditional 3 dB down points and are expected to vary, depending on the reference given. Some point midway between aperture extremes and beam coverage will probably be defined as the pattern axis. And the 2° spacing advisory committee indicates that "many" shaped beam satellite antennas are *not* designed for superior sidelobe performance, and may be beyond FCC specifications.

Nonetheless, shaped beam antennas in the Fixed Satellite Service do assuredly increase EIRP and G/T for the terrestrial area of coverage, minimize adjacent channel/satellite interference, and may even allow less stringent transmitter and receiver specifications.

POPULAR SATELLITE SPECTRUM DISPLAYS

Now we should be ready to work through a half dozen of the more popular satellites using odd/even transponders and derive a general idea of what satellite downlink signals are all about. But first, let's say that superior crosspole (the difference in amplitude between prime and adjacent transponders) should be some 20 dB down, with a 35 dB difference as something to strive for. With those figures in mind, let's see what one TVRO system shows, then *savor* the final comments:

SATCOM F4 (WL 84°). Six of the twelve transponders are evident, but skew is not satisfactory and there is hardly 10 dB difference between horizontal and vertical. Crosspole is easily detected since at 50 MHz/div. 36 MHz channels only 20 MHz offset will easily be detected with improper skew. Interference here does not appear to be a factor (Fig. 3-5).

TELSTAR T302 (WL 86°). For some reason this is a difficult "bird" to access in my part of the country, and this one has only a couple of transponders operating anyway at reduced levels. On the other hand, there are evidences of data activity but even these are not well defined (Fig. 3-6).

GALAXY 3 (93.5°WL). Three transponders are very distinct, and the two humps on either side of the transponder on the left are probably wideband digital since they seem to occupy about 36 MHz each, or the entire bandwidth of two channels (Fig. 3-7).

TELSTAR T301 (96° WL). Once again, not a clean pattern with lots of crosspole showing and possibly some terrestrial interference toward each end, considering the proximity of several of the car-

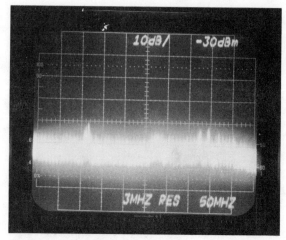

Fig. 3-6. Telstar T302.

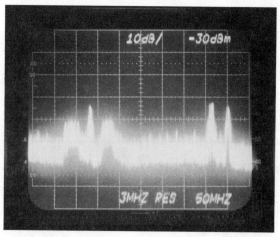

Fig. 3-7. Galaxy III.

riers which are certainly within 10 MHz of each other in several instances (Fig. 3-8).

SPACENET I (120° WL). Once more, sideband digital in the three humps, and a single well-defined transponder showing. Note, however, a probable transponder in the raised digital information on the left. If this is a video carrier, it's the universal problem currently interrupting data channels when one of these pops up in the *wrong* polarity and causes obvious information losses. (Fig. 3-9).

WESTAR V (122.5° WL). Fairly prominent prime transponder signals, reading from right to left (reversed), 2, 8, 15, 17, 20. In the middle, you're

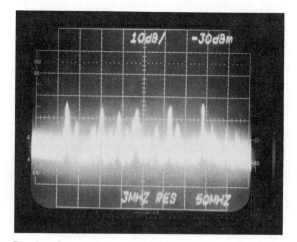

Fig. 3-5. Satcom F4.

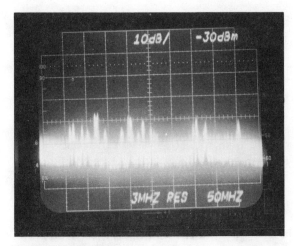

Fig. 3-8. Telstar T301.

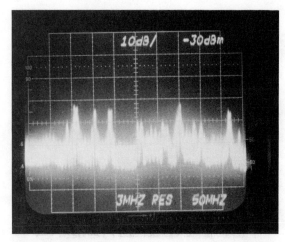

Fig. 3-10. Westar V.

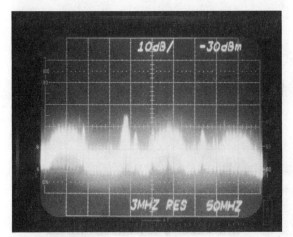

Fig. 3-9. Spacenet I.

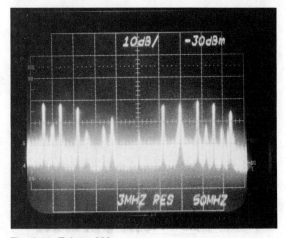

Fig. 3-11. Telstar 303.

probably seeing SCPC (single channel per carrier) information that can be either digital or voice (Fig. 3-10).

TELSTAR T303 (125° WL). Except what should probably pass as noise spikes in the lower banded (noise) portion of the pattern, you're seeing at least nine transponders, two or three of which are modulated, with only a small amount of crosspole creeping in on either end of the photo. There is no indication of anything else other than video transmissions among these odd-channel polarities (Fig. 3-11).

SATCOM F3-R (131° WL). Here you almost have your 20 dB down between adjacent tran-

sponders with nothing else to disturb. Along with Galaxy I, these two are the "scrambled" satellites, including HBO, etc. Unfortunately, you really can't tell from the modulation what's scrambled, but daily programming sheets—if not printed too far in advance—should supply the rest. Here, channels 22 (starting from the left) and either 12 or 13 (same pix) were used by HBO: *scrambled*, of course (Fig. 3-12).

SATCOM F1-R (139° WL). Has five or six apparently active video transponders operating, but there are crosspole indications on the left side and, apparently, more just to the right of center. At some 60 dB down from the LNB you wouldn't expect

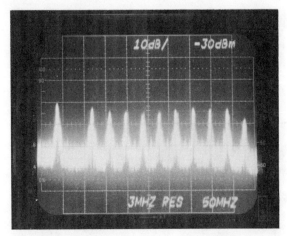

Fig. 3-12. Satcom F3-R.

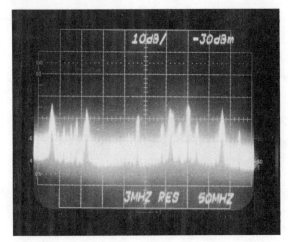

Fig. 3-13. Satcom F1-R.

startlingly clean pictures with this much "garbage" floating around. Note, especially, the third transponder from the right and its immediate crosspole that's only about 6 dB removed (Fig. 3-13).

THE BEST AND WORST

Naturally we saved a pair of special Polariods for the punch line so you would have no trouble in discerning the difference between great and lousy signals. In addition, if you should use or own an excellent spectrum analyzer that's capable of "reading" a single channel from among the clutter, we're also going to show you print-outs of what the Fed-

eral Communications Commission looks at when evaluating the various types of transmissions—all courtesy of the FCC. These latter signals are not easily seen with anything but $30,000 and up instruments, and such patterns are first stored in the analyzer's freeze frame and then reproduced by an X-Y plotter on well-defined graph paper. Nonetheless, however, they're *real* and may be reproduced exactly as shown on equavilent equipment such as a Tektronix 494 spectrum analyzer and attached printer.

In Fig. 3-14, the transponder display above is Canada's ANIK D-1, which delivers an excellent sig-

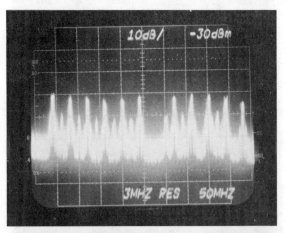

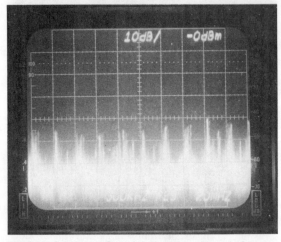

Fig. 3-14. On the top, Canada's Anik D1, with good C/N signal and passable crosspole. On the bottom, Galaxy 1 at its worst (in downtown Washington, D.C., surrounded by tall buildings and operating into an 8-foot reflector). Noisy, isn't it?

nal in the Washington, D.C.-Baltimore area. And even though there is obvious crosspole, the pattern is clean, carrier modulation good, and no great differences in transponder strength except the final transponder on the right, which is some 4 dB down from the one on the extreme left.

The second half of this figure, however, would commonly be called "a mess." And even though its signal strength seems to be rather high, there is all sorts of in-band interference among at least four of the channels, C/N ratios are not much greater than 10 dB in some instances, and the entire display is far too indistinct with noise to produce reasonable results. In short, transponders in the second photograph will *not* produce acceptable pictures on any-

one's receiver, regardless of make or parameters. It's lousy!

The final displays are those taken directly from FCC photos of the four prime transponder modulation methods. RF levels, attenuations/div., frequency range, resolution, center frequency, and frequency spans/div. are all given above and below the cross-grid printout. Therefore, if you have a superlative spectrum analyzer with peak detection and storage, you can duplicate what follows. If not, at least you know such techniques exist and can understand how valuable they are to ascertain precisely what each transponder on every satellite is doing at what time. Interpretations for the individual waveforms are included. See Figs. 3-15 through 3-21.

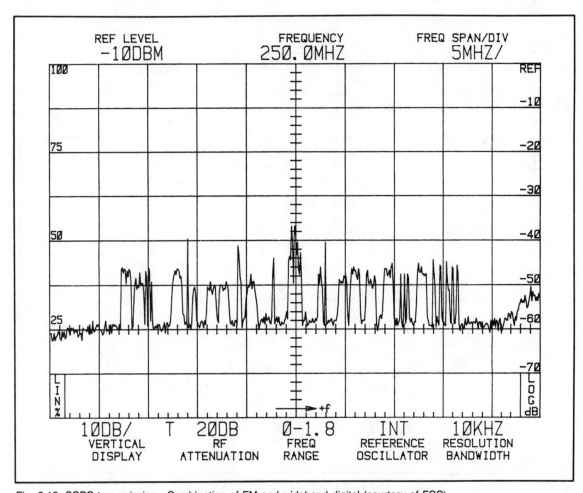

Fig. 3-15. SCPC transmission—Combination of FM and wideband digital (courtesy of FCC).

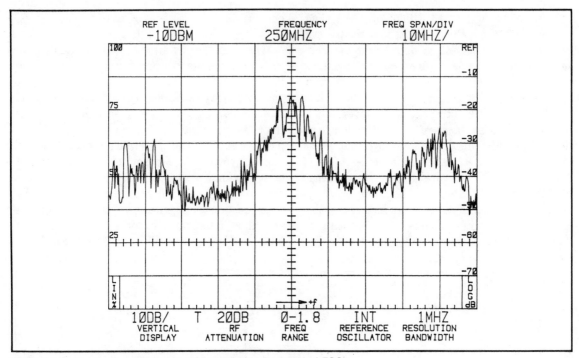

Fig. 3-16. Ordinary video FM baseband transmission (courtesy of FCC).

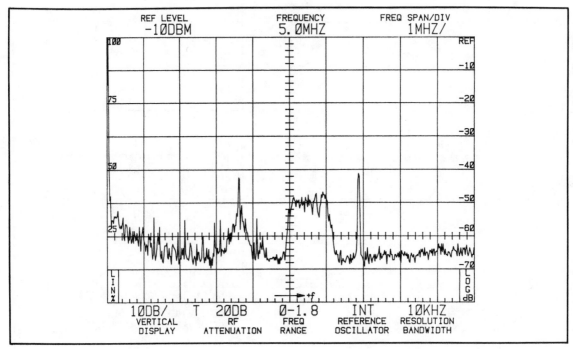

Fig. 3-17. Combination of video, digital, and audio information on a single transponder (courtesy of FCC).

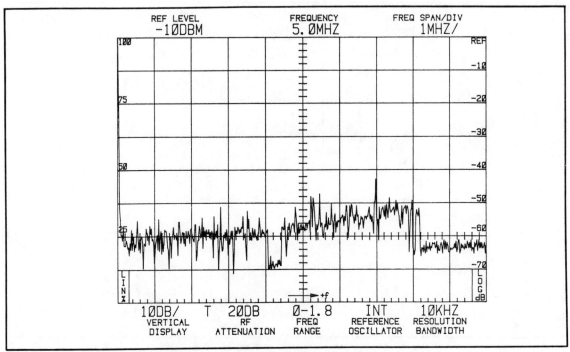

Fig. 3-18. Baseband FDM/FM at 1 MHz/div (courtesy of FCC).

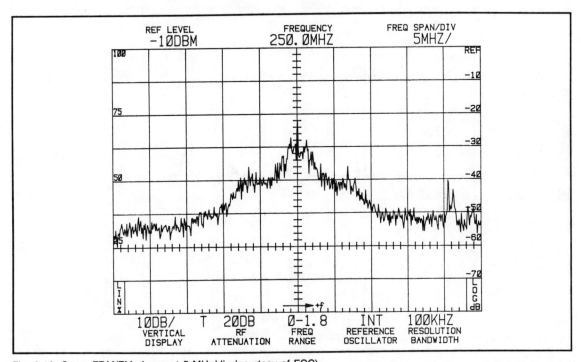

Fig. 3-19. Same FDM/FM shown at 5 MHz/div (courtesy of FCC).

51

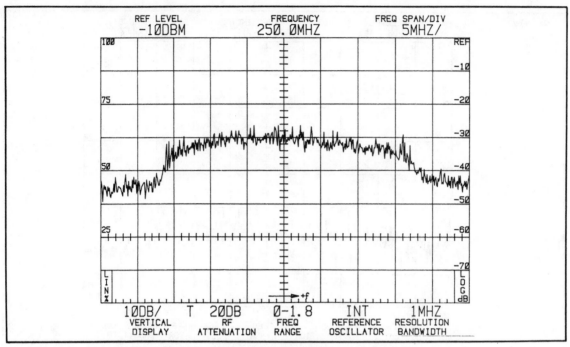

Fig. 3-20. Plain wideband digital, no audio or video (courtesy of FCC).

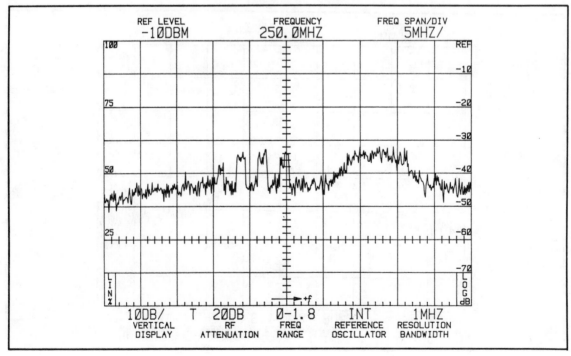

Fig. 3-21. More digital: possibly facsimile on left and digital on right (courtesy of FCC).

COMMENTS

Despite some of the "wise wags" shaking and quaking about crosspole, you pay a great deal more attention to carrier-to-noise, signal amplitudes and generally noisy displays where the carrier is both indistinct and noise levels are high. In-band and reasonable out-of-band interference you can usually defeat, but a noisy, low signal strength group of transponders is virtually hopeless unless your system badly needs tuning. Additional amplifiers may help, but filters must be added, too, for any worthwhile results. So, *beware the noisy signal,* because that's what really makes a lousy picture!

Now let's go VSAT for a bit and look at what commercial enterprise is doing under TVRO's very nose.

VSAT IS BLOOMING

While Ku appeals to urban dwellers because of small-sized terminals, business is possibly more attracted to the medium not only from the standpoint of size, but per-terminal cost is considerably less, and systems may also transmit and receive with proper FCC approbation. True, for the same size reflector, gain at Ku over C band for a 1.2-meter reflector will increase by over 9 dB, but we have to remember that the space loss factor is almost the same: 9.5 dB. Nontheless, with 45-60 W transponder power and these considerably smaller antennas, data and voice capacity has multiplied over Ku band even though some possible outage because of rain may be increased due to higher frequencies in the downlink. But this, of course, may be compensated to a large extent by antenna size and also earth terminal locations and the EIRP they receive. East and west coast regions of CONUS are especially vulnerable to both winter and summer moisture precipitation, as well as increased noise inherent in higher frequency transmissions and equipment resulting from shorter wavelength interference. Therefore, 1.8-meter Ku band receiving antennas are preferred in these areas for data and voice traffic, and even larger radiators for video. So for these reasons and the presently uncluttered orbit slots allocated (but not filled) for Ku, a number of major companies are electing to go the Ku route as rapidly as possible using very small aperture terminals called, for short, VSATs. These include such powers as: Federal Express; Southland Corp. (7-11 stores); the Associated Press; United Press International, Reuters, the stock exchanges; American Satellite Co., and Vitalink Comm., not to mention those who have since entered the market during late 1987 and 1988. Additions already would be: Microstar Networking Services; Comsat Technology Products; AT&T Communications, GTE Spacenet Corp., and Tymnet/McDonnell Douglas Network Services Co., which are all now VSAT competitors. Equatorial Communications, however, plans to stick with C band and has already installed thousands of earth terminals both here and abroad for its business sytems with discreetly downsized equipment.

EQUATORIAL EARTH STATIONS NUMBER IN THE THOUSANDS

Even though we are advertised as TVRO only, it would be a disservice to the satellite industry to pass up Equatorial Communications of Mountain View, California. With well over 30,000 earth stations already shipped and still growing strong, Equatorial provides satellite network services for many great U.S. corporations with vast data communications needs. It is also active in Australia, Brazil and, by now, probably other countries in and out of the hemisphere, including Canada and Hong Kong.

At this writing Equatorial owns 16 satellite transponders; 12 on Galaxy III (93.5° WL) and four on Westar IV (99° WL) that cover CONUS as well as Hawaii, Alaska, Canada, and the Caribbean basin. A $1.2 million order from Australia begins construction of a single "hub" earth station and micro earth stations for that country's interactive send-receive "Q-Net" enabling government department data sharing through its Aussat DOMSAT (domestic satellite) communications. A total of 4,000 micro earth stations are anticipated at an estimated $30 million expenditure. K-200 and other micro earth stations are to be used. Transmissions are by code division multiplexing (Fig. 3-22).

Equatorial's Brazilian enterprise consists of a potential $30 million contract with Victori Comunicacones LTDA, a Brazilian distributor of telecommu-

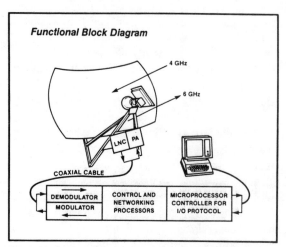

Functional Block Diagram

4 GHz

6 GHz

LNC   PA

COAXIAL CABLE

| DEMODULATOR / MODULATOR | CONTROL AND NETWORKING PROCESSORS | MICROPROCESSOR CONTROLLER FOR I/O PROTOCOL |

Fig. 3-22. Typical C-band receive-transmit commercial station and ancillary equipment (courtesy of Equatorial Communications).

nications equipment who will become the exclusive agent for Equatorial's interactive and point-to-point multipoint networks. Victori will also be licensed to manufacture Equatorial's equipment in Brazil. System users are to lease transponders on Brazil's new C-band satellites recently launched.

In the U.S., Equatorial serves such large companies as Financial Information Trust, Bridge Market Data, and others in financial transaction, process control monitoring, retail point-of-sale, branch office administration, and travel reservation industries. Further, the company has recently announced a $10,000,000 expansion program for new equipment to "support" an additional 20,000 two-way micro earth stations by 1988. Included is a third 11-meter control and master antenna, 2.5×10^6 amperes of additional power, more air conditioning and extra digital and microwave electronics for the larger network. In addition, a master earth station facility will be available in Brooklyn, N.Y. to back up the Mountain View, California facility and serve eastern U.S. traffic.

All this is part of the EquaStar network devoted to terminal-to-host computer and terminal-to-terminal communications with offices in Atlanta, Chicago, Dallas, Denver, Newark and 61 field locations with engineering response times of 4 hours for aid or repairs.

EQUIPMENT

Basic equipment for transmit and receive is the C200 micro earth station, having a reflector 72 inches wide and 42 inches high, and weighing 150 lbs. Cabling is supplied by Belden at maximum run lengths of 300 feet—all for C-band transmit at 6 GHz and receive at 4 GHz. Installation is said to consume less than one day, the antenna requires no ac power and only low dc voltage for the preamplifier and converter. AC, however, is required at the controller, but only 250 watts. The earth station has both UL and FCC approval and meets 2° satellite spacing requirements for T_x and R_x (Fig. 3-23).

Receiving network data at the published rate of 153.6 kilobits/sec., each of these micro earth stations have two basic assemblies: the transmit section contains an upconverter and power amplifier (PA); while the receive section has a low-noise amplifier and frequency downconverter (LNC) with signal leads to the controller of up to 300 ft. of coaxial cable. This controller consists of transmit and receive modems (modulators/demodulators), codec, control circuits, protocol and network processor, status monitor and power supplies.

Master earth stations are 11-meter reflectors with redundant (double) transmitters and receivers, including multiplexing and switching. For point-to-multipoint nets and outbound interactive networks, signals are received from customer data sources, combined, and transmitted by spread-spectrum transmissions to Equatorial's satellite transponders. Frequencies are then downconverted and messages are sent to receiving sites wherever located. In terminal-to-terminal processing, one or more micro earth station signals are amplified and retransmitted to the intended receivers. But in terminal-to-host interactive networks, masters pick up data from micro earth stations and transmit them to customer host computers.

Redundant electronics, constant power supplies and special interference resistant transmissions offer a bit error rate of better than $1:10 \times 10^6$; packet-switching uses variable length packets with error correction; network monitoring and diagnostics provide a network availability of greater than 99.9%; point-to multipoint network capacity ranges

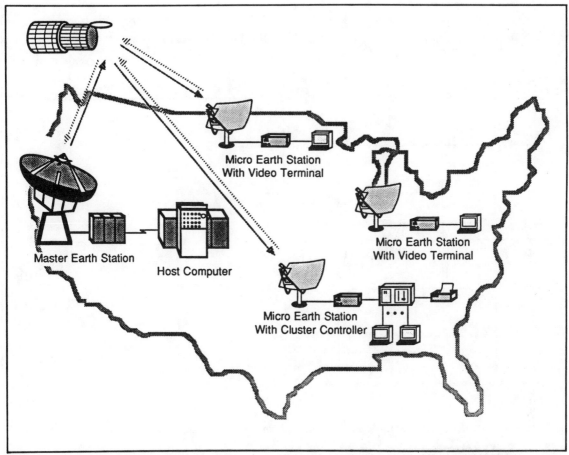

Fig. 3-23. System wide video/data network in U.S. with more stations abroad (courtesy of Equatorial Communications).

from 150 to 19,200 bits/sec.; while shared interactive network transmissions produce up to 153,600 bps/channel outbound and inbound, with micro earth stations 1,2000 bps inbound and 19,200 bps outbound. Each micro earth station identifies with a unique code and receives only those messages intended.

Monitoring facilities include: *Satmon* for transponder measurements and alarms; *Echos* compares customer data traffic to that transmitted; *CMS®* monitors transmissions from host computer to network control; Titan logs summary and status of Equastar network equipment and clearing house for alarms and other monitoring equipment; and *Ciclops* consolidates all monitor data then delivers summary reports and network performance evaluations.

CODE DIVISION MULTIPLEXING

Unlike frequency division multiple access (FDMA) and time division multiple access (TDMA) where specific uplink/downlink frequencies or channels with specific time slots are assigned, code division multiple access offers spread spectrum electronics with satellite power *on* only during micro earth stations transmissions. Typically, some 120 stations operate on a single shared channel at any one time within a bandwidth of about 3 MHz and a bit rate of 1.2 kbits/sec at 1 watt. Above 120 stations, bit error rates increase an order of magnitude for 25 percent overloads, but with no message losses to 50 percent.

Before data transmissions, information spreads to a bandwidth of as much as 2,000 times its origi-

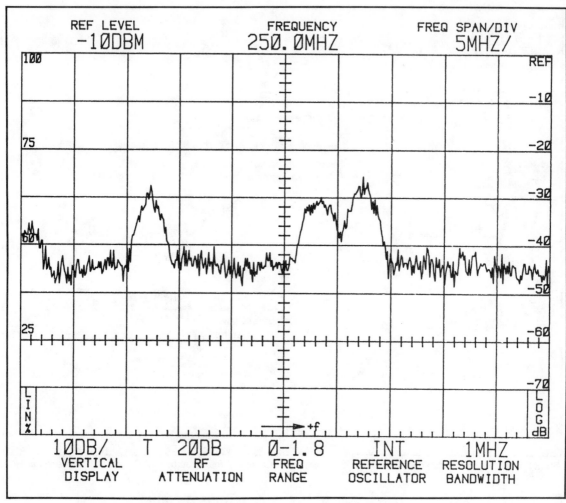

Fig. 3-24. Equatorial's data transmissions (courtesy of FCC).

nal dimensions by encoding each data bit in a binary sequence of thousands of microbits said to be contained in a psuedo-random noise sequence. Receivers decode this information in the same order and resolve it into original message content.

The master station, of course, can access multiple data channels, and then transmits one or more binary phase-shift-keyed (BPSK) carriers at a data rate of 153.6 kilobits per channel, still within the 3 MHz/transponder bandwidth. With reception up to 19.2 kbits/sec, every micro earth station then selects assigned information from the channel, according to specific addresses in the identical spread-spectrum coding (Fig. 3-24).

When transmitting, the micro stations collect information from user terminals, add the necessary coding, and transmit 6 GHz carrier signals to their respective satellites. Such signals are then frequency-translated to 4 GHz carriers and sent to the master station below. Such data streams may be redirected to other sections of the network at any time by the master earth station's packet switch.

Chapter 4

Satellite Receiver Systems and Circuit Analysis

FOR MOST CONSUMERS WITH BETTER SATELLITE systems, we've passed the days of the 120° LNA, followed by a single 4 GHz to 70 MHz "tuner" and downconverter, and advanced to dual heterodyne downconversion systems that take in the entire 500 MHz satellite bandspread making possible multi-receiver independent channel tuning. Fortunately, the same preamplifier gain of some 50 dB (at least) remains, but first i-f conversion is usually centered around 1 GHz, while the second i-f is probably less than half that, depending on the manufacturer. Happily, too, there are relatively few systems that do not use the 950-1450 MHz block conversion frequencies for 500 MHz C- and Ku-band spectrums now fully authorized by the World Administrative Radio Conference (WARC) and its subset, the Regional Administrative Radio Conference (RARC) of the Americas and approved by the Federal Communications Commission (FCC).

Furthermore, just as with combined TV and monitor television sets, TVRO positioners and tuners are becoming largely integrated into a single unit, and have already been augmented to some extent by built-in Video-Cipher decoders for those willing to pay an extra several hundred dollars for the privilege of subscribing to pay satellite television. In addition, the number of *original* equipment TVRO manufacturers in both Canada and the U.S. are stabilizing, with apparently less dependence on Japanese imports, although Toshiba remains a first-class source of earth station electronic products, while some of its lesser Oriental competitors are fading rapidly. All this, plus the inclusion of advanced electronics, more accurate positioners, and slightly better prices for the best systems, offer considerable promise for steady growth in a formerly volatile industry.

TUNING SYSTEMS

This area is the greatest departure from the LNA and single donwconverter days. Early systems had little more than a dozen or so diodes, a few tunable resistors, and somewhat regulated power supplies, much like the early videocassette recorders, but without varactors. As you see in Fig. 4-1 there are 13 diodes supplied with various dc potentials from the arms of 13 voltage-divider potentiometers. When a channel is selected, digital logic IC U1 "strobes" a particular potentiometer and its guide diode, which is then delivered through the U7 amplifier to a 70 MHz i-f board and thence up its coaxial connector to the single-stage downconverter at the antenna (Fig. 4-1).

Unfortunately, early tuning systems were not constructed of the best components, tended to drift, were affected by large temperature swings, and probably radiated considerably more local oscillator frequencies than they should have. Furthermore they were generally noisy, often subject to poor coupling between LNA and downconverter, and the 70 MHz system could be interfered with rather easily from competing television channels in that broad-

cast range. By now, we hope, most have already been replaced with block-down dual converters and C-Ku band compatible receivers. If not, here's a real opportunity for new business since eventual service charges and repeated tuneups could easily offset the cost of superior equipment.

In newer equipment (Fig. 4-2), any receiver may tune any of the (nominal) 24 C-band or currently 16 Ku-band (can be "split" to 32) channels if provided with video inversion for Ku, having the 950 to 1450 MHz spectrum passband. But those receivers having different bandspread frequencies for C and Ku, must have different local oscillators and separate C and Ku inputs. Otherwise, the initial downconverter local oscillator easily serves both via high and low side injections for C and Ku bands, respectively. This does not mean, of course, that i-fs of, say, 910 to 1410 MHz can't do the same thing

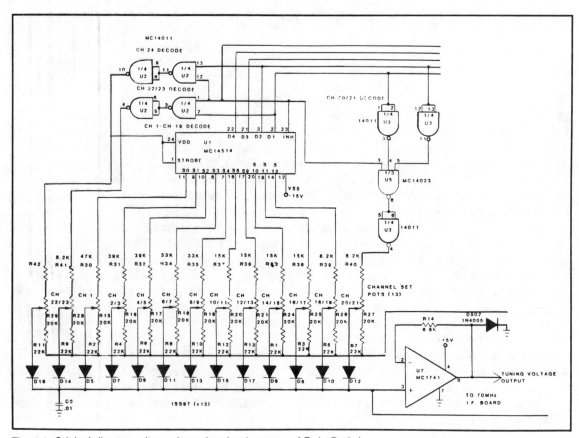

Fig. 4-1. Original discrete voltage channel tuning (courtesy of R. L. Drake).

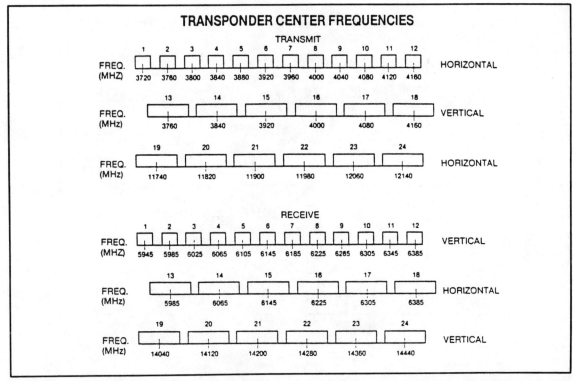

Fig. 4-2. Good example of "hybrid" channel frequencies for C and Ku bands on one satellite (courtesy of GTE Spacenet).

as the 950-1450 MHz variety; they can, but you may have problems with future block downconverters if not manufactured by the *same* company. You also should know that standard transponder bandwidths for C band are 36 MHz, but vary from 36 MHz to 120 MHz for Ku, with nonstandard center frequencies. Therefore, an AFC override with fine tuning may be preferable for Ku and also to compensate for any offset drift at C band, although SBS 3 and RCA's K-1, K-2 and GSTARs 1,2 so far don't require this particular addition nor any correction over many months of continuous access. Manual adjust for the *positioner,* however, is another matter entirely, and we'll talk about that later. The same is true for stereo sound reception, sorry to say.

LOCAL OSCILLATORS AND PLL

Local oscillators, as usual operate at the 2nd i-f *difference above* the initial channel center frequency, in this instance 1833 MHz since the 2nd i-f is 403 MHz. Center tally, therefore, is 1430 MHz for chan-

nel 1. This progresses in odd/even 20 MHz/offset steps all the way "down" to 970 MHz and channel 24. Notice that high channel numbers have the lowest center frequencies due to C band *high side* injection. At Ku band low side injection, channel 1 would become 970 MHz and read correctly if reverse receiver compensation hadn't already taken place. Therefore Ku reads backwards. Then at 403 MHz, the signal is SAW filtered to 30 MHz, preventing adjacent channel interference.

Phase-locked loop tuning now takes over, and here's how it operates. The tunable local oscillator (LO) operates between 686.5 and 916.5 MHz, buffered by × 1 unity gain amplifier with its output divided between the × 2 doubler and the 1/64 prescaler. Two additional unity-gain amplifiers then carry the LO doubled frequency to the mixer at between 1.373 and 1.833 GHz (Fig. 4-3).

In the meantime, the 1/64 prescaler has divided the original oscillator frequency accordingly so that it now becomes 10.727 MHz for channel 24 and

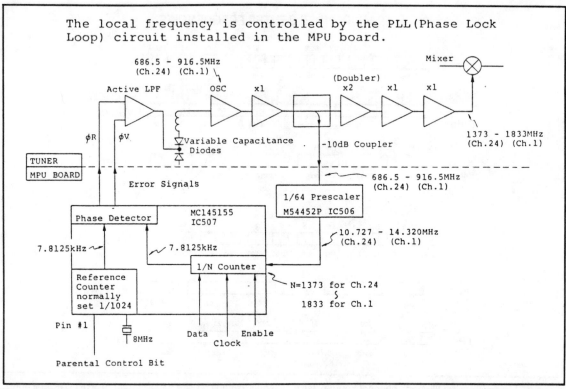

The local frequency is controlled by the PLL (Phase Lock Loop) circuit installed in the MPU board.

Fig. 4-3. Block diagram of PLL, the controlled tracking circuit for all channels (courtesy of M/A-COM and General Instrument Corp.).

14.32 MHz for channel 1 and IC507, the phase-locked loop frequency synthesizer. In the PLL, a 1/N counter further divides this frequency so that 1373 now represents channel 24 and 1833 stands for channel 1, responding to data, clock and enable inputs from other sources. The resulting 7.8125 kilohertz signal is then routed to one portion of the phase detector, while a crystal-controlled 7.8125 kHz signal from the reference counter enters another. This latter frequency results from an 8 MHz crystal-controlled clock that is then divided down by a 1/1024 counter.

Any phase difference is then transmitted to the tuner through an active low-pass filter and corrects the oscillator's frequency through dc-induced capacitative action of varactor diodes. If parental blockout is instituted, the reference counter is offset 1/16 division by an IC508 microprocessor, forcing local oscillator drift to its greatest freerun frequency, totally out of band.

The tuner block produces a maximum gain of 65 dB and is so AGC-controlled it produces a constant 0 dBm output to the following A/V board—A/V standing for audio/video.

FM VIDEO DETECTION

This is often glossed over in most writeups because satellite FM detection not only differs from the usual AM video processing, but also is considerably more complex. Here a phase-lock detector (PLD) with extended static threshold ability is evident, once again comparing any phase error information and returning it to the phase detector for dynamic correction.

In the illustration (Fig. 4-4) you see "suggested" negative-going sync pulses (in the black region to reduce noise), with video riding in the positive region above, described in terms of frequency since there is yet no baseband detection. As FM expands and contracts within the frequency

60

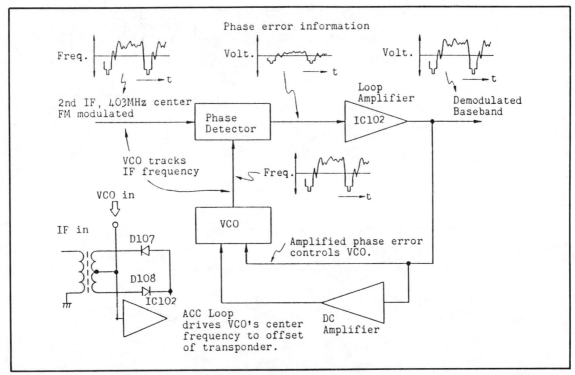

Fig. 4-4. FM video demodulation involves phase-lock detector, VCO and dc amplifier for accurate baseband output (courtesy M/A-COM).

envelope, the phase detector accepts this modulated information within the 403 MHz i-f carrier, which initially routes it to and through the loop amplifier for both feedback to the phase detector and also as completely demodulated baseband (Fig. 4-4).

DETECTION PROCESS

Typically you can consider the phase detector as a transformer-coupled discriminator that produces amplitude variations equal to frequency variations of the input. In this example, diodes are connected in *series* with respect to the centertapped secondary and appear much more like a ratio detector. When both diodes have equally applied voltages their outputs are identical, otherwise they are not. Conduction, of course, occurs on half cycles of the input in conjunction with the VCO input above.

On positive square-wave half cycles from the voltage controlled oscillator, D108 conducts, and on negative half cycles, D107 turns on. Where (Fig.

4-5) equal polarity inputs from the i-f and the VCO coincide, maximum current flows through the affected diode, while lesser matches produce diminished outputs. In this way, in-phase and out-of-phase signals are generated, which result in positive and negative detected averages. Effectively, these averages are the sum of the phase *differences* between the 403 MHz i-f and VCO, with the output also representing any phase-error signals.

Following detection, a differential video amplifier and seven additional transistors constitute IC102, the following loop amplifier, with a frequency range from dc to 8.5 MHz contains both 4.2 MHz video baseband as well as all the audio subcarriers.

Phase errors from the detector are now returned to the voltage-controlled oscillator (VCO) in the form of a control potential to maintain precise i-f phase tracking, thereby producing a linear FM to AM output. The loop amplifier also supplies a separate dc circuit which is actually a dual operational am-

61

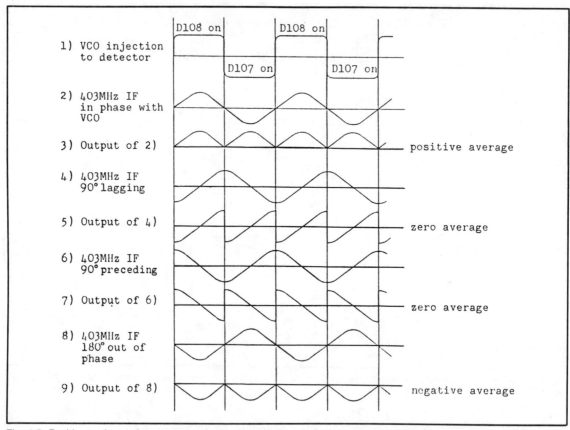

1) VCO injection to detector

D108 on   D108 on

2) 403MHz IF in phase with VCO

D107 on   D107 on

3) Output of 2)   positive average

4) 403MHz IF 90° lagging

5) Output of 4)   zero average

6) 403MHz IF 90° preceding

7) Output of 6)   zero average

8) 403MHz IF 180° out of phase

9) Output of 8)   negative average

Fig. 4-5. Positive and negative average outputs characterize phase detector FM/AM process (courtesy of M/A-COM).

plifier whose function develops automatic centering controls (ACC) for the VCO. Here, only the dc part of the detected FM is amplified by about 60 dB and then returned to the VCO so that it will adequately and automatically track offset transponder frequencies. When adjusted correctly, picture sparkes will be minimum as the noise portion of carrier-to-noise (C/N) reception decreases.

FM AUDIO SELECTION AND DETECTION

Because of the 5-8.5 MHz frequencies involving the audio subcarriers, a similar detection arrangement, at least for error correction, becomes comparable to that used in video. However, actual audio demodulation may be accomplished by discriminators, ratio detectors, quadrature detectors, etc., depending on the quality you may wish. This particular unit, however, has two independent au-

dio tuners identified as master and slave. Each is identical with local oscillator-controlled PLL, mixer, i-f amplifiers, selectable bandwidth filters, and a single IC detector. All this provides monophonic, direct left and right, or matrix L + R and L − R stereophonic sound. In addition, a National Semiconductor LM1894 supplies dynamic noise reduction to produce virtually noise-free audio.

The master tuner has a local oscillator that tunes between 15.68 MHz and 19.22 MHz in 20 kilohertz increments, producing the usual 10.7 MHz audio i-f as it transports the various audio subcarriers (Fig. 4-6). The VCO output is also returned to the divide by 1/N counter in IC507, resulting in 784 for 4.98 MHz to 961 for 8.52 MHz. The microprocessor then converts these counts through its data, enable, and clock inputs to a 20 kHz step signal that is phase-compared with the same frequency output counted

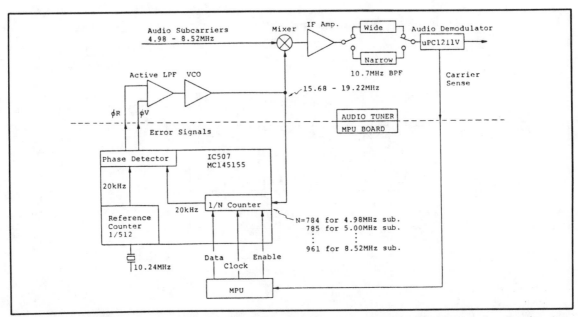

Fig. 4-6. Frequencies of 15.68-19.22 MHz mix with 4.98 to 8.52 MHz to form 10.7 MHz audio i-f with subcarriers (courtesy of M/A-COM).

down by 512 from a 10.24 MHz crystal-controlled reference oscillator. Any difference is then routed as 0 R and 0 V to an active low-pass filter (LFP) and the VCO itself, thereby correcting any out-of-tolerance from the mixer. Corrected audio subcarrier frequencies selected from the control panel and commanded by the microprocessor unit (MPU) continue on via an i-f amplifier through wideband or narrowband bandpass filter(s) and thence to the micro uPC1211V audio demodulator, whose output goes both to the audio circuits and provides carrier sensing for the microprocessor.

During up/down scanning, the microprocessor changes inputs into the PLL in 20 kHz steps at 50-millisecond intervals, completing a single all-frequency scan in about nine seconds. Any subcarrier existing tells the MPU to stop, and detected audio is made available as sound in any one of the three identified modes, amplified and outputted as standard audio via baseband or remodulated at rf for either TV channels 3 or 4, as customary.

AUDIO DEMODULATION

As previously stated, audio detection can take many forms, but today's version is usually an in-

tegrated circuit with peripheral RLC components and dozens to several hundred transistors, resistors, and diodes within. (See Fig. 4-7.) This particular one consists of a voltage stabilizer, quadrature limiter, AFC tuning meter driver, amplifiers, level detectors, signal meter driver, and mute. The actual FM-to-audio processor is a quadrature detector and RLC phase shifter, following a quadrature limiter to remove any residual noise. Usually a differential amplifier receives i-f both in direct and 90° offset phase, then peak detects these voltages forming the traditional ''S'' curve for FM-to-audio recovery. An RC de-emphasis circuit then restores pre-emphasized audio to its original state for further amplification.

In addition to basic audio detection, there is also a muting control for those circuits connected with audio channel selection. They are: S/N cutoff with weak signals, S-curve detuning, and muting for changes in input signal levels.

DYNAMIC NOISE REDUCTION

Developed by National Semiconductor for general audio noise quieting, this LM1894 circuit is now used not only in satellite receivers but high quality television receivers and probably audio receivers

63

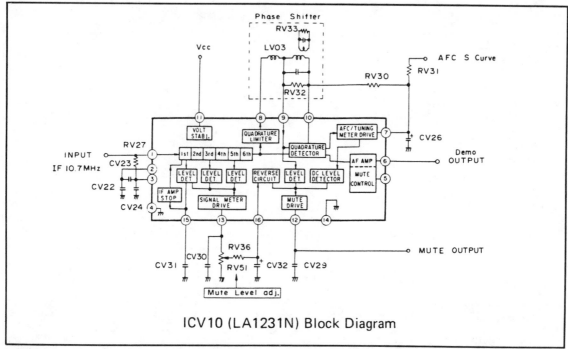

Phase Shifter

ICV10 (LA1231N) Block Diagram

Fig. 4-7. FM video detector block diagram contains many transistors and diodes (courtesy of M/A-COM).

too (Fig. 4-8). It is a single IC of 14 pins and can attenuate high frequency audio noise without disrupting program sound. It has both a main signal input and a bandwidth control path. The main signal enters an FM block followed by an operational amplifier acting as an integrator. The control entry generates a bandwidth control signal that follows the ear's sensitivity to noise as it hears tones. Right and left channels are added together in a summing amplifier. Capacitors between the summing amplifier and peak detector determine frequency weighting. The resulting voltage converts into proportional current reaching the gm blocks, where it develops as a variable bandwidth between 1 kHz and 30 kHz, depending on the frequencies processed. Bandwidth reduction to within 10 percent of minimum value occurs in approximately 60 milliseconds, permitting music passage but preventing audible noise.

THE T6 RECEIVER/POSITIONER

The M/A-COM T6 integrated receiver/positioner has proved a highly successful combination

of good design, proven electronics, and owner conveniences, contributing to a single, programmable unit internally handling all but the external LNB electronics skew, and actuator. Controlled by three microprocessors and numerous digital integrated circuits, the system, nontheless, commands both internal and external operations so that complete system control is maintained either by manual or remote control from a single receiver/positioner location—a considerable advance and convenience over nonintegrated separates whose dubious performance in the past has not always been a credit to the TVRO industry.

Factory preset for all 24 normal C-band channels, an *additional* 8 channels (25 through 32) are also programmable for Ku-more, also, if you wish to delete any of the original 24. In sum total, with the T6 there are 32 programmable channels available for insertion into memory.

As you might expect, all three of these microprocessors (Fig. 4-9) "talk" to one another via a communications line and are "influenced" in their decisions by a data bus, front panel enabling

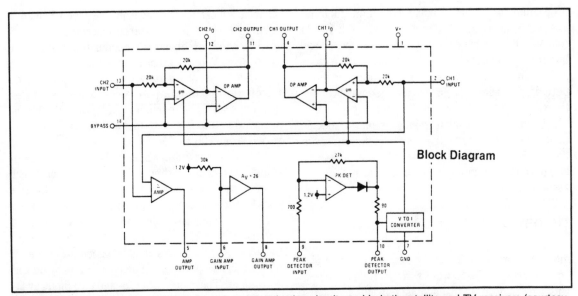

Block Diagram

Fig. 4-8. The LM1894 highly regarded dynamic noise reduction circuit used in both satellite and TV receivers (courtesy of National Semiconductor).

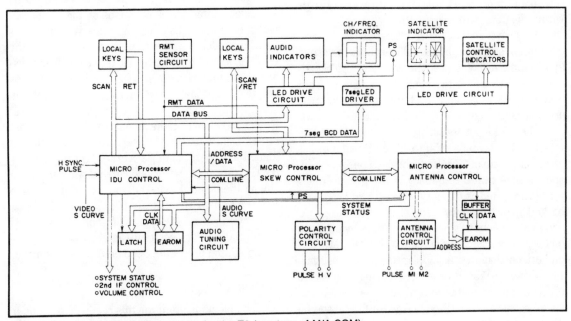

Fig. 4-9. The three control microcessors for the T6 (courtesy of M/A-COM).

keys, and the various tuning circuits. The Indoor Unit (IDU) is responsible for channel selection, memory, scan, audio tuning and bandwidth, local keys, PS control and C/Ku band selection. The Skew

microprocessor maintains proper skew, video switching output, auto polarity, communications, local keys, and favorite channel selection. And the antenna μP, sets azimuth limits, selects satellites and programming, actuator pulse counting, memory lock, error messages, and realignment. An EAROM (electrically alterable read-only memory) clocked and buffered, accepts antenna control satellite positions and retains them (unless discharged) for an indefinite period, providing access to the geosynchronous translators 22.3 kilomiles in the sky.

In effect, each microprocessor has a specific (and different) duty within the equipment, even though each is linked to the other by a well-defined bus permitting a common language and responsive association.

THEORY OF OPERATION

Now that you understand the "shakers and movers" portion of this satellite combo receiver and positioner, it's time to work through the entire unit with a block diagram that at least explains the signal flow since it contains some 37 integrated circuits and a number of discrete semiconductors which, on a schematic, represents little more than a very large wiring diagram with many pathways.

As always, receiver characteristics often tell an interesting story and are usually accurate if issued by a reliable manufacturer. Sometimes, the big advertisers do stretch the absolute truth a bit, but they're quickly found out in a hurry, especially if the product isn't quality.

The T6's input sensitivity is specified from −50 to −20 dBm from the 950 to 1450 MHz input, has an i-f bandwidth of 27 MHz (probably conservative), and a final i-f center frequency of 140 MHz. Tuning modes are listed as memory, carrier, and sync lock, backed up by frequency scan. The first two use AFC and sync detection, while sync lock is obvious, and on frequency scan, sync detection occurs alternately on horizontal and vertical polarities. The noise factor is given as 15 dB or less, with carrier-to-noise (C/N) of approximately 8.5 dB or less. Video and audio signal-to-noise (S/N) are quoted at 50 and 60 dB, respectively.

Video response extends from 30 Hz to 4.2 MHz from its baseband output, while audio ranges between 30 Hz and 15 kHz, with selectable bandwidths of 150 kHz or 330 kHz, and audio levels are ± 2.5 dB about 0 dB for signals with 75 kHz deviation.

Tunable subcarriers are available between 5 and 8.5 MHz to receive mono, stereo discrete, or stereo matrix, and if baseband is remodulated, the output is 66 dB, μV on channel 3 or 4.

Rotor polarizer drive amounts to + 5 Vdc reinforced with 500 mA for polar adjustments and/or frequency scan. The pulse to the polarizer also is specified at 0 to 5 V peak (ac) and its width may be varied from 700 to 2500 μsec.

Antenna positioner pulses also swing between 0 and 5 volts for either a reed or an Hall-Effect switch, and there is a positive 5 V supply for the Hall-Effect transistor. The isolated motor drive (M1-M2) is supplied ±36 Vdc, with drive currents *not* more than 5 amperes. Hookups for Warner, Saginaw, and Transmissions type actuators are all detailed in an operator's manual accompanying the equipment. There are both pre- and final-limits available to prevent linear actuator over-extension problems or damage to their shafts (Fig. 4-10).

Hookups for these different actuators, polarizer, and video switch are all contained on the single omnibus illustration that even includes various tables detailing specific connections from the IUD to the OUD (indoor-outdoor) portions of the combined system. Note that wire sizes, colors, and terminal strips are all labeled and there should be no difficulty in attaching appropriate wires to designated contacts. However, when or if the actuator should move east rather than west, or vice versa, instead of the intended direction, simply reverse the red/white 14 AWG motor drive wires and current will once again flow in the desired loop the way you want. Pulses and/or other drive controls take care of the rest; meaning the stop, start, and duration for each portion of the satellite position search. And once programmed, the procedure becomes totally automatic.

BLOCK DIAGRAM

The block diagram for this receiver/positioner seems simple enough at first glance, but it is somewhat more formidable when viewed in closer detail (Fig. 4-11). Some of the special circuits we have already discussed, but there is considerably more in this signal flow drawing that bears further examination. For example, there are mixers, surface-wave

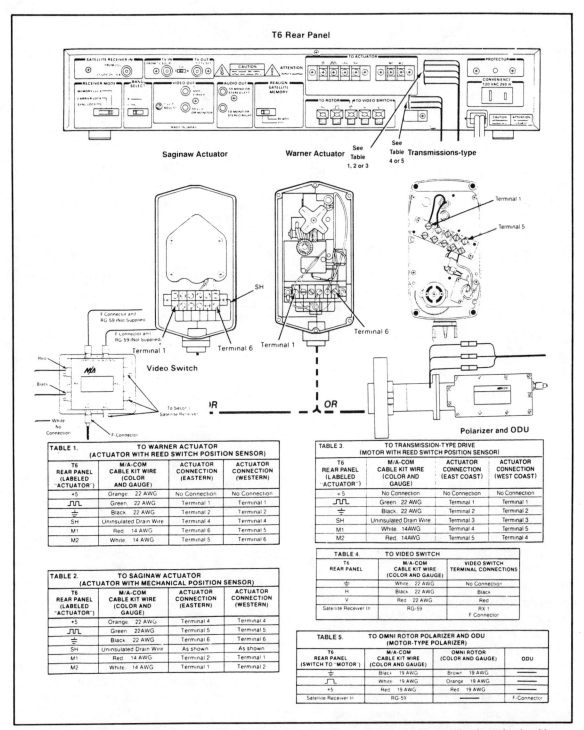

T6 Rear Panel

Saginaw Actuator   Warner Actuator   See Table 1, 2 or 3   See Table 4 or 5   Transmissions-type

Video Switch

Polarizer and ODU

TABLE 1.	TO WARNER ACTUATOR (ACTUATOR WITH REED SWITCH POSITION SENSOR)		
T6 REAR PANEL (LABELED "ACTUATOR")	M/A-COM CABLE KIT WIRE (COLOR AND GAUGE)	ACTUATOR CONNECTION (EASTERN)	ACTUATOR CONNECTION (WESTERN)
+5	Orange 22 AWG	No Connection	No Connection
⎍	Green 22 AWG	Terminal 1	Terminal 1
⏚	Black 22 AWG	Terminal 2	Terminal 2
SH	Uninsulated Drain Wire	Terminal 4	Terminal 4
M1	Red 14 AWG	Terminal 6	Terminal 5
M2	White 14 AWG	Terminal 5	Terminal 6

TABLE 2.	TO SAGINAW ACTUATOR (ACTUATOR WITH MECHANICAL POSITION SENSOR)		
T6 REAR PANEL (LABELED "ACTUATOR")	M/A-COM CABLE KIT WIRE (COLOR AND GAUGE)	ACTUATOR CONNECTION (EASTERN)	ACTUATOR CONNECTION (WESTERN)
+5	Orange 22 AWG	Terminal 4	Terminal 4
⎍	Green 22 AWG	Terminal 5	Terminal 5
⏚	Black 22 AWG	Terminal 6	Terminal 6
SH	Uninsulated Drain Wire	As shown	As shown
M1	Red 14 AWG	Terminal 2	Terminal 1
M2	White 14 AWG	Terminal 1	Terminal 2

TABLE 3.	TO TRANSMISSION-TYPE DRIVE (MOTOR WITH REED SWITCH POSITION SENSOR)		
T6 REAR PANEL (LABELED "ACTUATOR")	M/A-COM CABLE KIT WIRE (COLOR AND GAUGE)	ACTUATOR CONNECTION (EAST COAST)	ACTUATOR CONNECTION (WEST COAST)
+5	No Connection	No Connection	No Connection
⎍	Green 22 AWG	Terminal 1	Terminal 1
⏚	Black 22 AWG	Terminal 2	Terminal 2
SH	Uninsulated Drain Wire	Terminal 3	Terminal 3
M1	White 14 AWG	Terminal 4	Terminal 5
M2	Red 14 AWG	Terminal 5	Terminal 4

TABLE 4.	TO VIDEO SWITCH	
T6 REAR PANEL	M/A-COM CABLE KIT WIRE (COLOR AND GAUGE)	VIDEO SWITCH TERMINAL CONNECTIONS
⏚	White 22 AWG	No Connection
H	Black 22 AWG	Black
V	Red 22 AWG	Red
Satellite Receiver In	RG-59	RX 1 F Connector

TABLE 5.	TO OMNI ROTOR POLARIZER AND ODU (MOTOR-TYPE POLARIZER)		
T6 REAR PANEL (SWITCH TO "MOTOR")	M/A-COM CABLE KIT WIRE (COLOR AND GAUGE)	OMNI ROTOR (COLOR AND GAUGE)	ODU
⏚	Black 19 AWG	Brown 19 AWG	——
⎍	White 19 AWG	Orange 19 AWG	——
+5	Red 19 AWG	Red 19 AWG	——
Satellite Receiver In	RG-59		F-Connector

Fig. 4-10. Rear panel hookups include polarizer, video switch, actuator and motor for T6 combined receiver/positioner (courtesy of M/A-COM).

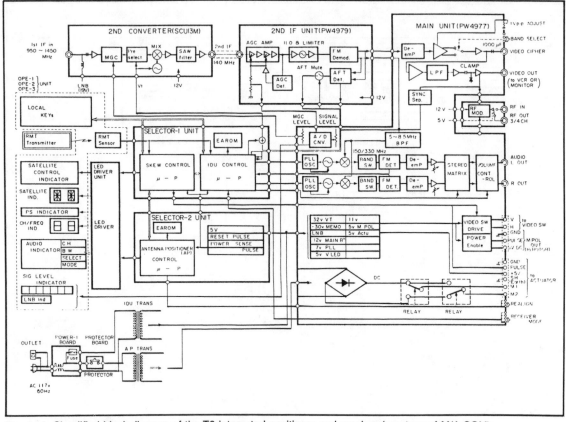

Fig. 4-11. Simplified block diagram of the T6 integrated positioner and receiver (courtesy of M/A-COM).

acoustical filters, AFT and AGC circuits, band-switches, stereo modes and controls, the power supplies, and the various outputs.

Readily apparent are the remote transmitter, control indicators, LED drivers, skew and IDU controls, as well as the antenna positioner electronics, and the second i-f unit. By the time signals reach the main unit, they have been FM detected, and are already supplying automatic fine tuning and automatic gain control. Of course, being FM, both video and audio higher frequencies have been de-emphasized and filtered and sync separation is about to occur.

For the video portion, low-pass filtering and an electronic clamp clean up the wideband composite output with its multiple subcarriers, while the detector's audio output goes directly to a bandpass filter limiting frequencies there to between 5 and 8.5 MHz. Observe also that there are two sets of band

switches, two FM detectors, and one stereo matrix that will reproduce both types of stereo sound.

The Selector unit below contains skew and positioner controls and the various pulse and operating voltage supplies for azimuth reflector aiming. Other than the power supplies, which we'll detail later, that's about the block diagram reading, at least from a signal-flow standpoint, accompanied by a few additional insights for extra interest. We're now ready to become specific once again.

THE FRONT END (Fig. 4-12)

The front end is an old television nomenclature that remains applicable to current satellite receivers since all tuning and initial filtering is done in the 2nd converter (Fig. 4-12), the first set of stages following block downconversion between 950 and 1450 MHz (for most receivers). Initially there is the usual

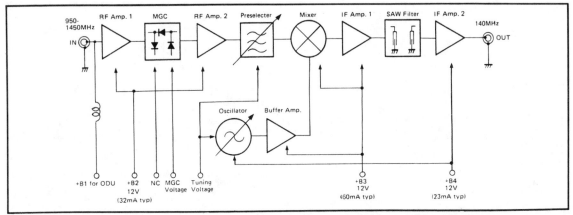

Fig. 4-12. The second converter and transponder tuning "frontend" of the T6 (courtesy of M/A-COM).

rf amplification, followed by a set of PIN diodes in a double-tuned circuit designed to reject image frequencies within oscillator voltage ranges. Tuning is dependent on an AGC *2* voltage ranging between 0 and 12 volts, which varies directly with that of the 3-25 V tuning voltage applied to the local oscillator and used to select various transponders as they are accessed. B + for ODU, of course, is the dc supply for the LNB at the reflector feed; B2 is another regulated supply for the rf; and B3 furnishes operating voltage for the i-fs.

After dual amplification and requisite attenuation and image rejection, the oscillator receives tuning voltages from the IDU microprocessor and its output is mixed with that of 950-1450 MHz preselector inputs from the LNB. Transponder channels are then selected within the bandpass of the resulting i-f which has now been heterodyned to 140 MHz center frequency. The product is amplified, bandpass-limited by a surface wave acoustical (SAW) filter, and amplified once more for the 140 MHz composite output, whcih is now the resulting final receiver intermediate frequency carrier.

I-F, AGC, AND DETECTION

These are contained in the 2nd i-f circuit block, which develops automatic fine tuning, signal levels, video output, and further signal processing. Following i-f amplifier No. *2*, video levels are detected and returned to a dc amplifier, riding continuous gain on both gain control amplifiers 1 and 2 at their transis-

tor bases, which is called forward AGC since large inputs increase through-current lowering their collector (and therefore signal) outputs and decreasing gain. Lesser signals reduce forward bias and therefore increase transistor amplifier signal output. Reverse AGC would have positive potentials applied to the emitters of NPN transistors, *reducing* output by limiting current flow. See Fig. 4-13. And even though forward biasing may affect input impedances and drive some transistors rather hard, this method is commonplace and often preferred since possible cutoff is unlikely, as may occur with reverse bias in unusual circumstances.

AGC is designed for a 140 MHz i-f at a bandwidth of 27 MHz between − 50 and − 20 dBm, and it also drives the signal level meter on the front panel.

Injection-locked oscillator Q106 and tunable coil L103 operate synchronously with input signal frequencies, and free-running frequency adjusted to approximately 140 MHz. According to M/A-COM, it then becomes both a limiter and tracking filter with narrowed beamwidth and output of some − 16 dBm into a 50-ohm load. The two cross-coupled diodes in Q106's base-collector electrodes are, of course the limiters, with L103 serving as the tuning element. The following guide diodes are center biased, passing only desirable signals to the following i-f and driver amplifiers and on into the video demodulator.

Although this type of detector has been previously described at the beginning of the chapter, we'll

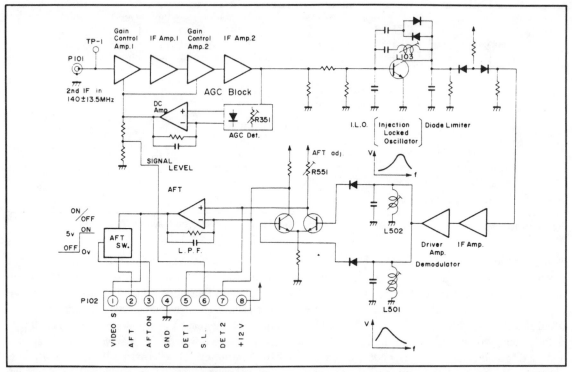

Fig. 4-13. Control voltages such as AGC and AFT are generated in the 2nd i-f followed by video detection (courtesy of M/A-COM).

add a few more pertinent details since it is slightly different as shown but adheres to the identical principles. Just like the Foster-Seeley discriminator, one input through the L502LC tuned circuit and diode is tuned to a frequency slightly higher than the carrier and the other input via L501. The capacitor and diode is tuned lower than the carrier. The resulting output into the differential amplifier becomes what is know as an "S" curve, but behaves actually more like a ramp with curved tails top and bottom. If the frequency deviation into such a circuit has an appropriately limited range, the rectified output potential approximates that of the oncoming FM. The circuit, of course, delivers a zero output when the instantaneous input equals that of the carrier, thereafter delivering a more positive or negative output as deviation increases or decreases.

Such well-designed circuits are quite linear, with this one swinging between 95 and 185 MHz at either S-curve ends. Outputs of the following differential amplifier are connected in "push-pull" to a

succeeding amplifier and its low-pass filter, then on to the off/on automatic fine tuning switch and also to the video signal level "S" connection at pin 1 of P102. AFT final output emerges through pins 2 or 3, either on or off.

Video S is then routed to the IDU microprocessor for further control operations, while composite video takes two paths: DET 2 goes directly to several buffers, drivers and differential amplifiers where, with all subcarriers, it eventually appears at the composite (video cipher) output at the chassis rear approximately 6 MHz wide. But it also is routed through heavy filtering and a 5-transistor clamp and drive circuit to remove both subcarriers and the carrier-spreading factor required by the FCC to prevent adjacent carrier interference when normal modulation ceases. This output, then, is suitable for baseband video at a minimum bandpass of 4.2 MHz, including vertical and horizontal sync as well as color burst, all of which is then coupled to the rf modulator or regular sync circuits in the T6 receiver. DET

1, on the other hand, couples directly to a highly restrictive bandpass filter and thence into dual sets of audio detectors required for stereo. Video polarity reversal is also available for the Ku band switch.

AUDIO DETECTION PROCESS

Preset audio frequencies normally occur at 6.2 and 6.8 MHz, but must be tunable for any offset subcarriers that may be arbitrarily inserted, deliberately or otherwise. Usually, however, most audio is satcast over the 6.8 MHz subcarrier, with discrete stereo and matrix subcarriers tunable where required. See Fig. 4-14.

DET 1, therefore, delivers positive-going composite video-audio to the 5-8.5 MHz bandpass filter, followed by dual 10.7 MHz sound carrier bandswitching and the two FM phase-locked oscillators, all video having been securely filtered out.

The 10.7 MHz i-f results from mixing the audio subcarrier with the local oscillator, and is the difference between the two frequencies since LO operates between 15.7 MHz and 19.2 MHz. Bandswitching simply amounts to audio bandwidth selection between 150 or 330 kHz, both of which are fixed frequencies. PLL control originates from the IDU

microprocessor, subject to operator commands.

The two audio detectors appear to be conventional quadrature demodulators originally developed in the days of the vacuum tube but modified for semiconductor usage so that differential amplifiers and switches fully detect audio information from the i-f carrier. Another method used in the U.S., especially by RCA, is differential peak detection, which is also accomplished with differential amplifiers and produces much the same results.

Once the carrier has been stripped from incoming audio, originator uplink high frequencies are de-emphasized and the two channels (if stereo) proceed to the matrix for stereo recombination. From there they pass through a volume control and then on/off muting, if and when required. Muting pulses from the IUD can cancel audio outputs whenever selected by the system operator.

POWER SUPPLIES

The final circuit description for the T6 involves its several power supplies and their interesting origins. Once again we'll use a block diagram to illustrate, sparing you some of the filter and routine

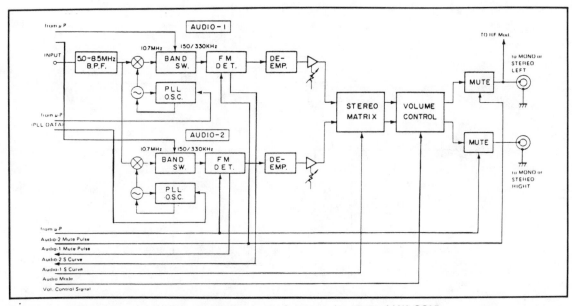

Fig. 4-14. A block diagram of the T6's dual audio circuits for stereo (courtesy of M/A-COM).

reference details generally known to most technical people in the industry. You must remember, however, that this single power supply delivers generally regulated direct current (dc) to *both* the receiver and positioner, contains two power transformers, one having a 2-A ac circuit breaker and the other a 1-A ordinary glass encapsulated metal element. At 120 Vac, this means that the positioner could draw in excess of 200 watts—it does supply the 36 volts for the actuator and various relays—and the other as much as 100 watts for the receiver and LNB. You should therefore be prepared for an ac current drain of as much as 3 amperes anticipating the usual surge on startup (Fig. 4-15).

Although there is only half wave and full wave rectification for the 22-30-volt dc sources, the other three dc units are served by full-wave bridge rectifiers, delivering substantial outputs and maximum current for everything else, including the highly regualted 19.4-volt LNB source. A number of neon and other signal lamps establish that various supplies are operating. All dc regulators consist of similar discrete transistor units having reference zeners, feedback samplings and base current changes to pass transistors to maintain the correct output voltage. In such arrangements, current fluctuates but voltage should remain relatively constant, probably within 1 or 2 percent. Additional fusable resistors are also found in the 19-V and 12-V regulators.

The diagram as shown is reasonably explanatory and offers a good guide to the various sources and the circuits they serve. Whenever troubleshooting some portion of the receiver or positioner that has more than a single stage affected, always suspect a power supply and measure its potential immediately! Hardware and semiconductors will absolutely not operate without the necessary operating sources. For the actuator, M1/M2 and the +5V supplies are always suspects if the reflector won't move; unless, of course, its linear shaft is bent

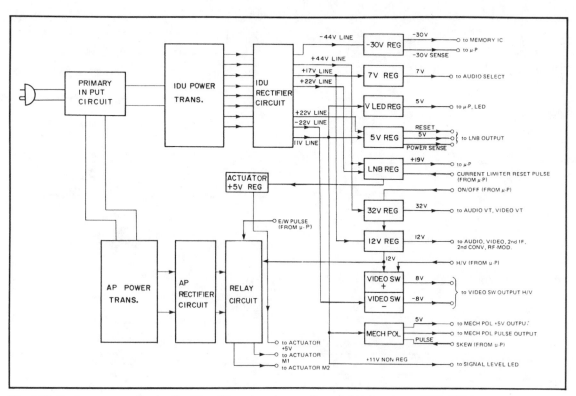

Fig. 4-15. Dual power supplies for the T6 positioner/receiver— all regulated (courtesy of M/A-COM).

or a worm gear in the horizon-to-horizon mount has broken.

ZS-4000 RECEIVER/POSITIONER

Marketed by Zenith but still manufactured by Japan's Toshiba (and very similar to the M/A-COM T6 just described) this satellite receiver/positioner combination does most of the same things equally well but its service manual has certain descriptive material not included with its competition, which may add just enough additional topics to neatly ice the electrical cake. We note immediately that this one uses a 24-V, 3.5-A nominal motor power (M1,M2) supply for the actuator and + 5 V for a Hall or reed switch sensor. Of course it has a video reversal polarity switch for C and Ku bands, along with the usual 8.5 MHz audio and 4.2 MHz video bandwidths. The second i-f frequency remains filtered at 27 MHz, usually at −3dB down. Audio may be narrow or broad banded at either 150 kHz or 330 kHz, with frequency response between 30 Hz and 15 kHz. On Zenith's remote control, however, there is fine tuning for channels as well as for antenna E or W incremental movement in the Auto mode. However, satellite locations, polarity, skew, and reflector E and W limits must be stored in memory from the receiver only, not the remote tuner. But once you have mentally fixed locations of the various audio, bandwidth, channel, and audio mode indicators, along with overall satellite location programming, you should feel right at home with a very responsive and automated system.

PLL TUNER UNIT

Part of the frequency synthesizer, the phase-locked loop portion consists of a wideband preamplifier, a divide-by-two high speed prescaler, and a crystal-controlled Colpitts oscillator (Fig. 4-16). The PLL IC (by itself) has a wideband amplifier, divide-by-8 prescaler, a programmable counter containing a ÷ 12 reference counter, phase detector and charge pump. A three-line input receives channel data in 14-bit segments from the IUD microprocessor.

In operation, the entire channel selector is made up of a non-volatile memory, audio PLLs, channel PLLs, digital and LED indicator circuits. As you can see, there is a large, central 64-pin CMOS (Fig. 4-17) microprocessor with two crystal-control circuits, the antenna positioner microprocessor, readouts, 16-segment LEDs, and the dual-circuit audio load pulse pair at the lower right with data output. Dual buses permit constant information flow with the antenna positioner and also memory storage for the various satellite programmed positons. Other services include those for audio mute, bandwidth, mode, and audio volume. Crystal controls at pins 18-19 and 21-22 have frequencies of 4 MHz and 32.768 kHz, respectively.

Output of the voltage-controlled oscillator is first prescaled by 1/16, then again to 1/(32M + S) in the programmable counter—M and S being integral numbers in the programmable counter's frequency divison. This enables the microprocessor to calculate the value (Fig. 4-18) of M and S so it can be com-

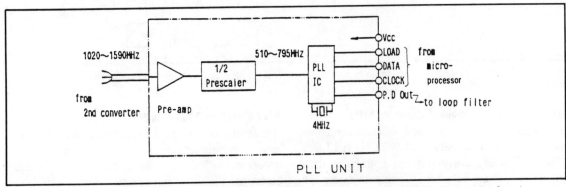

Fig. 4-16. The ZS-4000's phase-locked loop oscillator frequency control (courtesy of Zenith Electronics Corp.).

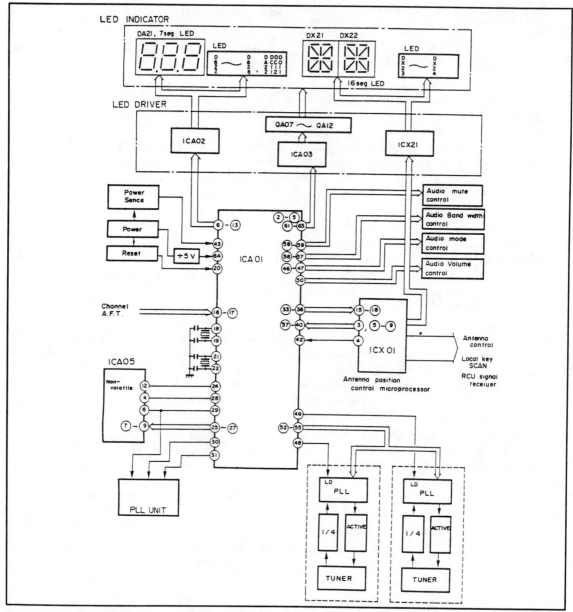

Fig. 4-17. The complete channel selector in block diagram—all controlled by ICA01 (IUD) microprocessor (courtesy of Zenith Electronics Corp.).

pared with 1/512 divided down 4 MHz crystal-controlled oscillator, as the local oscillator continues operating somewhere between 1.085 GHz and 1.620 GHz at C band. Correct tuning voltage is then produced by phase detector D/A output causing the VCO to track accordingly.

ANTENNA POSITIONER

Zenith also offers a significant insight into the antenna positioner and its operations, along with an excellent block diagram supporting the listed data behind it. We'll try and interpret (Fig. 4-19).

The ICXO1 microprocessor responsible for all

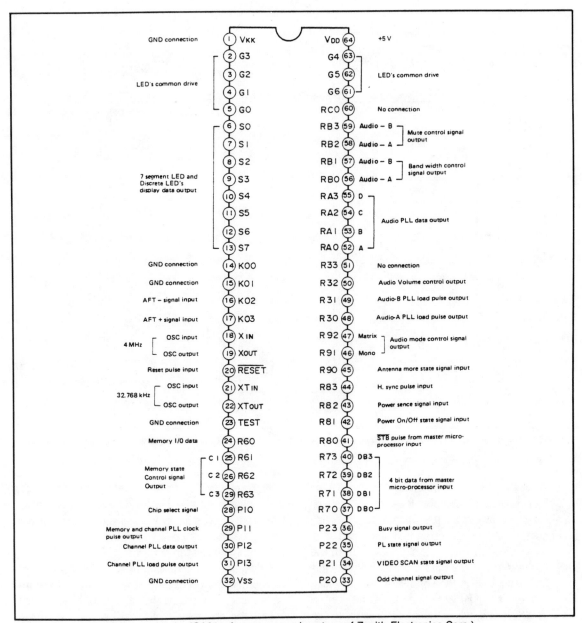

GND connection	① Vκκ	Vᴅᴅ ⑥₄	+5 V		
	② G3	G4 ⑥₃			
	③ G2	G5 ⑥₂	LED's common drive		
LED's common drive	④ G1	G6 ⑥₁			
	⑤ G0	RC0 ⑥₀	No connection		
	⑥ S0	RB3 ⑤₉	Audio – B	Mute control signal output	
	⑦ S1	RB2 ⑤₈	Audio – A		
	⑧ S2	RB1 ⑤₇	Audio – B	Band width control signal output	
	⑨ S3	RB0 ⑤₆	Audio – A		
7 segment LED and Discrete LED's display data output	⑩ S4	RA3 ⑤₅	D		
	⑪ S5	RA2 ⑤₄	C	Audio PLL data output	
	⑫ S6	RA1 ⑤₃	B		
	⑬ S7	RA0 ⑤₂	A		
GND connection	⑭ K00	R33 ⑤₁	No connection		
GND connection	⑮ K01	R32 ⑤₀	Audio Volume control output		
AFT – signal input	⑯ K02	R31 ④₉	Audio-B PLL load pulse output		
AFT + signal input	⑰ K03	R30 ④₈	Audio-A PLL load pulse output		
OSC input 4 MHz	⑱ X IN	R92 ④₇	Matrix	Audio mode control signal output	
OSC output	⑲ XOUT	R91 ④₆	Mono		
Reset pulse input	⑳ RESET	R90 ④₅	Antenna more state signal input		
OSC input 32.768 kHz	㉑ XT IN	R83 ④₄	H. sync pulse input		
OSC output	㉒ XTOUT	R82 ④₃	Power sence signal input		
GND connection	㉓ TEST	R81 ④₂	Power On/Off state signal input		
Memory I/O data	㉔ R60	R80 ④₁	STB pulse from master micro-processor input		
C 1	㉕ R61	R73 ④₀	DB3		
Memory state Control signal Output C 2	㉖ R62	R72 ③₉	DB2	4 bit data from master micro-processor input	
C 3	㉗ R63	R71 ③₈	DB1		
Chip select signal	㉘ PI0	R70 ③₇	DB0		
Memory and channel PLL clock pulse output	㉙ PI1	P23 ③₆	Busy signal output		
Channel PLL data output	㉚ PI2	P22 ③₅	PL state signal output		
Channel PLL load pulse output	㉛ PI3	P21 ③₄	VIDEO SCAN state signal output		
GND connection	㉜ Vss	P20 ③₃	Odd channel signal output		

Fig. 4-18. Functional pinouts for the ICA01 microprocessor (courtesy of Zenith Electronics Corp.).

this is a 64-pin shrink CMOS type that contains the antenna positioner control, electrical and mechanical polarizer, LED readouts, decoder remote control and local keys, communication bus, and external program memory. Coupled to it is a non-volatile memory storing satellite positions, actuator limits,

skew and format, priority view information, volume, power on/off and auto/manual response for azimuth positioning.

As you can see, microprocessor ICX01 operates with two demultiplexers. One is to decode phase gating and read/write instructions, and the

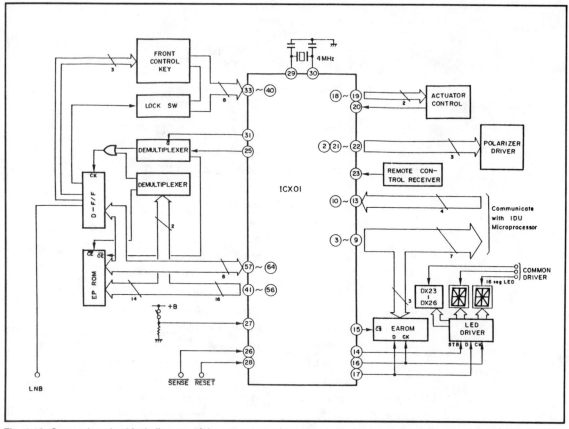

Fig. 4-19. Comprehensive block diagram of the antenna positioner and allied subsystems (courtesy of Zenith Electronics Corp.).

other to access the various memory addresses from 0 to 15. This latter demultiplexer as well as the pins 41 through 56 bus from the microprocessor also reaches the electrically programmable read only memory (EPROM), as do the 8 data bits from the microprocessor and the data flip-flop circuit. Outputs from the D-F/F then proceed to the block downconverter (LNB) as well as the front control key and lock switch, which then processes these signals as Key returns between 0 and 7 bits to pins 33—40 in ICXO1. Power sense and reset commands are also received by the processor through pins 26 and 28, with processor mode source voltage entering via pin 27. Demultiplexer commands are shown OR-gated into the data flip-flops (Fig. 4-20).

Atop the ICXO1, the 4-MHz crystal clock connections are obvious, while motor controls for the

actuator exit from pins 18 and 19, as return *counting* pulses are received at pin 20. Skew outputs originate from pin 2, polarity vertical and horizontal from pin 21 and another skew from pin 22. Remote control commands enter pin 23.

Two-way communications with the Indoor Unit microprocessor occur between pins 3 and 13 and include mute, power, strobe, four data bits, a busy signal, odd channel, scan and PL. The first three commands and four data bits also reach the electrically addressable read only memory (EAROM), as do data and clock pulses from pins 16 and 17, which also are received by the LED display drivers energizing the 16-segment LEDs, in addition to a strobe pulse from pin 14.

To aid in further understanding these microprocessor actions, we note the pin functions of the

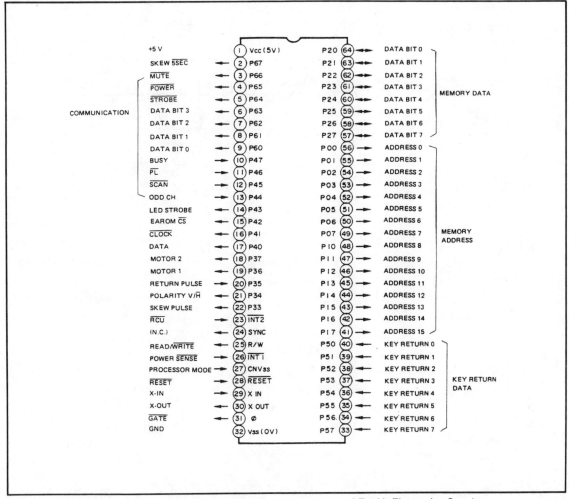

Fig. 4-20. The ICX01 LSI IC with complete functional pinouts (courtesy of Zenith Electronics Corp.).

ICXO1 microprocessor so you'll have this information and also include the actuator and polarizer timing charts (Fig. 4-21). So as we know it, this should pretty well wrap up the total information on these Toshiba-built receiver-positioners. We hope you'll find the contents considerably more inclusive than that heretofore available.

One additional note and/or observation. Because of the 0.25° minimum accuracy tuning requirement for the actuators, the horizon-to-horizon manufacturers are favoring reed switches and potentiometers over other options, considering that these two are the best choices (at least for now) over other competition. Reed switches, of course, may double the number of internal counting magnets and derive double resolution well within Ku-band azimuth tuning requirements. We have yet to check a name-brand linear with enough accuracy to do the same.

The 24-volt positioner/actuator systems do seem a mite slow in arc traverse and have trouble pushing heavy reflectors. On the other hand, a 30-V system *into* load with approximately 4 amperes of current, seems to do rather well under ordinary circumstances. Underwriters Labs or not, we still prefer and endorse the 36-V, 4-A systems generally accepted throughout the industry.

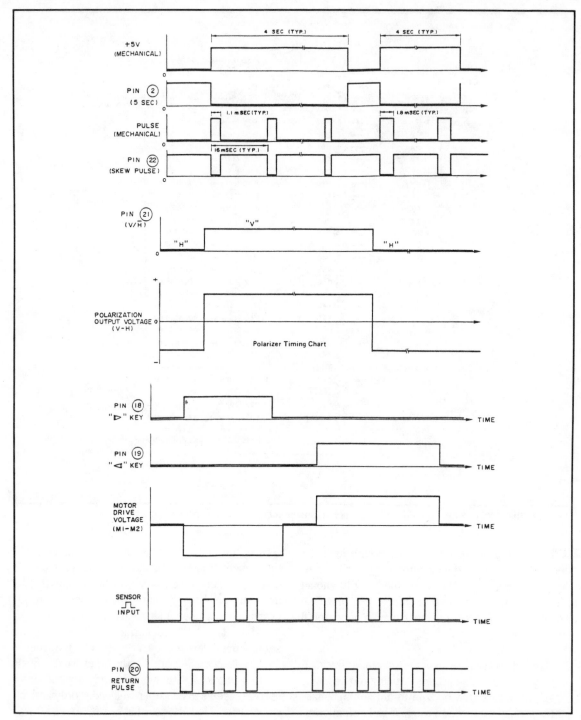

Fig. 4-21. Combined polarizer and actuator tuning charts (courtesy of Zenith Electronics Corp.).

Chapter 5

Testing Basics for Downconverters and Receivers

BLOCK DOWNCONVERTERS OF INITIALLY GOOD quality are probably the most reliable component in any satellite ground station—at least if they are the standard 950 to 1450 MHz variety. And preceding them were the single conversion 70 MHz amplifier/converters, which now appear only in the less expensive TVRO systems or where additional gain is needed in some very low signal areas with limited orbit access. Here both LNA and LNCs are coupled together, offering some 18 dB of additional gain over a single converter and amplifier by itself—if most samples are indicative of general measurements. Consequently, if you need additional gain, or would like lightning to hit the LNA first *before* possibly blowing the converter, use the two in tandem. Be sure, however, that coupling between them is very non-leaky and secure because of individual channel-oscillator tuning and the extra slug of gain. This same arrangement may also apply to wideband amplifiers and block downconverters, but seldom does since the combination of good gain and stepped i-f conversion requires little additional assistance.

The common denominator guaranteeing satisfactory operation for both types, however, is adequately shielded and jacketed cable with (preferably) an 18 AWG center conductor. Our preference every time for satellite downlead is always RG6/U, especially types fabricated by M/A-COM or Belden. We'll continue to stress these same points throughout the text. There is no substitute for suitable cable!

CHARACTERISTICS ARE IMPORTANT

While such receiver preamplifiers and converters offer very little in the way of problems they are major contributors to system noise, therefore considerable care should be paid to their characteristics and receiver matching qualities. Being very high gain, they can be driven into saturation and must have adequate current and voltage on which to operate. In the past, many installers (but not necessarily servicers) have attempted to quick-match any old preamp with whatever receiver may be handy. These are always questionable procedures since impedances, standing wave ratios, gains, and noise factors all differ among many types, and the receiver is usually matched with only one by competent engineers. True, some of the cheap systems seem to try and cheat, but better quality components are normally matched as closely as adequate electronics and comparative costs required by the original vendor/manufacturer.

In some "get-by" situations you may be lucky temporarily, but with the passage of time and unusual weather conditions, undesirable results are bound to appear. When they do, you may have to shell out a free replacement or create a bad reputation, either of which costs both time and money. Furthermore, don't blame an LNA/LNB or the receiver; marginal operation at gigahertz frequencies isn't the same as a 2-kHz amplifier in some nursing home. Either you have precision components admirably suited to one another, or there are problems galore. In addition, with extra wideband video and additional audio carriers on the way, poor quality equipment won't carry the load, especially when there's carrier-to-noise (C/N) or carrier-to-interference (C/I) factors with which to contend, particularly with the smaller reflectors.

Now, since there are so few actual preamplifier and converter breakdowns, you had best send them back to the manufacturer/distributor for repair since a considerable amount of very expensive test equipment is necessary to do a competent job. Here you'll need a microwave signal and sweep generator combination, special temperature chambers, precision tools and expensive gallium arsenide (GaAs FET) semiconductors, possibly printed circuit boards, and a few bipolars thrown in. Not to mention oscillator components and special alignment facilities. Fortunately or unfortunately, only corporation shops can afford these very expensive pieces of test gear, all of which could easily amount to over $100,000. So, in the best interest of everyone, do send them back, and don't be suckered into cheap replacements!

LOCAL TESTING

There are, however, several local (field) checks possible with some less expensive equipment that can be helpful. Of course, the easiest check is sub-

stitution, but marginal conditions may well arise that require a few numbers to back up any good-bad claim. Further, if the LNB still retains good sensitivity, will respond to full dc voltage range, and hasn't obvious casing cracks, it probably is perfectly good. The problem then resolves itself either to wiring, reflector positioning, or your receiver—all of which we'll expound upon in due time.

You could use a sensitive meter, such as Pico Peaker, or one of the considerably more expensive CRT display testers that sell for some $1,500. These, however, don't normally generate CW and modulated signals. They only receive what's on a single given transponder at any one time. But they're certainly better than nothing.

Naturally, we'll go the deluxe route since Wiltron and Tektronix have made excellent (and expensive) test gear available for just such purposes, and we do have standard gain feedhorns, transmit reflectors, a laboratory 4-foot receiver, and various bar and color bar generators. With these, of course, it isn't difficult to pin numbers on the gear under test and verify their operational abilities with relative ease. This is done deliberately as examples of general testing so you will understand the difference between superior and run-of-the mill instrumentation. Many of the mobile uplinks may well opt to stretch an extra $60,000 mile for the sweep/signal generator and special portable spectrum analyzer. Small TVRO operators won't be able to afford it, unfortunately. But large service organizations should invest more than nominal amounts for professional equipment and immediately learn to use it. Our reports suggest that less than 2% of all LNA/LNBs fail in their first several years of life. Later, however, there will be many failures due to both man-made causes and the elements, and manufacturers will not look too kindly on returns that are perfectly good. Perish the thought—you might even be charged.

Probably the easiest way to check an LNA/LNB is with a transponder signal into a power divider. Even if you have a loss of 4 dB, as Channel Master's Model 6215 does, sensitivity through the transponder from one end to the other on block converters may easily be evaluated by either some spectrum display device or a genuine spectrum analyzer, provided the former has its amplitude calibrated in dBm. Just remember, however, you're dealing with power when evaluating microwaves not simply voltage or current, and a 3 dB loss, as always, means half power—50% rather than 70% remaining. Therefore, each decibel is a relatively precious commodity when working at gigahertz, since a little goes a long way.

Current and voltage requirements for the LNA/LNB are also of special importance since they will indicate GaAsFET leakage, opens, or partial operation. This procedure requires no more than a 10- to 25-V power supply capable of suppling up to 250 dc milliamperes. Be careful, though, since the bipolar/GaAsFET combinations do draw current almost immediately and swing into operation sometimes more quickly than you'd want them to. At this point, you must be careful of overvoltage conditions, but don't be alarmed if the current reaches only its normal drain. The dc swing on this particular Drake model was virtually on-the-nose for both voltage and current: +14 to +24 V and 120 mA of current. Almost any two meters (or even one used separately) will monitor these inputs almost exactly, but do try and use meters with at least 20 Kilohm/volt ratings rather than lower values that will decidedly load the circuits being measured. This is especially true in

any dB or ac measurements where impedance-balancing is vital for believable readings. You must also remember that frequency response of such meters at ac are also highly important since many don't go beyond a few kilohertz and this is not helpful for higher value audio measurements and is useless in video. Once again, know your instrument and use it within the manufacturer's published parameters for decent results.

DELUXE TESTING

Using a Wiltron Model 6647A-40 (a 10 MHz to 18.6 GHz) sweep and signal generator that may be either FM or AM modulated, and a Tektronix 492A or my own Tek 7L12, you can do most any video measurements needed to following the LNA/LNB (Fig. 5-1). However, to take off CW or modulated signals directly from the feed horn, the 492A is required since our 7L12 has a top end response of only 1.8 GHz. Then add a color/bar generator for specific chroma and bandpass measurements, and you're almost completely in business. Of course, there should be a couple of good digital meters around, and even a power meter if you haven't complete confidence in the spectrum analyzer—but do remember that a power meter measures *all* incoming signal magnitudes non-selectively, and you may want to single out specific portions that can only be seen with a

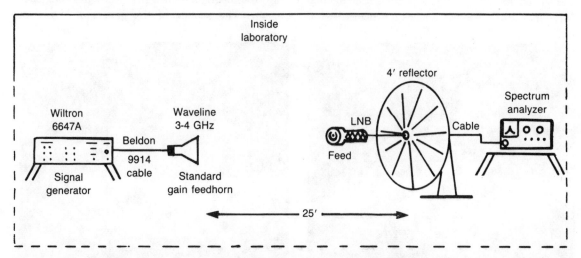

Fig. 5-1. LNB and receiver checkouts in the laboratory using standard gain feedhorn and common prime focus feeds. Wiltron 6647A delivers microwave signals and Tektronix 492A or 2710 (low cost) display.

spectrum analyzer. That's why this particular piece of equipment is so extremely valuable. I would be unable to work without one. What else, for instance, can "see" signals up to 350 gigahertz? That's 350 × 10[9] cycles/second! Somewhat rapid for even computer eyeballs.

Now, if your signal generator has an attenuator of better than 80-100 dB, you may possibly be able to handle the low end of the LNA/LNB input. If not, a standard gain feed horn connected to the generator and a space of some 25 feet between it and 4 ft. reflector will do nicely. Then, with feed and LNA/B firmly connected, measurements may begin that are *not* precise but will certainly indicate the *range* of the LNA/B and its ability to downconvert to a suitable i-f. Especially do you want to watch for spurious (spurs) and any harmonics (Fig. 5-2) that might appear under normal inputs, but which most certainly will pop up with *deliberate* signal overload. At the top end, you'll be able to tell immediately when more than the proper amount of signal is reaching the LNA/B, and on the bottom end, when the normal signal begins to fall off more than 10 to 20 dB. The final test should occur with the mating receiver connected and a modulated signal put to the LNA/B under test. This will not only establish the preamplifier's operation, but also that of the receiver as well since this is an absolute operational check and should be made at several points within the 500 MHz span for C band using block downconverters.

With the 70 MHz LNAs, you'll have to pick certain channels and run tests individually, watching most carefully for any unusual conditions often apparent with *single* i-f frequency conversions such as image reflections and strange, unfiltered intrusions.

The actual generator/analyzer hookup requires an immediate calibration check between the two instruments via a short, low-loss cable, preferably with less than 1 dB loss. If there is any discrepancy between generator attenuator (presuming it has one, and it better) and the analyzer, this must be recorded and used in all ensuing measurements. In this instance, there was no appreciable difference in the short piece, which is now connected to the standard-gain feed horn, but a loss of 2 dB was evident in the 30-foot cable between the reflector feed and the spectrum analyzer. So that requires consideration and *addition* (since it's a loss) in all forthcoming measurements.

However, when measuring the signal-handling ability of the LNB (Fig. 5-3); readings are relative to the extent that you actually require both high and low operational readings to establish an operating swing. In this instance, at −51 dBm the 50 dB gain (rated) cut on and began showing overload at +8 dBm. Therefore the swing/gain of the amplifier amounts to 58 dB, which is the (added) difference and 7 dB more than that specified to allow (probably for temperature changes and possibly component aging). The setting of the generator, however,

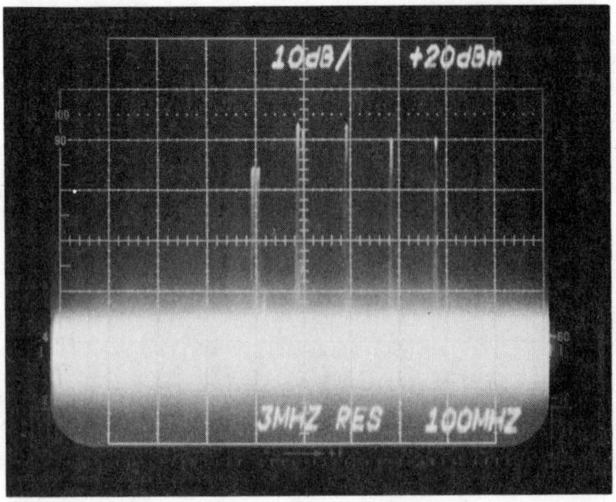

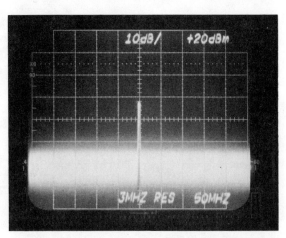

Fig. 5-2. Marker points must be clean and have no spurs as shown here.

Fig. 5-3. A −12 dB out of LNB shows excellent CW pattern at 3 MHz signal resolution, and a 50 MHz/div display.

amounted to −30 dBm, but then you have to calculate in this equation the 15 dB feedhorn gain, space loss, and reflector gain. Nontheless, since we know more than one part of the equation, then −30 dB + 15 dB − Space loss + antenna gain = −51 dB. Assuming a modest antenna gain of +25 dB, −30 + 15 − Space loss + 25 = −51 dB, or 61 dB.

Therefore, Space loss amounts to 61 dB. And that should be fairly close since we're within 1 or 2 dB of antenna gain.

Now, if the LNB reads 7 dBm on the spectrum analyzer when connected and supplied with at least 15 volts dc and 125 mA of current, you have an obvious gain of 58 dB. Using the generator's attenuator, there was no obvious loss (20 dB or more) until it read 57 dB. Therefore there was an easy 30 dB or more to work with, indicating a probable low end of some −80 dB or slightly better, depending on the signal required to adequately "fire" the receiver.

TESTING RECEIVERS

It is time now to hook up the block downconverter to the receiver and see how well the two respond. Unfortunately, however, a great deal depends on the sweep/signal generator's ability to FM modulate, since that's the audio/video exciter mode of all satellite receivers designated as TVRO. Most of this variety of test equipment will pass only audio and other low-value baseband signals, which makes such necessary video evaluation somewhat restricted since it is blocked by narrowband deviation. Any CW signal, of course, has already been stripped (as carrier) by the receiver's detector and only modulation remains; consequently, if there's little worthwhile video it's impossible to evaluate any receiver's complete operation, at least for video. The audio portion we'll come to later, including an experiment with multichannel sound as well as standard audio. Here, receiver bandpass, fortunately, poses no problem and this *most* revealing parameter is easily evaluated through baseband video and possibly even the composite output that *retains* the usual audio frequencies, if present, usually on a test pattern only (Fig. 5-4).

After the preliminary block/ receiver test, the signal generator is then connected *directly* to the re-

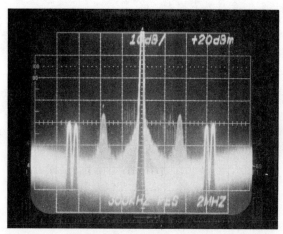

Fig. 5-4. Spectrum baseband display illustrating chroma and the two 6.2 and 6.8 MHz stereo tones.

ceiver to establish sensitivity, audio response, overloads, etc. These specific parameters, therefore, should certainly tell the remainder of the story, at least in the definitive measurements category. You'll then know for sure how good this satellite equipment has been designed and if it actually meets published specifications. The esoterics, such as cosmetics and special functions are left to user selection; we only want to know how good the receiver is and its expected performance in terms of definition, signal-handling ability, and image resolution. If it has 300-channel storage and 21 satellite go-gettum recognition, so much the better. But that, of course, is determined by the positioner and its electronics operating through either a horizon-to-horizon (140°) or linear (about 90°) actuator controlled in any one of three ways as we'll soon describe.

In this test, we continue the original generator/feedhorn setup, with the Wiltron 6647A set for −30.5 dBm, cable loss of 2 dB, and another 4 dB loss through a power splitter. As we continued down, sparklies began at −43.8 dB showing up at an average value of −15 dB in the 6 to 10 MHz slot. With a radical increase up to +19.2 dB on the generator, there was no overload visible in the picture and only a modes change of gain approximating +5 dB. All the while, of course, color bar input was held constant (Fig. 5-5).

When we did increase and decrease color bar modulation, the display either widened or narrowed

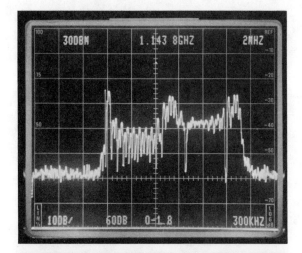

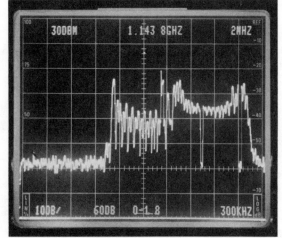

Fig. 5-5. Examples of constant color bar generator modulation with −43.8 dB and +19.2 dB signal amplitude settings. Changes are only relative.

in opposition to greater or lesser gain. In other words, the more modulation, the less signal bandwidth was displayed. All this is becuase the power output from FM transmissions does not change, but the frequency of the carrier does. And any *deviation* in frequency is proportional to the magnitude of the modulating signal. Said another way, maximum frequency shift (Δf) is called frequency deviation and frequency range variation directly represents the modulation amplitude, with Δf being *independent* of the signal frequency. In a simple

equation, the instantaneous frequency of the modulating wave amounts to:

$$f = f_c + \Delta f \cos \omega_s t$$

where f_c is the carrier frequency and always amounts to $2\pi f$, with "s" representing a sinewave.

The *bandwidth* of any FM signal, consequently, represents all components slightly more than equal or greater than one percent of the unmodulated wave's amplitude.

If then, any signal with "n" significant sideband pairs appears on the modulating sinusoidal voltage identified as f_s, the bandwidth is:

$$BW = 2nf_s$$

You should also know that the ratio fo the frequency deviation to that of the modulating signal equals the modulation index:

$$m \text{ (modulation index)} = \Delta/f_s$$

And this modulation index is further described as the deviation ratio and depends both on the amplitude of the modulation as well as the signal frequency. Different frequencies within the FM information such as A_0 through A_3, and A_n are directly related to values of the modulation index (m_f) and may be evaluated by using Bessel function charts as shown (Fig. 5-6).

That ought to be enough to become familiar with FM-casting as practiced by radio, mobile and/or microwave carriers, and satellites. The principles are all the same regardless of the carrier, although detection methods vary considerably between video and audio due to obvious frequency differences. Quadrature detectors and discriminators are partial to audio whereas diode bridges that look like ring modulators/demodulators are popular in most satellite receiver designs (Fig. 5-7).

DIRECT TESTING

We now leave the block downconverter to posterity and hook up our signal/sweep generator directly to the receiver under test, with the output

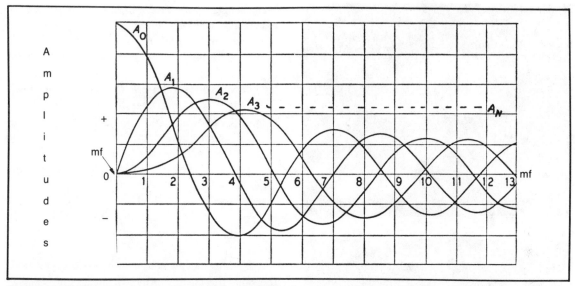

Fig. 5-6. Bessel function chart showing carrier components from A_o to A_n between 0 and $\pm$ relative values.

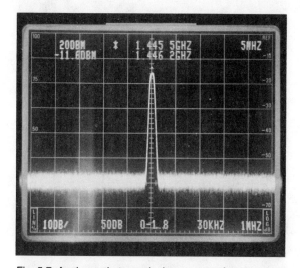

Fig. 5-7. Analyzer photograph shows center frequency out of LNB with generator set at 3.7 GHz and unmodulated carrier. There was only a 2 dB cable loss in 25 feet.

going to either an oscilloscope or spectrum analyzer to determine the final receiver test parameters. We'll first inject high and low carrier signals, modulation, then finally sweep. That shoud tell as much of the entire story as required here to this point. Modulation, of course, will be monitored on a television receiver screen, too, so that picture quality,

plus spectrum display visual quality may be simultaneously observed.

Unfortunately, you're in for a negative surprise. Because of impednace mismatches (50 ohms versus 75), an 8 dB cable and power splitter combined loss, and capacitative coupling to prevent analyzer front-end damage, the results are not nearly as comprehensive as previous signal waveforms. In addition, both crosshatch and color bars were shaky and ragged—not nearly as solid and clean as those projected through the LNB and its satellite-type feed. And whether entering the receiver at + 11.2 dBm or at − 43 dBm, the results are virtually the same with the exception of diminished amplitudes and lesser signal-to-noise. So although the LNB/signal generator dBm inputs pretty well checkout, the image produced doesn't compare (Fig. 5-8).

It therefore stands to reason that electronics in *any* satellite system should be checked as a unit rather than simply as distinct parts. One would also add that over-the-air, transponder emission type checking, even with a calibrated feedhorn is *considerably* better than attempting direct hookups with cable. In this way, signal pickup, sensitivity, overload, and almost anything else has a reasonable chance of accurate, meaningful measurement, not

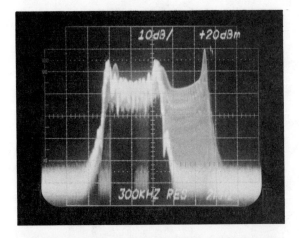

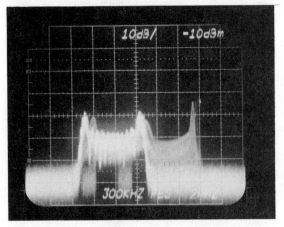

Fig. 5-8. Signal generator connected directly through dc block, 75-ohm power splitter, etc. Signals not so clean and well defined.

oscilloscopes could come in handy if they are of reasonable accuracy.

As predicted, the mono sound portion was quite easy, and you see in the illustration a pretty good representation of peak detected sound (maximum level) from 1 kHz to 20 kHz, at about 15 dB down (Fig. 5-10). This is considerably better than 90 percent of the television receivers. The upper 10 percent, of course, have multichannel sound and their baseband measurements regularly exceed 100 kHz because of the various carriers that extend to better than 100 kHz: 15,734 Hz × 6.5 (the professional carrier) equals 102.271 kHz. You must, however, have at least video sync going into the FM input to coordinate transmitter and receiver; otherwise, audio becomes simply a jumbled mess.

Any attempt to couple either AM or FM into the video FM channel proved fruitless with this par-

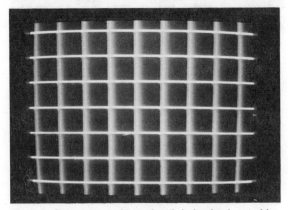

Fig. 5-9. Color bars and crosshatch help check out video portion of system.

to mention actual operational conditions so important to final analysis test-proven results (Fig. 5-9). Once again we *must* emphasize system checkout rather than measurements of individual parts. For most engineer/technicians these waveguide frequencies are too tricky to attempt to separate by amplifier/receiver function. Put it all together, then take your readings with good, calibrated test gear. There's no substitute!

The *audio portion*, of course, is easy provided you stick to monophonic rather than stereo. If stereo measurements are required, than a low-frequency spectrum analyzer and stereo generator(s) are essential. Even standard low frequency

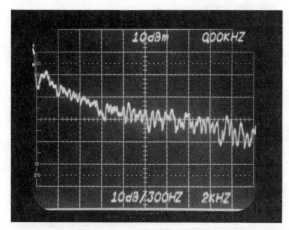

Fig. 5-10. Audio response to 20 kHz readily visible in this Tektronix 7L5 analyzer photograph.

ticular setup, and we were unable to use either a standard FM signal generator or our B & K-Precision 2009 MTS generator, although the various kilohertz signal tones were plainly visible. This particular Drake receiver, also, doesn't have stereo, so no measurement was possible, as anyone might readily conclude (Fig. 5-11). Nontheless, we tried everything just to make sure nothing was deliberately overlooked. We'll have to confess that audio measurements are still the most difficult part of our work most of the time since they're not always familiar and sometimes downright elusive. Regardless, the audio portion of this receiver compares favorably with video so that all measurements are well within accepted limits and even beyond.

To satisfactorily complete the audio examination, we once again tried coupling various instruments into the FM channel without a great deal of success. And even though the multichannel sound 2009 generator did produce a stereo lamp light through a monitor connected to the receiver, tones were not pure, and overall results were inconclusive as the illustration shows. Remember that you must have 6.2 and/or 6.8 MHz carrier(s) to adequately deliver audio to the satellite receiver. Standard FM or FM/stereo generators will not do the job. This is where we'll have to dig down in our bag of tricks and find some way, eventually, of exciting this *delightful* stereo. Frankly, you haven't heard great stereo until a good musical program has been transpondered by satellite. Records and standard radio broadcasts just won't do at all. And to have clean audio tones, all that "garbage" in the photo must be removed and only pure sinewaves should appear with signal-to-noise ratios of 45-55 dB. Then, you'll hear some real music.

CONCLUSIONS

In any realistic assessment of these receiver/LNB examinations with basically a spectrum analyzer and a sweep/signal generator, most of the parameters you need to know can be measured fairly easily, provided you know cable losses, have a good feedhorn and are careful. The exceptions, of course, being adequate video bandwidth and the 6.2 and 6.8 MHz audio carriers. However, all this will probably be overcome in almost the immediate future with somewhat lower priced and more functional equipment on the way—some of which we already know about. Fortunately, low cost test sets for the TVRO industry are indispensable, and several manufacturers were well on the way to developing such instruments, but are now distinctly slowed by our old bugaboo—scrambling.

Now, just to leave you with a good taste in your mouths before and after dinner, we'll show two photographs (Fig. 5-12) that show both the 4 MHz video or composite audio/video outputs of the R.L. Drake receiver. At 3 dB down, the upper trace shows

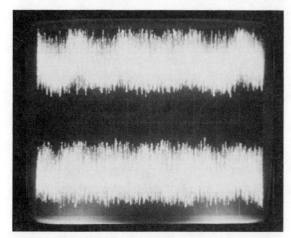

Fig. 5-11. Stereo portion not outstanding using a separate stereo receiver with L and R outputs (inconclusive).

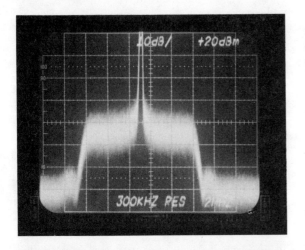

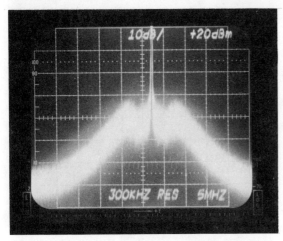

Fig. 5-12. Baseband video (top) and composite video/audio outputs (bottom) illustrate filtering and bandwidths.

about 10 MHz of bandwidth, while the bottom illustration has almost 20 MHz. Unfortunately, to be used by most receivers, considerable filtering is required of the composite output, especially at C band where a low frequency *dispersal* wobbulator has been mandated by the FCC to prevent terrestrial interference as transponder modulation nears zero.

Oh, we almost forgot to tell you, a good *signal* generator with CW and adequate modulation and output (+10 to +20 dBM) can do the analysis job nicely; a sweep function is *not* necessary since the spectrum analyzer will easily reveal both filtered and nonfiltered bandpasses that were just illustrated.

EQUIPMENT CHECKOUTS

When using either new or well-used test equipment—especially if rented or borrowed—always make preliminary checks to see if it is really working. This is especially important for waveguide-to-N connectors (leakage or damage), LNA or LNBCs (for gain, harmonics, spurs, etc.), cabling losses or bad connectors, and whether your signal generator and spectrum analyzer approximately agree on both frequency readouts and leveled emissions. Then, if there is compensation, a few pencil notes on paper does the rest for reference as you continue your investigations.

You will, however, have to keep feeds in the same positions for qualitative measurements, and such measurements are best made in the transmit-receive mode. In other words, use a *good* generator such as Wiltron's 6647A, and an agreeable spectrum analyzer that's either a Tektronix 492A or its equivalent (if there is one) that can handle inputs between .01 and 21 GHz. You'll be working with frequencies between 3.7 to 12 GHz, covering both C and satellite K bands now in commercial use, even though each retains a spectrum of 500 MHz wide for the C, Ku and allied bands. And although we have not fully checked 17.3-17.8 high power DBS, it will fall in the higher of these categories, at least for the uplink. Downlinks for Ku are 11.7 to 12.2 and 12.2 to 12.7 GHz for dBs. Primarily, of course, we're basically interested in the downlink since that's what the terrestrial reflector and its electronics sees.

The setup for this measurement is extremely simple! You probably have some sort of Polarotor® laying around that may or may not respond to skew stimulus. If not, no matter, since you can turn it over (rotate) on its side to produce maximum gain. About 10 to 15 feet away, line up an opposing feed mated with only a waveguide-to-N adapter. Then, using some good cable, such as Belden 9914 or equivalent, connect the first feed to a signal generator and the second feed to the spectrum analyzer. Taking into account any obvious cable losses, you have an immediate set of numbers, in this instance −48.6 dBM at a resolution of 1 MHz and 5 MHz/division. Frequency readout, of course, is at the transmitter frequency of 3.953 GHz (Fig. 5-13).

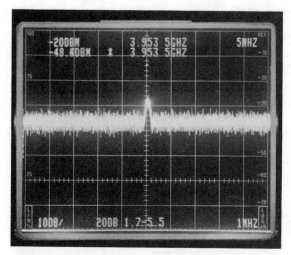

Fig. 5-13. CW signal measured from non-amplified feedhorn. Note rf level shift upwards and diminished C/N ratio.

Next, connect a block downconverter (in this application) or another microwave amplifier, put a dc voltage on line to operate the electronics and a dc block between this voltage and the spectrum analyzer. With a voltage between 15 and 20+ volts along the signal line to the LNBC, the results should approximate those illustrated in Fig. 5-14. Observe that you're working at a starting figure of +20 dBm instead of −20 dBm as shown previously. And also note that the LNBC's output is 1.196 GHz rather than 3.953 GHz appearing in the original frequency.

Therefore, the first downconversion has already made a difference of almost 2.8 GHz, and other heterodyne actions will further decrease these carriers to i-fs somewhere between 140 and 500 MHz.

The gain difference between the straight feed and amplified feed with LNBC then becomes −48.6 dBm − (+7.6 dBm), for a total difference of 56.2 dB. This is pretty close to being exact with our initial (Fig. 5-14) feed measurements with a standard gain feed horn. So this, really, is the simpler way and can be done in half the time and with much more basic equipment you may already have on hand. In addition, both feed and block downconverter are checked simultaneously so that you know for a fact that they are operating as they should.

The principle of all this is that a feed (within reason) may be used both as a power transmitter and as a receiver. But don't try more than 20 dBm on many feeds or you could do damage, especially if the generator's output fluctuates. Ours is safely leveled and doesn't move. In addition, the Wiltron has an electric attenuator that is invaluable when certain low and high levels are necessary. Manual attenuators have been known, unfortunately, to deliver a shock to LNA/Bs that blows fuses in their dc supplies resulting from sudden signal surges as attenuation levels change. So do use electronic attenuators if at all possible, supplied as part of the generator by the original equipment manufacturer.

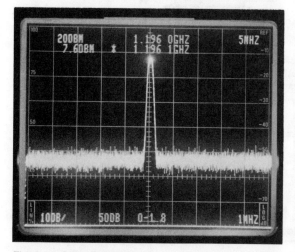

Fig. 5-14. Same CW voltage as amplified by good LNB/C connected to same feedhorn with excellent C/N.

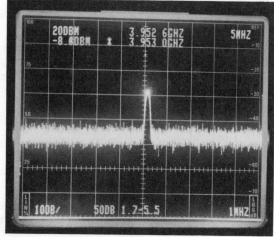

Fig. 5-15. CW signal comparison as amplified by an old 40 dB LNA. C/N here is only fair.

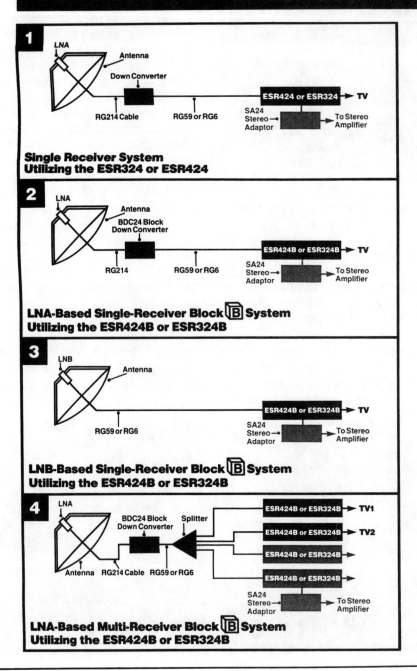

TYPICAL INSTALLATION

1

LNA
Antenna
Down Converter
ESR424 or ESR324 → TV
RG214 Cable
RG59 or RG6
SA24 Stereo Adaptor → To Stereo Amplifier

**Single Receiver System
Utilizing the ESR324 or ESR424**

2

LNA
Antenna
BDC24 Block Down Converter
ESR424B or ESR324B → TV
RG214
RG59 or RG6
SA24 Stereo Adaptor → To Stereo Amplifier

**LNA-Based Single-Receiver Block 🅱 System
Utilizing the ESR424B or ESR324B**

3

LNB
Antenna
ESR424B or ESR324B → TV
RG59 or RG6
SA24 Stereo Adaptor → To Stereo Amplifier

**LNB-Based Single-Receiver Block 🅱 System
Utilizing the ESR424B or ESR324B**

4

LNA
BDC24 Block Down Converter
Splitter
ESR424B or ESR324B → TV1
ESR424B or ESR324B → TV2
ESR424B or ESR324B
ESR424B or ESR324B
Antenna
RG214 Cable
RG59 or RG6
SA24 Stereo Adaptor → To Stereo Amplifier

**LNA-Based Multi-Receiver Block 🅱 System
Utilizing the ESR424B or ESR324B**

Fig. 5-16. Single or multiple receiver hookups, depending on downconverters and power splitters (courtesy of R.L. Drake).

CONFIGURATIONS

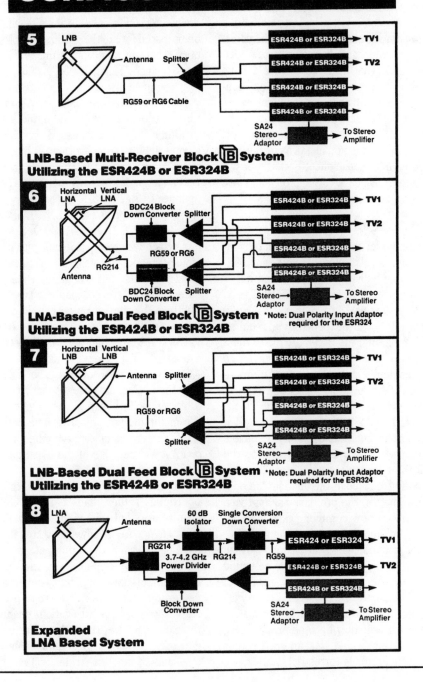

5

LNB

Antenna   Splitter

RG59 or RG6 Cable

ESR424B or ESR324B → TV1
ESR424B or ESR324B → TV2
ESR424B or ESR324B
ESR424B or ESR324B

SA24 Stereo Adaptor → To Stereo Amplifier

LNB-Based Multi-Receiver Block Ⓑ System
Utilizing the ESR424B or ESR324B

6

Horizontal LNA   Vertical LNA

BDC24 Block Down Converter   Splitter

RG59 or RG6

RG214

Antenna

BDC24 Block Down Converter   Splitter

ESR424B or ESR324B → TV1
ESR424B or ESR324B → TV2
ESR424B or ESR324B
ESR424B or ESR324B

SA24 Stereo Adaptor → To Stereo Amplifier

LNA-Based Dual Feed Block Ⓑ System   *Note: Dual Polarity Input Adaptor required for the ESR324
Utilizing the ESR424B or ESR324B

7

Horizontal LNB   Vertical LNB

Antenna   Splitter

RG59 or RG6

Splitter

ESR424B or ESR324B → TV1
ESR424B or ESR324B → TV2
ESR424B or ESR324B
ESR424B or ESR324B

SA24 Stereo Adaptor → To Stereo Amplifier

LNB-Based Dual Feed Block Ⓑ System   *Note: Dual Polarity Input Adaptor required for the ESR324
Utilizing the ESR424B or ESR324B

8

LNA

Antenna

RG214

60 dB Isolator   Single Conversion Down Converter

3.7-4.2 GHz Power Divider   RG214   RG59

Block Down Converter

ESR424 or ESR324 → TV1
ESR424B or ESR324B → TV2
ESR424B or ESR324B

SA24 Stereo Adaptor → To Stereo Amplifier

Expanded
LNA Based System

There is also a third circumstance (Fig. 5-15) in this particular feed/amplifier series of which you should be aware. Connecting an old-style LNA to the unamplified feed photo shown originally, you will notice only a difference of 40 dB. And this, added to vastly increased noise characteristics, is the difference betwen many amplifiers obtainable on the "distress" market and what you really should have connected in your better systems. Noise temperature and good gain are two absolute essentials when working with gigahertz microwaves. Decent results are not obtainable otherwise—believe it or not! Think it over the next time you install a cheapie and walk away with a guilty conscience. Sometimes it's better to lose a sale than have to sleep on it and face the consequences sooner or later.

SINGLE AND DUAL CONVERSIONS

More as a reminder than a recitation of new information, in single satellite signal conversions following the feed, one individual oscillator and mixer convert all signals directly from the 500 MHz C band spectrum down to the final i-f frequency, usually 70 MHz. While this method is inexpensive and requires many fewer components, the oscillator/mixer must tune both the satellite and its various channels, so that it really does double duty. For low i-f frequencies such as 70 MHz, an image-rejection type of mixer is needed which even then is in the 20 dB down category rather than the usual 50 dB needed for pictures approaching studio quality. Tunable preselection filters are also desirable prior to the preamplifier if the cost isn't prohibitive.

All this is why (to remove the undesirable possibility of mirror images) the professional approach of dual conversions is now common practice in the late 1980s. Although more expensive, the first converter/oscillator is fixed, while the second now in the receiver, is tunable, making possible selection of any individual satellite along with the capability of tuning all of its 24 channels selectively with very little local oscillator radiation. Should said radiation around the reflector assembly become pronounced, nearby TVRO systems could pick up such spurs, resulting in more undesirable terrestrial interference

than usual. Now, a simple bandpass filter provides any required image rejection and local oscillator re-radiation to the outside world.

So if you're *determined* to use a 70 MHz single downconversion scheme despite all the warnings, be prepared for anything from poor pictures to neighbors complaints and often unsatisfactory all-round performance. Here, cheap just isn't good!

You must also understand that in the single conversion systems, multiple television sets must all tune to the same transponder and satellite that the "mother" TV has accessed through the satellite. Conversely, systems with dual, block downconversions, may have switching for several satellite receivers and tune *any* of the 24 available transponders (Fig. 5-16).

Good examples of the LNA/LNB/C systems are included in R.L.Drake's 1985 Dealer Product Planner, which we are reproducing with permission. Obviously you don't have to use all this manufacturer's good products, but the general idea for additional receivers and stereo adapters is wholly accurate. Splitters, by the way, you may know as power dividers, and take signals from the block downconverters, often amplify, and then distribute to other satellite receivers serving additional television sets. Note there is none of this type signal distribution with the LNAs, and observe that RG59/U or RG6/U cable is specified between preamplifier and receiver. We might add you will always be better off with 18 AWG center conductors than the smaller ones at 20 or 22 AWG because of the usual per hundred-foot losses.

In the not-too-distant future, you may be using fiberoptics rather than coaxial cable if the prices aren't out of line when commercial distribution begins. Higher/frequency analog limitations apparently have been largely overcome, at least for TVRO applications below 1,500 MHz. Individual receivers, too, without skew or polarity reversal, can be connected through power dividers to provide separate television receivers with various channel pictures on the same satellite. But if this is the case, skew, audio, etc., should be programmed into a ROM beforehand so most overrides will not be necessary.

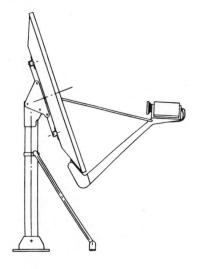

Chapter 6

The Ku-Band Picture

OPERATING UPLINK BETWEEN 14 AND 14.5 GHZ AND downlink from 11.7 to 12.2 GHz, the steadily expanding Ku band of frequencies is becoming a highly important part of the U.S. Fixed Satellite Service, often called DOMSAT for domestic satellite service. With 30 orbit "parking" spaces set aside for Ku operations, there are already 8 "pure" Ku satellites parked in geosynchronous orbit, and three C- and Ku-band hybrids having a total of 70 transponders available for operations, some with bandwidths of 72 MHz (soon 120 MHz). Others such as RCA's K-3 and GSTAR 3 are almost on the launch pads awaiting lift off to allocated positions in assignements 22,300 miles above the equator, sharing the Clarke Orbit or Clarke Belt with C-band satellites some of which have already been retired. Among these are WESTAR I, SATCOM I, COMSTAR D1, COMSTAR D3 and SATCOM II. Those remaining, occupy orbit slots between 69° West Longitude (WL) and 143° WL, although SBS-6 and SATCOM-7 will occupy 62° WL later and Aurora-1 has been assigned 146° WL and is already in position. A listing of all orbit assignments currently allocated by the Federal Communications Commission (FCC) are shown in Tables 6-1 and 6-2.

With a nominal design life of some 10 years, principally because of limited station-keeping fuel, retired satellites are usually replaced with newer and often more powerful units, with some in the C band category having 10-watt transponders instead of the 5-watters originally flown. That's about as high as they'll go, however, because of the probability of their signals generating extra terrestrial interference. So far, this is not true of K-band satellites, however, and these will become 60W transpondered in time, generating peak efficiency there.

For those who wish to remember, Canada's ANIK B was the first hybrid C/Ku commercial satellite launched in 1978 and SBS-1 was the U.S.'s initial Ku "bird" entering orbit in Nov. 1980.

Ku BAND REASONING

In late 1985, RCA Astro-Electronics and RCA Americom offered some interesting information on

Table 6-1. FCC Orbital Assignments.

Position	Satellite	Frequency
146° W.L.	Aurora-1	4/6 GHz
144° W.L.	Westar-7	4/6 GHz
142° W.L.	Aurora-1	4/6 GHz
140° W.L.	Galaxy-4	4/6 GHz
138° W.L.	Satcom-1R	4/6 GHz
136° W.L.	Spacenet-4/GSTAR-3	4/6/12/14 GHz
134° W.L.	Unassigned - vertical	4/6 GHz
134° W.L.	Comsat General-B	12/14 GHz
132° W.L.	Galaxy-1	4/6 GHz
132° W.L.	Westar-B	12/14 GHz
130° W.L.	Satcom-3R	4/6 GHz
130° W.L.	Galaxy-B	12/14 GHz
128° W.L.	ASC-2	4/6/12/14 GHz
126° W.L.	Telstar-1	4/6 GHz
126° W.L.	Martin Marietta-B	12/14 GHz
124° W.L.	Westar-5	4/6 GHz
124° W.L.	Fedex-B	12/14 GHz
122° W.L.	Unassigned-vertical	4/6 GHz
122° W.L.	SBS-5	12/14 GHz
120° W.L.	Spacenet-1	4/6/12/14 GHz
105° W.L.	GSTAR	12/14 GHz
103° W.L.	GSTAR	12/14 GHz
101° W.L.	Ford-1	4/6/12/14 GHz
99° W.L.	Westar-4	4/6 GHz
99° W.L.	SBS-1	4/6 GHz
97° W.L.	Telstar-2	4/6 GHz
97° W.L.	SBS-2	12/14 GHz
95° W.L.	Galaxy-3	4/6 GHz
95° W.L.	SBS-3	12/14 GHz
93° W.L.	Ford-2	4/6/12/14 GHz
91° W.L.	Westar-3/6S	4/6 GHz
91° W.L.	SBS-4	12/14 GHz
89° W.L.	unassigned - vertical	4/6 GHz
89° W.L.	unassigned	12/14 GHz
87° W.L.	Spacenet-3	4/6/12/14 GHz
85° W.L.	Telstar-3	4/6 GHz
85° W.L.	RCA-A	12/14 GHz
83° W.L.	ASC-2	4/6/12/14 GHz
81° W.L.	Satcom-4	4/6 GHz
81° W.L.	RCA-B	12/14 GHz
79° W.L.	Westar-3	4/6 GHz
79° W.L.	Martin Marietta-A	12/14 GHz
77° W.L.	Fedex-A	12/14 GHz
76° W.L.	Comstar	4/6 GHz
75° W.L.	Comsat General-A	12/14 GHz
74° W.L.	Galaxy-2	4/6 GHz
73° W.L.	Westar-A	12/14 GHz
72° W.L.	Satcom-2R	4/6 GHz
71° W.L.	Galaxy-A	12/14 GHz
69° W.L.	Spacenet-2	4/6/12/14 GHz
67° W.L.	Satcom-6	4/6 GHz
67° W.L.	RCA-C	12/14 GHz
64° W.L.	ASC-3/4	4/6/12/14 GHz
62° W.L.	Satcom-7	4/6 GHz
62° W.L.	SBS-6	12/14 GHx

Assignment of Orbital Locations to Space Stations in the Domestic Fixed-Satellite Service, 50 Fed. Reg. 35228 (August 30, 1985)

Notes: WL = West Longitude position. 4/6 or 12/14 GHz are the down-link and uplink frequency assignments

Table 6-2. United States Domestic Satellite System.

Satellite	Orbit Locations West Longitude	Frequency Band (GHz)	Date Launched	# of Xpdrs/ BW (MHz)
SATCOM V	143°	4/6	Oct. 1982	24/36
SATCOM I-R	139°	4/6	April 1983	24/36
GALAXY I	134°	4/6	June 1983	24/36
SATCOM III-R	131°	4/6	Nov. 1981	24/36
ASC-1	128°	4/6; 12/14	Aug. 1985	12/36 & 6/72 6/72
TELSTAR 303	125°	4/6	June 1985	24/36
SPACENET 1	120°	4/6; 12/14	May 1984	12/36 & 6/72; 6/72
WESTAR V	122.5°	4/6	June 1982	24/36
GSTAR II	105°	12/14	March 1986	16/54
GSTAR I	103°	12/14	May 1985	16/54
SBS IV	101° (temporary)	12/14	Sept. 1984	10/43
SBS I	99°	12/14	Nov. 1980	10/43
WESTAR IV	99°	4/6	Feb. 1982	24/36
SBS II	97°	12/14	Oct. 1981	10/43
TELSTAR 301	96°	4/6	July 1983	24/36
SBS III	95°	12/14	Nov. 1982	10/43
GALAXY III	93.5°	4/6	Sept. 1984	24/36
WESTAR III	91°	4/6	Aug. 1979	12/36
TELSTAR 302	86°	4/6	Sept. 1984	24/36
SATCOM Ku-1	85°	12/14	Jan. 1986	16/54
SATCOM IV	84°	4/6	Jan. 1982	24/36
SATCOM Ku-2	81°	12/14	Nov. 1985	16/54
WESTAR II	79°	4/6	June 1974	12/36
COMSTAR D$_2$ & D$_4$	76°	4/6	Sept. 1976 & Feb. 1981	24/36 24/36
GALAXY II	74°	4/6	Sept. 1983	24/36
SATCOM II-R	72°	4/6	Sept. 1983	24/36
SPACENET II	69°	4/6; 12/14	Nov. 1984	12/36 & 6/72; 6/72
WESTAR I	retired (8/83)	4/6	April 1974	12/36
SATCOM I	retired (5/84)	4/6	Dec. 1975	24/36
COMSTAR D$_1$	retired (9/84)	4/6	July 1976	24/36
COMSTAR D$_3$	retired (8/85)	4/6	Sept. 1978	24/36
SATCOM II	retired (2/85)	4/6	March 1976	24/36

In Orbit as of April 3, 1986

SATCOM - RCA American Communications, Inc.
WESTAR - Western Union Telegraph Company
SBS - Satellite Business Systems
GALAXY - Hughes Communications Galaxy, Inc.
COMSTAR - owned - Comsat General Corporation
- operated - AT&T Co.
TELSTAR - AT&T Co.
SPACENET - GTE Spacenet Corporation
GSTAR - GTE Satellite Corporation
ASC - American Satellite Company

Planned Launches in 1986

Shuttle	Ariane
Westar IV-S	Spacenet F3
GSTAR 3	SBS-5

"Why Ku Band" which is worth summarizing and updating as substantiation for this new and important service. Following this, we'll devote additional space to many of the technical details involved and try to combine uplink and downlink operations so that you may understand exactly where TVRO belongs and how to deal with it. Prime entrants in this Service—Satellite Business Systems (SBS) and the Radio Corporation of America (RCA, now GE/RCA)—pretty well represent a great deal of the ongoing technology, even though substantially upgraded SBS satellites are now awaiting launch due to the Challenger disaster in early 1986 and a subsequent Ariane (European) failure that halted all U.S. commercial launches for many months.

THE RCA Ku STORY

Because RCA recognized the service-expansion potential of the 12/14 GHz spectrum for business, government, and consumer applications, engineering and marketing decided on a series of 16-transponder satellites having bandwidths of 54 MHz, each capable of serving either the entire U.S. or half of CONUS, whichever is required. All are 3-axis stabilized spacecraft with transponder power of 45 watts for K-1 and K-2, with K-3 increased to 60W/transponder. Satcom K-2 reached orbit aboard Space Shuttle Atlantis on November 22, 1985, and K-1 was lofted by Columbia on Jan. 12, 1986. Launch date for K-3 has been set for sometime in 1989, with delivery probably by Ariane to its orbital parking space of 67° WL. On the FCC's assignment sheet, these RCA K satellites are identified as RCA A, B, and C, respectively, and not K-1, K-2, and K-3.

Satisfactory terrestrial signal pickup for most regions of the country should require only 1.2 meter reflectors at the least and 1.8-meter antennas for studio-grade reception. F/D ratios, however, could amount to between 0.375 and 0.4 for best results, with offset feeds beneficial in preventing feed support blockage, rapid snow and rain runoff, desirable gain, and minimum sidelobes. Above 2.4 meters, however, focal lengths on offset reflectors become extremely long and generally undesirable.

Solid reflectors, customarily fiberglass, are preferable at Ku for both longevity and retention of accurate rms curvature—an absolute necessity at Ku. Usually these are one-piece antennas constructed on critically-engineered molds that must retain tolerances between 0.010 and 0.025-inch rms, some 3 to 6 times tighter than standard C-band reflectors. At 0.015 inch rms, such reflectors may also transmit as well as receive and are to be used extensively for business as well as home communications.

For frequencies better than double those of the 4/6 GHz service, terrestrial interference will become considerably less, though probably not totally eliminated, and signals are powerful enough to overcome rain outages in most, if not all parts of the country. In addition, there may yet be more room for parking slots, even though most have already been assigned, due to possible "due diligence" tardiness on the part of prior assignees. This FCC regulation requires full contract construction entry and launch within specified periods, or the applicant loses his orbit allocation—a condition especially noticeable among Direct Broadcast Service (DBS) applicants in the forthcoming 12/17 GHz band, which is still essentially dormant.

At launch the RCA K series (Fig. 6-1) will weigh 4,245 lbs., measure 98 inches tall and, once it has attained orbit, a weight of 2,255 lbs., a maximum array span of 65 feet, and an array area of 280 ft.². Its core (body) structure, measures 67 × 84 × 60 inches, and contains all electronics, batteries, in addition to propulsion and attitude control equipment on eight honeycombed panels. Transponders and

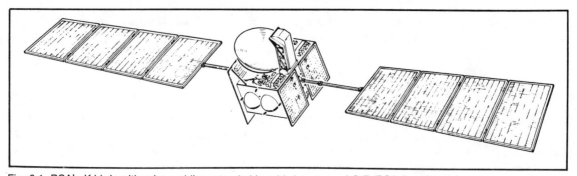

Fig. 6-1. RCA's K-birds with solar paddles extended in orbit (courtesy of G.E./RCA Americom).

satellite "housekeeping" components are mounted on four panels, divided equally between the north and south sides of the spacecraft, with more housekeeping equipment on a base panel facing upward. A lower earth-facing panel contains the communications antenna mount and feed assembly, a telemetry antenna, and earth sensors for attitude sensing. And in addition to the 16 channels having 45-watt traveling-wave-tube amplifiers, there are also six redundant TWTAs in case of failures amoung the other 16. Dielectric antenna reflectors have orthogonal conducting grids to double channel capacity for frequency reuse and crosspole isolation, magnetic torquing corrects roll and yaw errors, and an auxiliary control loop maintains antenna pointing accuracy. Command security for these satellites is guarded by a 12-bit preamble sync message in addition to a 6-bit spacecraft address, ground-verified, and then authorized by an execute tone from master control.

Satellite power originates with eight solar array panels generating a bus voltage of between 24.5 and 35.5 volts, with dc/dc conversions for specific power feeds. During eclipses or other outages, three parallel-connected 50 ampere/hour nickel-hydrogen batteries, which are continuously charged during normal flight, supply spacecraft power. For stationkeeping, four electrothermal hydrazine thruster engines do the job for north-south control in addition to the usual reaction control system of eight dual sets of thrusters.

Specific details of upgrading the K-3 satellite to 60W/channel have not yet been made available. We do know that it has been purchased by RCA Communications and Home Box Office. Named the Crimson Satellite Associates, it will serve both the CATV industry and the "home market", probably delivering virtually all-scrambled "subscriber" programs to suitable paying participants. Footprints for the K series are shown in Fig. 6-2.

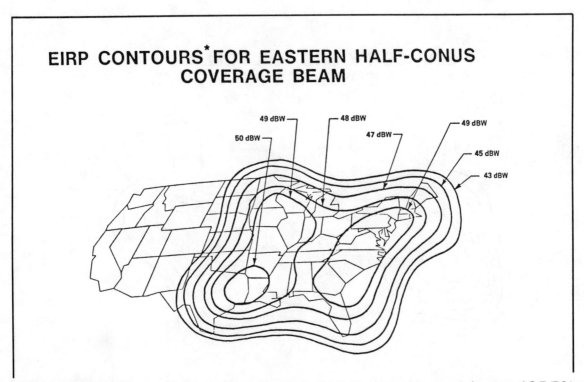

EIRP CONTOURS*FOR EASTERN HALF-CONUS COVERAGE BEAM

49 dBW — — 48 dBW

50 dBW — — 49 dBW

47 dBW —

— 45 dBW

— 43 dBW

Fig. 6-2. Anticipated EIRP partial and full CONUS coverage for RCA's Ku group of spacecraft (courtesy of G.E./RCA Americom).

EIRP CONTOURS*FOR WESTERN HALF-CONUS COVERAGE BEAM

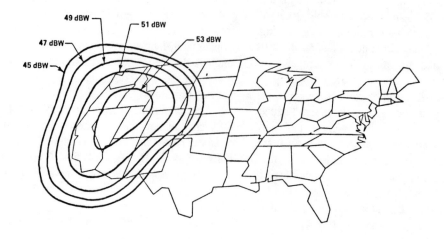

EIRP CONTOURS*FOR FULL-CONUS COVERAGE BEAM

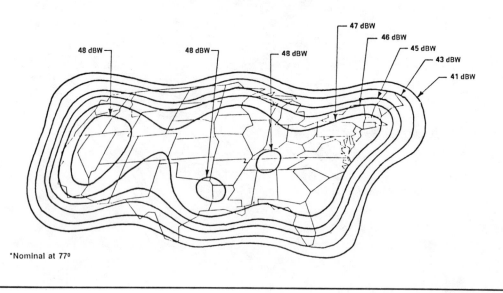

*Nominal at 77°

Fig. 6-2. Anticipated EIRP partial and full CONUS coverage for RCA's Ku group of spacecraft (courtesy of G.E./RCA Americom). (Continued from page 97).

THE GSTARS

Another of the GTE Spacenet series, these 12 −14 GHz satellites are also built by RCA Astro Electronics. They operate at 103° WL and 105° WL. GSTAR I went aloft on May 1985 and GSTAR II in March, 1986, boosted by Ariane III from French Guiana. Launch weights are 2667 lbs., and in orbit this is reduced to 1577 lbs. Stabilization is described as 3-axis, and stationkeeping specifications indicate a high accuracy of 0.05°. Life design expectancy: 10 years (Fig. 6-3).

Part of the three hybrid SPACENET and two GSTAR spacecraft group for GTE, a fourth SPACENET and third GSTAR approvals are expected from the FCC in due time. These satellites will operate both single and multi-carriers for both FDM/FM analog, SCPC/FM, TV/FM and digital such as TDMA, SCPC/PSK, spread spectrum, etc. Designed primarily for business interests, they are said to be the first DOMSATS supplying full frequency reuse and full CONUS Ku-band coverage. Tracking, telemetry, command, and service centers are located at McLean, Virginia (headquarters), as well as Oxford, Connectitcut, and Grand Junction, Colorado.

Each GSTAR has 16 tranponders with bandwidths of 54 MHz, 14 of which have TWT (traveling wave tube) power outputs of 20 watts, and two deliver 27 watts for the 50-state coverage. There is also ground-commanded east or west spot beam facility for specific coverage and smaller earth terminals. For redundancy in case of failures, one spare 27 W TWT and five spare 20 W TWTs offer protection for active channels on the satellite. Linear or limiter modes may be programmed for multicarrier or peak saturation modes, respectively, accomodating a number of different carriers and signal characteristics.

EIRP levels referenced are for typical transponders in saturation with a single carrier "within the central" 36 MHz of any GSTAR transponder. And vertical polarization is defined by GTE as "lying in the plane formed by rotating 26° counterclockwise from the plane of the satellite's N-S axis and the center of the earth." Receivers on the satellite have step attenuator settings between 0.5 and 4.5 dB in half dB steps to adjust gains and are ground adjustable. Frequency differences between uplinks and downlinks are 2300 MHz, being held to within accuracies of ± 10 parts/million over the transponder design life. Crosspolar isolation amounts to 33 dB when illuminated by any CONUS terrestrial antenna (belonging to the system).

Users may buy or lease transponders, according to a 1985 announcement, and minimum service periods are 15 minutes for occasional use, or high capacity channels may operate 24 hours a day 7 days a week.

A block diagram of the GSTAR system is shown in Fig. 6-3, illustrating its circulators, attenuators, receivers, switches, TWTs, etc. Note that there are East and West regular and enhanced ports as well as one for Alaska/Hawaii. Uplink and downlink frequency assignments are shown below. Diagrams illustrating EIRP in dBW for CONUS or selected coverage are shown in Fig. 6-4. These should be valuable in determining the size reflector and areas where best reception appears possible. Maximum antenna height *off* the ground becomes advantageous in many instances since earth temperature effects are thereby largely avoided. (*Our Ku band reflector is mounted on the roof*).

THE SPACENETS

The second portion of GTE's Spacenet grouping involves the 4/6 and 12/14 GHz hybrids that serve both C and Ku bands, which are also constructed by RCA Astro Electronics. Spacenets I and II were orbited successfully in May and November of 1984 by Ariane, but Spacenet III, scheduled for June 1986 was lost during September when the first stage of an Ariane rocket failed. Consequently, only two Spacenets and two GSTARS are now on station, the former at 120° WL and 69° WL for the two respective Spacenets (Fig. 6-5). When Spacenet III flies again, it's parking slot will be 87° WL.

Weighing over 2600 lbs. at launch and 1526 lbs. in orbit, these spacecraft are 3-axis stabilized, require peak power of 1,212 watts, have nickel-hydrogen batteries for eclipse periods, keep station within 0.05°, and respond to earth stations at Woodbine, Maryland, San Ramon, California, with headquarters control at McLean, Virginia.

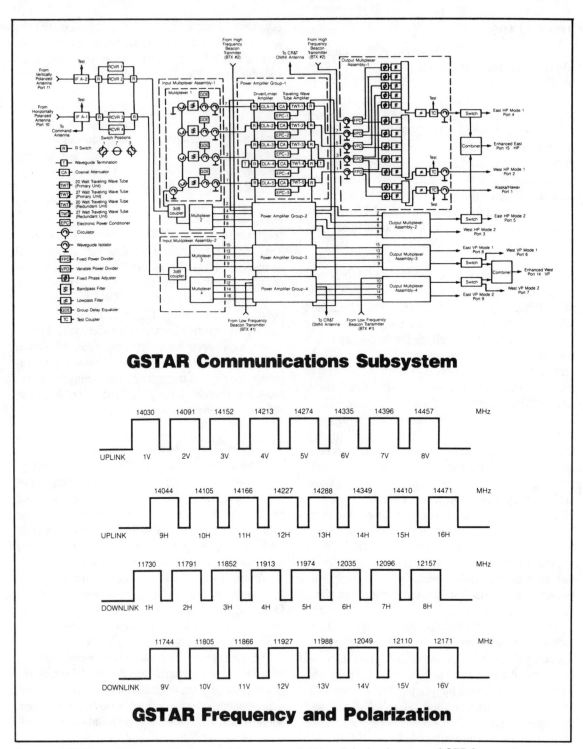

GSTAR Communications Subsystem

GSTAR Frequency and Polarization

Fig. 6-3. GSTAR satellite communications and frequency uplink/downlink plan (courtesy of GTE Spacenet).

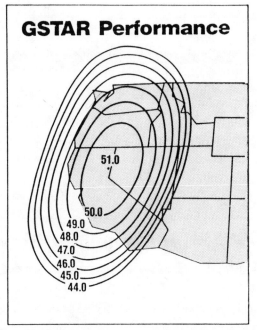

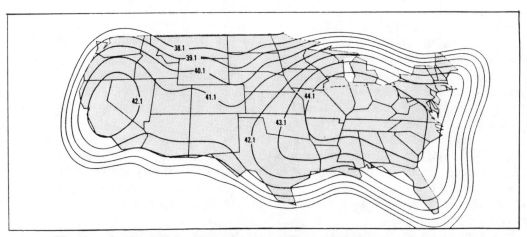

Fig. 6-4. GSTAR footprints in different configurations (courtesy of GTE Spacenet).

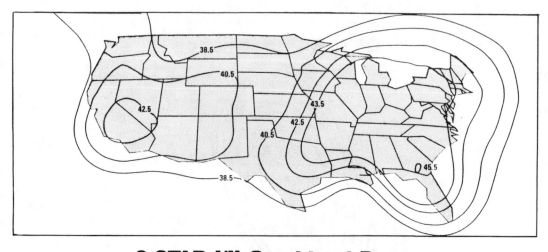

G-STAR I/II Combined Beam
Typical EIRP (dBW) Performance in CONUS

Fig. 6-4. GSTAR footprints in different configurations (courtesy of GTE Spacenet). (Continued from page 101.)

In the C-band configuration there are twelve 36 MHz transponders having 8.5 W solid-state power amplifiers and six 72-MHz transponders with 16 W TWT amplifiers. At Ku, there are six 72-MHz transponders powered by 16 W TWT amplifiers.

For satellite coverage, Spacenet I will cover all 50 states at C band and CONUS at Ku. Spacenet II illuminates CONUS and Puerto Rico at C, and CONUS at Ku. And Spacenet III will do the same as Spacenet II, but provide East and West spot beams instead of CONUS for Ku. Frequency difference between uplinks and downlinks for C band transponders is 2225 MHz and 2300 MHz for Ku band and may not drift more than ± 10 parts/million over transponder design life. Polarization isolation at C band is guaranteed at 30 dB except for "some areas" of Hawaii and Alaska, regarded as fringe areas, especially for C band.

These satellites are prominent in news gathering, private channel services, telephone traffic, etc. Terrestrial coverage and its transponder frequency and polarization plans are included in Figs. 6-6 and 6-7. Transponder service permits uses as small as 15 minutes, over 24-hour periods, 7 days/wk. Footprints for both C and Ku bands are shown in Fig. 6-7 for the SPACENET II satellite. These probably represent prime examples of many more such dual-frequency spacecraft to follow—at least those engineered and constructed by RCA.

SATELLITE BUSINESS SYSTEMS (SBS)

Built by Hughes Aircraft Company's Space and Communications Group, SBS I began operations in March 1981 delivering voice, data, electronic mail, and video over the first all-digital DOMSAT system in the $^{12}/_{14}$ GHz Ku band. Positioned at 99° WL, this spacecraft was followed by SBS II at 97° WL, launched in October of that same year, and further supported by SBS III at 95° WL, orbited in November, 1982. All were originally owned by a consortium of IBM, Comsat General Corp, and Aetna Life and Casualty Co. These satellites were primarily communications vehicles until RCA-NBC established a coast-to-coast video network link in late 1984 early 1985, which became the forerunner of their K-1 through K-3 series now taking most, if not all, their satellite network traffic. SBS 3, we are told, was the prime video carrier at that time.

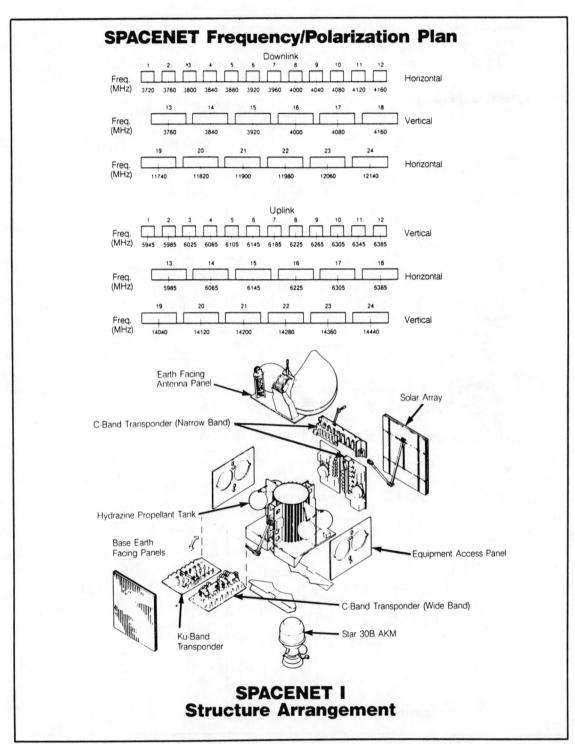

Fig. 6-5. Spacenet frequency plan and exploded structural spacecraft view (courtesy of GTE Spacenet).

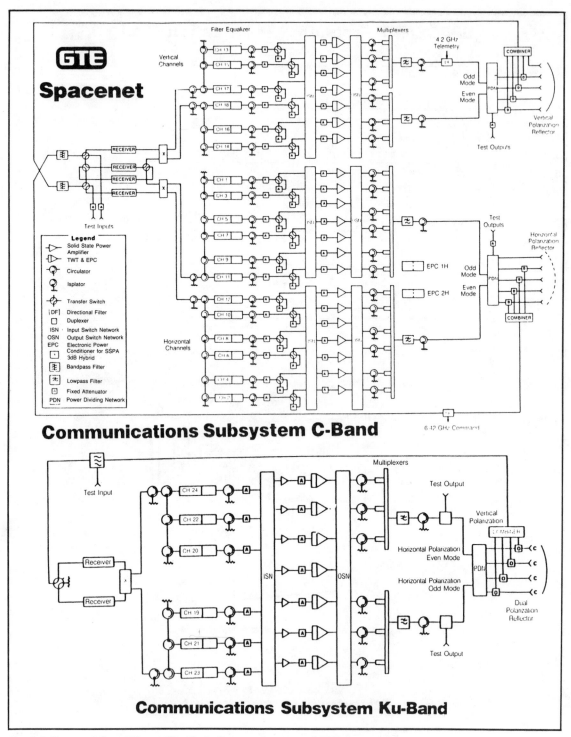

Fig. 6-6. Spacenet C and Ku satellite block diagrams (courtesy of GTE Spacenet).

SPACENET II (69° WL)

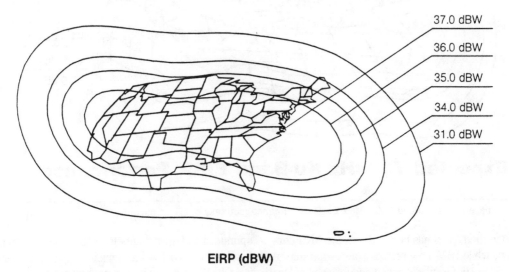

37.0 dBW
36.0 dBW
35.0 dBW
34.0 dBW
31.0 dBW

EIRP (dBW)

Expected 36 MHz C-Band EIRP Performance

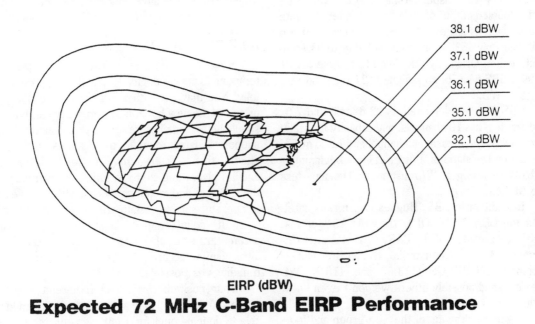

38.1 dBW
37.1 dBW
36.1 dBW
35.1 dBW
32.1 dBW

EIRP (dBW)

Expected 72 MHz C-Band EIRP Performance

Fig. 6-7. Spacenet II C/Ku and 36/72 MHz EIRP performance (courtesy of GTE Spacenet).

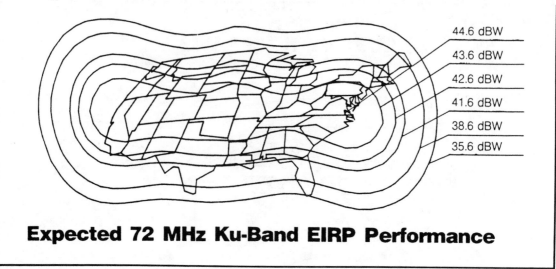

Expected 72 MHz Ku-Band EIRP Performance

44.6 dBW
43.6 dBW
42.6 dBW
41.6 dBW
38.6 dBW
35.6 dBW

Fig. 6-7. Spacenet II C/Ku and 36/72 MHz EIRP performance (courtesy of GTE Spacenet).

Since then, SBS has been sold to the MCI corporation, while IBM now retains sole ownership of SBS 4, 5, and 6. Originally scheduled for orbit in December 1987, SBS F6 Prime will use the Hughes HS 393 upgraded spacecraft, having a design life of 10-12 years, 19 transponders, a payload of 1870 lbs., and a doubled output of 40 W/transponder. Despite being twice as large as the HS 376 series, SBS 6 will cost only 15% more to launch due to its compact design. Originally scheduled to replace SBS 1 at 99°, SBS 6 has been assigned 62° WL, and SBS 5, 122° WL.

SBS 3, when deployed, is 22 ft. tall, and 7 ft. in diameter, has 10 channels, and capacity for 1,250 two-way phone messages/channel and/or color TV frequency translations. Power at life's beginning is 1118 W supplying 20 W/transponder. Headquarters are McLean, Virginia.

In addition to SBS, Hughes also makes satellites for LEASAT (DOD), the GALAXY series, ANIK C (Canada), TELSTAR, PALAPA-A,B (Indonesia), AUSSAT (Australia), INTELSAT (International), MORELOS (113.5° and 116.5° WL Mexico), and possibly others we don't even know about.

A general drawing of the SBS group and footprints for SBS 3 and 4 are included in Fig. 6-8. On SBS 5, we are told, there will be ten 43 MHz tran-

sponders and four channels of 120 MHz bandwidth. In addition, two TWTA amplifiers may be paralleled for a 40 W output. These satellites are all spin stabilized and their antennas are independently controlled. SBS 5 will contain the two polarities, but SBS 4, like SBS 3, will have only horizontal polarity and the same power output of 20 W/transponder.

Ku INSTALLATIONS

How do you do these? Without in the least attempting to appear dogmatic: you do them *very* carefully! You may use either a special linear actuator or one of the new horizon-to-horizon types, but you should be extremely careful that your concrete mast support is large enough, the mast is sufficiently sturdy, that it is *absolutely* perpendicular to the earth's plane, and there is sufficient clearance for the reflector and mount so there is little or no earth temperature noise pickup. Here, every T°K and each dB counts almost double that of C band parameters since these are smaller reflectors and ultra pointing accuracy is required in as quiet surroundings as possible.

Your positioner will aslo require a counting range approaching 1,000 and the actuator should be able to double-count for accuracies equal to or better than 0.15°. The usual 2.5° to 3° taken for granted at C band will not reliably pick up Ku con-

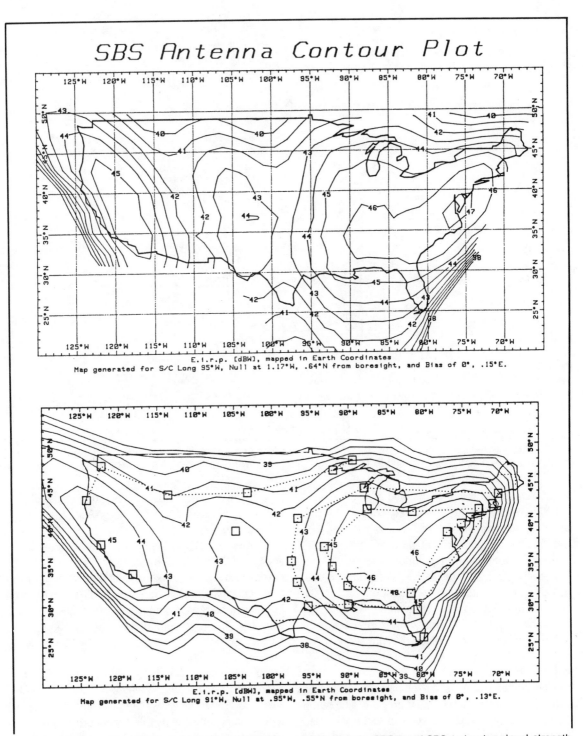

SBS Antenna Contour Plot

E.i.r.p. [dBW], mapped in Earth Coordinates
Map generated for S/C Long 95°W, Null at 1.17°W, .64°N from boresight, and Bias of 0°, .15°E.

E.i.r.p. [dBW], mapped in Earth Coordinates
Map generated for S/C Long 91°W, Null at .95°W, .55°N from boresight, and Bias of 0°, .13°E.

Fig. 6-8. General configuration for the SBS satellite series, and footprints for SBS 3 and SBS 4 showing signal strength in dBW (courtesy of SBS; SBS3 owned by MCI and SBS 4 owned by IBM).

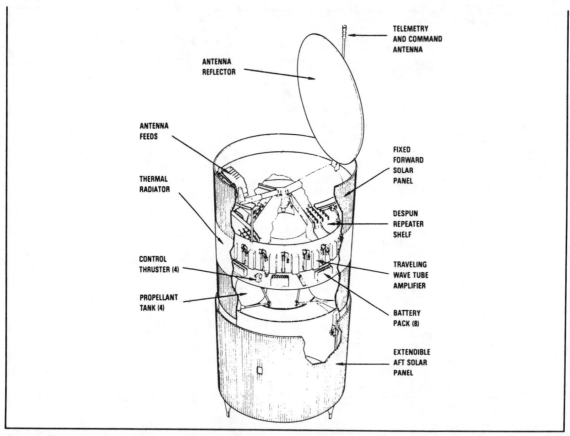

Fig. 6-8. General configuration for the SBS satellite series, and footprints for SBS 3 and SBS 4 showing signal strength in dBW (courtesy of SBS; SBS3 owned by MCI and SBS 4 owned by IBM). (Continued from page 107.)

sidering gear slop, wind effects, and positioner pulsing. Therefore, is using a reed sensor on the actuator, for instance, this will have to become two, and placed in parallel so that they will now double count and improve your resolution at least 0.1°, to approximately 0.15° cumulative. Then, should you be using one of the earlier positioners with, say a range of only 100 counts, the counter will have to be disabled so that a horizon-to-horizon mount may be used, or even a linear since the counter now actually sees 90 counts in the same period it formerly saw 45.

Thereafter, there's the installation of a new prime focus feed horn that must properly illuminate the reflector for both high- and low-frequency bands, if you are attempting to access both C and Ku. Should the installation serve Ku only, then the task

is somewhat easier with the exception of the older type mount which may be strictly AZ/EL and not polar at all.

There are probably several ways to undertake such installations. Consequently, we had best demonstrate our methods and let you work out the rest. Our installations, however, will involve *only* horizon-to-horizon mounts, and the reflectors are primarily fiberglass, although we do have both perforated and solid, spun aluminum 1.2-meter reflectors from Winegard.

The first approach (Fig. 6-9) to combined C and Ku reception has to be the mount followed by a suitable feed. And while we wait for a "confocal" coaxial feed from Boman that will have both C and Ku waveguides at center prime focus, a new "piggyback" feed from Gerry Blachley and National A.D.L.

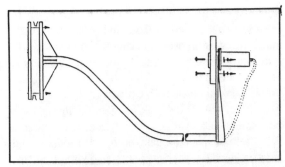

Fig. 6-9. Typical buttonhook feed support. Hacksaw can enlarge feed slot for piggyback C and Ku feeds. Keep Ku at boresight.

Enterprises will do for starters (Fig. 6-10). Designed for 0.375 to 0.4 f/D ratios, at C band, and the usual multi-ringed corrugated, tiny receptor for Ku, a double skew arrangement moves the feed probes separately, while the Ku feed, itself, mounts in a predetermined position just behind the hybrid C portion, and the waveguide cylinder passes through the front scalar portion at a slight angle from the C feed, itself. Visualize a saucer, cut a hole to the right of center and stick a pencil through—that's what the combined feed looks like.

Mounting instructions require dead centering for the Ku waveguide and offsets of 1-2 inches for the

Fig. 6-10. The hybrid C- and Ku-feeds in an integral mounting manufactured by National A.D.L. Enterprises.

C-band collector, depending on reflector size. Since we elected to use an 8-foot, 0.375 f/D fiberglass reflector, the C-band portion was shifted approximately 1.5 inches off dead center, then securely attached to a buttonhook feed holder that was handy and cut exactly for reflector f/D and offset. In this instance, it wasn't even necessary to drill additional holes in the scalar but two were required for the mounting plate.

The mount, in the meantime, should be remeasured for both perpendicularity and true North-South position. These specifications are especially important in horizon-to-horizon mounts because of their 140°+ coverage and the large arc they serve. Next, bracing cords may be attached to the feed and rim of the reflector to maintain feed position throughout the long H/H arc if there is any apparent sway due to the additional weight of the feed itself and extra block downconverter/preamplifiers.

Thereafter, find a fairly strong satellite (say Galaxy I) in the west sector, and perhaps F4 that's close to due south. If the setup is precise, you should track whatever you wish, although some elevation adjustments may still be required for the more difficult and weaker-signal spacecraft.

You may, however, encounter two prime difficulties. The 1-90 position counter on some of the older positioners, may prevent swinging through the entire arc without resetting. In these circumstances, the counter will have to be disabled and position programming done by the "seat of your pants." This condition will become doubly aggravating if you parallel two reed sensors for best stop-start resolution—which you will probably have to do for satisfactory Ku operation. Then, the counter will only permit arc movement of some 25 degrees before you have to reset it again and again. Newer positioners, we are told, will not have this aggravating problem and require no modifications at all. Our solution was to shunt a single-pole double-throw switch across the reset circuit and take it out of action altogether, immobilizing the counter.

Another problem that may slow you down a bit is the double skew, one for C and another for Ku. Most positioners, apparently, don't supply enough "stiff" pulses to operate both, therefore, you'll have to find an unused wire (perhaps in the actuator hookup) and connect (Fig. 6-11) one end to a switch at the positioner so that either, but not both, skews will move upon command. Then, separate C and Ku signal feeds are required so there's no interference or interaction between the two. These will also have to be connected to an analog switch that has sufficient bandpass to accomodate them as well as excellent isolation of at least 70 dB; perhaps more. Recall, too, that you're operating between 950 and 1450 MHz for the usual block downconverters and just any analog switch won't do. Fortunately, the ground and +5 or +6 volts required for skew dc applications may be jumpered betwwen the C and Ku feeds, so only the drive pulses need be routed on individual wires.

Later, of course, when dual concentrics have been further developed, a single feed and skew will handle both, *provided* there is sufficient isolation between the two to prevent undesirable interference. At that point, return to the true prime focus positions for the two C and Ku electromagnetic inputs will be feasible and most desirable. Temporarily, however, it will be necessary to make-do with whatever there is at hand as we combine the two bands.

Fortunately, most of the major problems appear to have been overcome already, and only a bit of tidying up remains before emerging with first-rate systems and salutary results. By the time this book is in general distribution such coaxial feeds will be in production and available at relatively modest cost. After that, we should look for general antenna improvements such as a 9-foot reflector of suitable dimensions including beamwidth, f/D ratios, C and Ku gain, good C/I characteristics, and very-low noise temperatures mounted on a superior H/H mount, with installation requiring no more than 20 minutes. Do, however, be positive the H/H mount will support your chosen reflector. Some are flimsy.

If you think the foregoing is a tall order, just reflect on what the TVRO industry must do to survive. Either these H/H polar mounts are set up quickly, easily, and accurately, or sales and service will rapidly accumulate the same problems the television folks have experienced; and their numbers are *decreasing* daily. There's no reason for this to occur in TVRO since the industry is young and fairly steady growth is apparent. Nontheless, you must be both technically competent and competitive. Scrambling has already been an unpleasant equalizer.

Fig. 6-11. National A.D.L. feed with C and Ku block downconverters mounted.

AZIMUTH AND ELEVATION AT K BAND

To make setups a little easier and more convenient for TVRO installers everywhere, we will repeat an earlier pointing diagram (Fig. 6-12) using a Maryland latitude and longitude (ours) but directing the AZ/EL angles to RCA's very popular and effective K-2 spacecraft that seems to have no more than a 4 dB attenuation factor (at least on the east coast) during heavy rainfall. Consequently, in most climates and CONUS regions, the K series should be readily accessible. Not so, unfortunately, with the 20 W transponder group which will often washout completely when viewed on 1.2-meter antennas upon encountering severe moisture conditions. Broadcast stations use 9.1-meter receptors for the weaker Ku spacecraft.

Our latitude and longitude is approximately 39° N and 76.5° W, and K-2 orbits at 81° W. The difference between the longitudes, therefore, is 4.5°, while our latitude is given as 39° N. Using the chart, proceed with the degree numbers, run dotted lines from the bottom and right sides of the figure until they intersect. Then read the curved lines for an elevation angle of 44.5° and an azimuth of 7° + 180°, which is vertually due south. And that's all there is to it! An extremely simple procedure and accurate enough to be within a couple of degrees of your target.

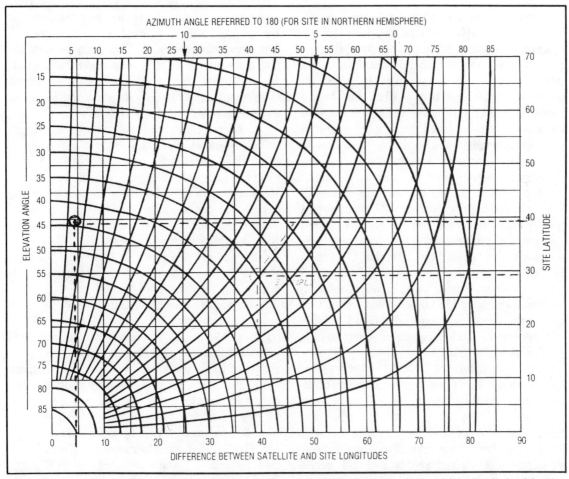

Fig. 6-12. Universal azimuth and elevation diagram requires only site latitude and longitude, and the longitude of the accessed satellite for accurate elevation and azimuth angles.

Afterwards, add or subtract any easterly or westerly *variation* and then point your compass. Should you be working with a M/A-COM offset reflector, deduct 22° from the 44.5° and you'll be on target. Other offsets may possibly vary, we don't know. Simple enough for all seasons? Unfortunately, the oval shapes of some of these offsets preclude polar mounts.

All you need now are clear fields west to south, taking into account the various elevation angles, and you're home free provided the mount and double reed count are accurate and the positioner is accomodating.

LOW SIDE INJECTION

While local oscillators in block downconverters operate at 5.150 GHz for C band, providing high side injection—*above* the 3.7-4.2 GHz 500 MHz frequency band—most Ku band oscillators have low side injection oscillators that run at 10.75 GHz and generate the usual 950-1450 MHz band by up-converting the 11.7 to 12.2 GHz frequencies. Consequently, two events occur that are different from C band: *video* must be *inverted* due to the low injection characteristic and Ku band channels are exactly reversed from those identified at C band.

For instance, channel 1 at C is now channel 24 at Ku, channel 2 becomes channel 23, etc. So to receive Ku transmissions, you will need not only a different block downconverter but also a satellite receiver with switchable video inversion to compensate for the up-conversion. Receiver tuning will remain the same, but you'll simply have to mentally reverse the ensuing LED designations as the various channel numbers appear. If Ku high-side injection were used, the local oscillator would have to operate at 13.15 GHz.

Channel numbers for 10- and 16-channel satellites, naturally, won't precisely match those of the 24-channel C-band spacecraft, so you'll have to learn transponder numbers for the various programming. And because of wider band characteristics of several of the Ku satellites, it was originally thought that center frequency fine tuning would be absolutely necessary. So far, we haven't found that to be true at all. A good AFC on the better receivers will usually pull

in a Ku channel within 2 seconds or less, and that's usually fast enough. Some of the cheapies without a phase-locked loop probably won't respond properly, but that's another problem altogether. The better ones will, especially those manufactured by Toshiba for the different distributors. If, however, there's *drift* in the receiver's second converter, then fine tuning and skew controls are essential!

Ku TROUBLESHOOTING

Fundamentally the same as C band, troubleshooting Ku will still have several differences. In the first place, terrestrial interference in-band and out-of-band should be substantially absent unless some mobile rig or other uplink is poorly aimed and maintained in your local area; test patterns on fewer transponders and some weaker satellites present some initial inconveniences. There may be considerably more scrambling on Ku eventually than C band, especially with SBS and RCA's K birds. Ku should have comparatively more commercial traffic than its sister service.

Conversely, reflectors and mounts will certainly be lighter and smaller. Many—if not most—of the commercial installations are single satellite AZ/EL mounts. Receivers designed specifically for Ku should occupy less space and be simpler in design. Installations and servicing should probably be much more rapid. Additional emphasis will be placed on adequate training for operators and installers. And those who have had a year or two in the business should become a professional cadre upon which others may lean and learn.

Already, the Electronic Industries Association has published a new PN-1661/TR 34.2 entitled Electrical and Mechanical Characteristics of Earth Station Antennas for Satellite Communications, an update of EIA standard RS-411, published August 1973. The new version is intended to offer an industry standard for terms, definitions, and concepts for mechanical and rf earth station antenna design, as well as means to verify rf performance. Shortly, too, SOUTC (Satellite Operators and Users Technical Committee) which followed the FCC's 2°, 70-engineer advisory committee, will publish its own detailed manual for setup, maintenance, and working standards for uplink/downlink earth terminals, including a strong recommendation for single satellite identification signals on designated transponders with operator phone numbers to contact in case of defective operations.

While not applying strictly to Ku, but C band, too, these guide rules and industry regulations should further the advancement of responsible satellite operations. We would also forecast some direct industry training as a result of these collective efforts. Eventually we can see a SOUTC-type organization working directly with EIA for the good of the spacecraft and terrestrial-based satellite manufacturers and distributors. Despite all the happy talk about fiberoptics wideband cable, satellites, too, will remain a major avenue of the world's system of communications. Competition and circumstances make room for all.

Other than those relatively few observations, there's not much more to servicing Ku band than C band. The elevated 12 GHz frequencies may require more expensive test gear, but if you use a block downconverter following the feed, a 1.8 GHz spectrum analyzer with accurate markers and adequate dynamic range will serve just as well because any satellite may be blocked down to 950-1450 GHz, with the rest being routine since cabling and receivers are either identical or similar in the better lines of equipment. Among the cheapies there will always be short cuts.

Signal generators that may be modulated to at least 2 MHz with FM are our greatest concern. At the moment, there's no such animal available among ordinary sweep-signal generators on the market. Apparently YIG oscillators are tough to deviate, and some sharp engineer is going to have to find a better way of handling these microwave frequencies so adequate test equipment in the modest price range can be made available for everyone. There has already been some movement in this direction, but a considerable number of improvements are sorely needed.

LATE DEVELOPMENTS

Several late developments of significance to Ku operations occurred just before the publisher re-

ceived this manuscript and we thought they should both be included because both will have a significant impact on the industry. One being a brand new spectrum analyzer, Model 2710, on the market by Tektronix; and another, a B-MAC receiver developed by engineering Vice President Bill Rowse of Private Satellite Network, Inc. (PSN) and the Sony Corp. of Japan.

A NEW SPECTRUM ANALYZER

Model 2710 (Fig. 6-13), designed as a low-cost instrument for general industry use by Tektronix and costing less than $9,000, offers an 80 dB dynamic range, 1, 5, and 10 dB log scales, a frequency span of 10 kHz to 1.8 GHz, 50/75 ohm switchable inputs, and sensitivity of -143 dBm (with option 1 at 300 Hz). Option 1 also includes a high stability phase-locked loop 5×10^{-7} frequency accuracy, and bandwidth resolution of 300 Hz. There are markers for peak find, center marker, and next right and left signals, in addition to four-trace digital storage for maximum signals comparison.

If you wish, there is also a video monitor mode that permits seeing a TV picture on the CRT and a 5 MHz system bandwidth. In addition, there are AM/FM audio detectors with amplifier, speaker, and headphone jack. Calibration of the instrument is automatic, and selectable reference levels include dBm, dBmV, dBμV, and dBμW, along with a noise normalization mode—all microprocessor controlled, of course.

While we haven't used this equipment extensively, we know its capabilities and accuracies, and specifically recommend it for satellite uplink and downlink use, as well as in the TVRO (and other) earth stations. Portable, the weight is less than 20 lbs.

A NEW LOW-COST OSCILLOSCOPE

The Tektronix Model 2225 50-MHz dual-trace oscilloscope becomes a worthy companion instrument to the 2710 spectrum analyzer; and between the two, virtually all useful satellite earth station measurements are possible (Fig. 6-14).

Primarily an rf (radio frequency) instrument not designed for baseband audio/video measurements, the analyzer is supplemented in TVRO audio/video

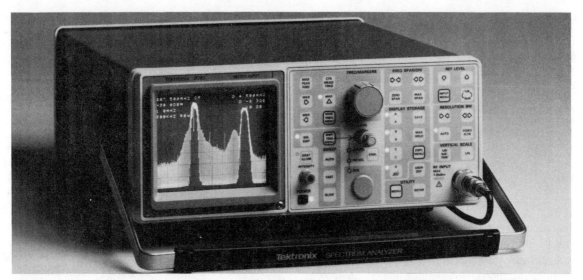

Fig. 6-13. The Tektronix new, low-cost Model 2710 spectrum analyzer with frequency response from 10 kHz to 1.8 GHz, special markers, it is self-calibrating, and has a bandpass of 5 MHz for detected video-audio (courtesy of Tektronix, Inc.).

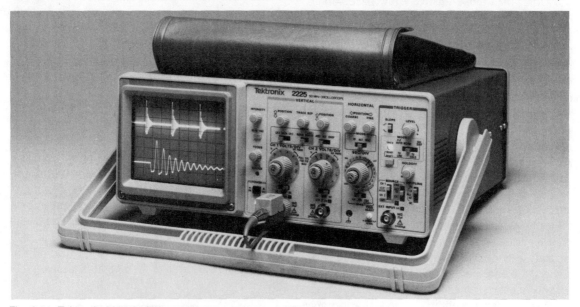

Fig. 6-14. Tektronix 2225 50-MHz oscilloscope (courtesy of Tektronix, Inc.).

measurements by a medium-frequency oscilloscope that can be highly useful in video and test pattern displays, pulse timing evaluations, dc level measurements and, in this instance, also permits selective triggering on either television lines or fields along with variable trigger holdoff.

Designed and built in United Kingdom factories, the 2225 has maximum sensitivity of 500 microvolts/division, independent trace triggering, 10× modular probes, a 12.6 kV accelerating potential, and alternate displays of magnified (×5, ×10, or ×50) and nonmagnified signals. With the 10× probe, maximum vertical deflection amounts to 50 V/div., or 400 volts max. Backed by a 3-year parts and labor warranty, the scope is only 15.2 inches wide, 5.4 inches high, and 20.3 inches long (with carrying handle). Net weight is 14.3 lbs. Sweep speeds are from 0.5 nsec to 5 nsec/div. High voltage, subminiature, $10\times$ FET, and current probes are among many available accessories.

The instrument's initial price is under $1,000 (but not much), and was specifically manufactured for such applications as field service, production testing, communications, classroom and laboratory uses, and television servicing. We think its price and features are also appropraite to the satellite earth station trade, as well.

THE PSN B-MAC RECEIVER

A 24-MHz bandwidth commercial receiver built for the Private Satellite Network (USA) by Sony, the PSN-785 is an innovative Ku-band-only receiver that checks both frequency and incoming signal strength, has *four* audio outputs, an independent AM/FM modulator, and an excellent block downconverter. It is marketed by Northsat and manufactured in Japan.

Small lamp indicators on the front panel light as the various video/audio/signal conditions are selected, and there are select buttons available for exact channel frequency entries and checks as well as *relative* incoming signal strengths between L00 and L45. In external hookups, the LNB may be mated to the receiver with quality coaxial cable in up to 600-foot lengths and F-type connectors. Double-shielded RG6/U with at least 18 AWG center conductors would seem to be recommended.

Signal/noise characteristics should be very good considering the i-f bandwidth is 24 MHz. Threshold sensitivities range between -30 dBm and -63 dBm, and up to 24 channels of information and selected audio can be stored in memory. An AGC output on the rear terminal permits voltmeter hookups to check dc levels proportional to rf signal strengths. Apparently forward AGC is used since high AGC readings denote larger incoming signal magnitudes. Out-of-band (11.7-12.2 GHz) channel settings produce an "ERROR" readout on the front panel and the receiver then reverts to a previously tuned channel number with display blinking. Front and rear panel drawings with explanatory notes are shown in the illustration as well as a highly simplified block diagram (Fig. 6-15). Power requirements, 1.9 W, Weight, 1 lb. 9 oz.

RF Ku spectrum signals are initially downconverted to 950-1450 MHz conventional i-f frequencies and capacitatively coupled into a tuning-controlled tracking filter, removing any spurious or image frequencies. This 500 MHz spectrum is then mixed with a front-panel, keypad-entered channel selection, which then results in microcomputer tuning control. Led indicator drives, and frequency selection for the voltage-controlled oscillator above. Signal mixing then occurs, with results establishing specific channel selection of 24 MHz bandpass into a filtered 2nd i-f of 402 MHz.

At this point, automatic frequency control feedback is established and routed back to the voltage-controlled oscillator to keep it on frequency. At the same time, video becomes phase-locked loop detected and delivered through a baseband amplifier to one output, or de-emphasized, low-pass filtered, and steered to a second *unclamped* output. Thereafter, video may be clamped (to avoid nonmodulation 30 to 120 Hz carrier dispersal), and routed to the *switcher* for final clamped video output or the rf channel 3-4 remodulator.

Since video still may contain the three 5.41, 6.2, and 6.8 MHz audio subcarriers and their modulation, these are selectively detected in the audio (probably quadrature) demodulator portion, with outputs going either to discrete 1,2,3 audio outputs or to the switcher for the channel 3-4 remodulator. All switch selection is done manually since the receiver has no remote control.

The various outputs are printed on the right of the block diagram. On the upper left you will see that the block downconverter receives a $+18$Vdc operating voltage through an rf choke and the rf-in, dc-out F-connector terminal.

Although fully equipped to handle B-MAC transmissions with various outputs and controls, the analog multiplexing system is not shown since it belongs to Scientific-Atlanta and not PSN.

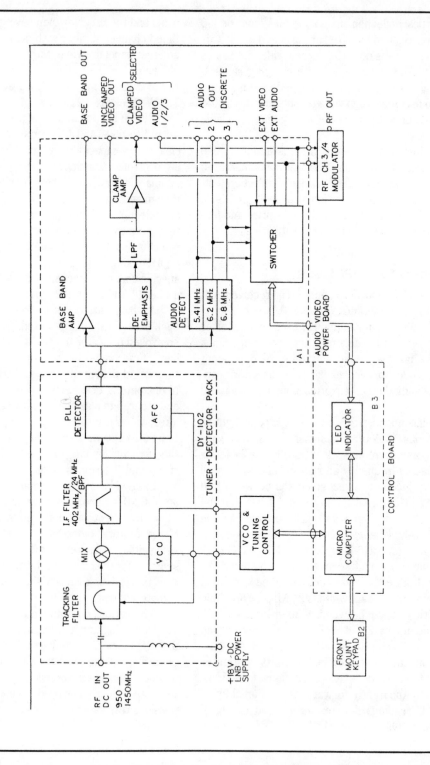

BASE BAND OUT

UNCLAMPED VIDEO OUT

CLAMPED VIDEO

SELECTED

AUDIO 1/2/3

AUDIO OUT

DISCRETE

1
2
3

EXT VIDEO

EXT AUDIO

RF OUT

BASE BAND AMP

DE-EMPHASIS

LPF

CLAMP AMP

AUDIO DETECT

5.41 MHz

6.2 MHz

6.8 MHz

SWITCHER

RF CH 3/4 MODULATOR

AUDIO VIDEO POWER BOARD

A 1

PLL DETECTOR

AFC

DY-102 TUNER + DECTECTOR PACK

I.F FILTER 402 MHz/24 MHz BPF

MIX

VCO

VCO & TUNING CONTROL

TRACKING FILTER

MICRO COMPUTER

LED INDICATOR

B 3

CONTROL BOARD

FRONT MOUNT KEYPAD

B2

RF IN DC OUT

950 — 1450MHz

+18V -DC LNB POWER SUPPLY

116

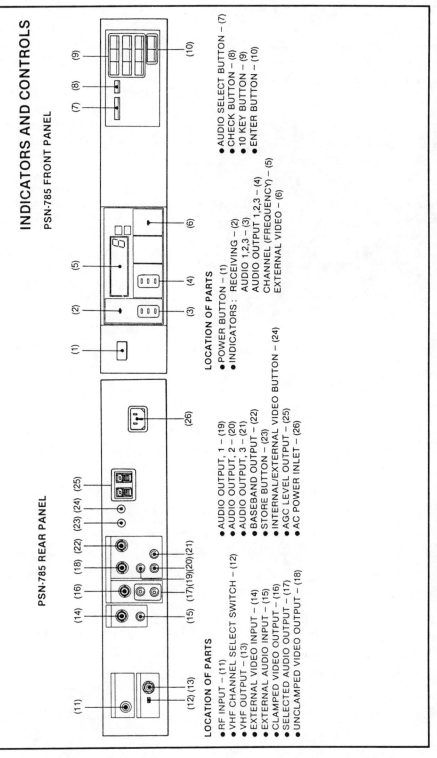

INDICATORS AND CONTROLS

PSN-785 FRONT PANEL

LOCATION OF PARTS
- POWER BUTTON – (1)
- INDICATORS: RECEIVING – (2)
  - AUDIO 1,2,3 – (3)
  - AUDIO OUTPUT 1,2,3 – (4)
  - CHANNEL (FREQUENCY) – (5)
  - EXTERNAL VIDEO – (6)
- AUDIO SELECT BUTTON – (7)
- CHECK BUTTON – (8)
- 10 KEY BUTTON – (9)
- ENTER BUTTON – (10)

PSN-785 REAR PANEL

LOCATION OF PARTS
- RF INPUT – (11)
- VHF CHANNEL SELECT SWITCH – (12)
- VHF OUTPUT – (13)
- EXTERNAL VIDEO INPUT – (14)
- EXTERNAL AUDIO INPUT – (15)
- CLAMPED VIDEO OUTPUT – (16)
- SELECTED AUDIO OUTPUT – (17)
- UNCLAMPED VIDEO OUTPUT – (18)
- AUDIO OUTPUT, 1 – (19)
- AUDIO OUTPUT, 2 – (20)
- AUDIO OUTPUT, 3 – (21)
- BASEBAND OUTPUT – (22)
- STORE BUTTON – (23)
- INTERNAL/EXTERNAL VIDEO BUTTON – (24)
- AGC LEVEL OUTPUT – (25)
- AC POWER INLET – (26)

Fig. 6-15. PSN's Model 785 Ku band B-MAC receiver block diagram and front/rear panel controls and connections (courtesy of Private Satellite Network).

BOMAN'S CONFOCAL FEED

According to the manufacturer, this is a lightweight 4/12 GHz prime-focus feedhorn that has both adjustable scalar rings and adjustable GHz focal lengths (Fig. 6-16). There's little insertion loss, cou-

Fig. 6-16. The Boman C- and Ku-band CONFOCAL feed for prime focus installations (courtesy of Boman Industries).

pled with high gain, and features a single heavy-duty servo motor. Boman Industries further states it is lightweight and easy to mount. Should performance support all claims, this may well be the answer to easily-mountable, good quality performance in a prime-focus feed that's almost equally suitable for either satellite spectrum.

Should this particular feed become successful, along with a similar-type product that should be available by the time you read this chapter—developed by National A.D.L. Enterprises—you will find C and Ku bands considerably easier to access with reliable mounts and actuators. Our experience with ''piggy back'' offset Ku- and C-band feedhorns has *not* been satisfactory. These new ones will mount in their *original* prime focus positions and *not* require various degrees of experimental offsets that probably vary antenna-by-antenna and f/D-by-f/D. Furthermore, they should mount easily on buttonhook feed supports, something the ''piggies'' couldn't handle successfully, even with the determined application of a hacksaw.

Chapter 7

Satellite and Cable TV Scrambling

AT THE MOMENT, THERE ARE FOUR PRIME SIGNAL scrambling schemes for satellites in existence, with several more serving cable and possibly a few MATV systems in the wings. By adopting or originating various algorithms (enciphering procedures) video and audio transmitted signals are encoded and then decoded, masking carrier information between points of origination and reception so that you and I are excluded from receiving anything but severely distorted transmissions. Most of these systems hard-scramble audio, reducing it to noise, with some mild interruptions to video. Other systems pay more attention to concealing video and massaging sync, along with obscured sound, creating double trouble for those who might wish to break the code and look/hear the programs. For the moment, we understand that 21 C-band channels may possibly scramble, but so far, only about half have already done so. HBO plans to move to RCA's K-3 (which the two now jointly own) sometime after launch in 1988 or 1989. So signal scrambling may, eventually, prove highly expensive for everyday tastes, and generally subside as advertisers see millions of viewers who refuse to pay $395 or something equivalent for standard decoders plus a sizeable monthly fee-per-view for programs, many of which are intended strictly for the "adult" market.

Prime scrambling systems for satellites in the U.S. for now are the VideoCipher® Linkabit® arrangement and B-MAC, with Orion holding forth in Canada. And since there has been no cross licensing between the two countries one country could not purchase decoders to view the other. One wonders if such enciphering will eventually cover the world, even if language barriers don't. What price entertainment, corporate secrets, and pure exclusion?

Eventually, however, someone's going to discover that very wideband video/audio can be dispatched probably more inexpensively over fiberoptics cable than satellites—at least between the major cities, and this could reduce sky traffic considerably. Temporarily, though, the competing services will go head-to-head until economics and convenient delivery terminals prevail. Even then, there's probably room for all, depending on need and continually advancing electronics.

VIDEOCIPHER®

Originated by west coast Linkabit®, bought out by M/A-COM, then by General Instrument Corp., Video Cipher II® has certainly been, to date, the most popular U.S. mode of video/audio encryption and is now used by many cable companies at their headends, as well as a number of pay entertainment mediums that must usually purchase movies or taped material to deliver continuous programming to their substantial audiences. Home Box Office (HBO), Showtime, the Disney Channel, CNN (Cable News Network), Cinemax, and others are all involved in scrambling their wares and taking greenstamps (as the highway truckers say) for audience viewing. A total of 21 transponder users say they're going the same route. Considering that video channels on SBS-3, K-2, K-1, GSTAR, and the Spacenets—all operating at Ku band—are not yet included. Less than 12 out of *more* than 150 video channels isn't necessarily alarming, even though some have been rather popular. We suspect the viewing public with their rooftop or backyard TVRO systems can manage to survive, and even prosper, considering the huge amount of continuing educational, religious, sports, and amusement material remaining. Meanwhile, the U.S. Congress is expected to do little more than offer sanctimonious gestures and an occasional "hold the scrambling" bill that has no chance clearing committee much less legal passage.

Therefore, the fewer decoders purchased by the public, the sooner scrambling could go away.

VIDEOCIPHERS® I AND II

VideoCiphers® I and II scramblers/descramblers originated from a special algorithm developed by the National Bureau of Standards, called the Data Encryption Standard (DES). Secure address and control signals are transmitted to each descrambler over regular video at a 250,000 rate-per-hour, along with other system "support" features. Multilevel con-

trols permit descrambler grouping into common program types, or tiers, and all may be authorized for individual programs by a single message. Such messages may control up to 56 independent tiers of programming, which can mean a single pay-per-view sanction or all available programs, depending on message content. Each descrambler, then, will respond only to those tiers previously authorized and cannot be interrupted or switched to other unauthorized programs without specific consent from the originator. However, tiering changes may be made easily at regular or irregular intervals, depending on customer preference.

VideoCipher® II operates on a 56-bit DES key that may amount to as many as 72.058×10^{15} permutations, many of which must be satisfied before the unit is authorized, with each descrambler having a special DES key stored on a solid state IC. During each billing interval the key is transmitted to individual descramblers, along with requested programming in the form of tiers. Thereafter, programs change at the end of program boundaries, approximately each half hour, permitting delinquent terminations, tier changes, new programming, etc (Fig. 7-1).

When one attempts to receive video without either descrambler or proper authorization, the picture appears as an out-of-sync color swirl that has no recognizeable form. This is because of video inversion, the centering of 3.58 MHz color burst away from the hoizontal blanking pulse, and removing both vertical and horizontal sync, leaving only a digital sync recognition pattern, which must be activiated to reproduce the 11 μsec and 1.3 msec blanking and sync intervals so familiar to those in television. Video S/N is specified at 57 dB(weighted) to 4.2 MHz.

Audio, on the other hand, is much more severely treated since it is digitized as two audio channels placed in the now empty horizontal blanking interval. Digital samples are then added to random binary sequences and combined with error coding bits. Any mistakes occurring during transmission are thereby corrected and noise-free audio is decoded and reproduced for the listener at the receive terminal, within a range of 20 Hz to 15 kHz with a dynamic range of 80 dB and no more than 0.5 percent

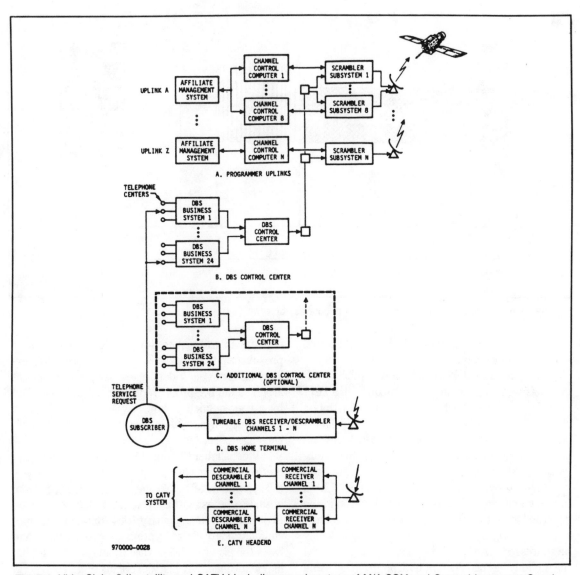

Fig. 7-1. VideoCipher® II satellite and CATV block diagrams (courtesy of M/A-COM and General Instrument Corp.).

harmonic distortion—at least that's what the specs say.

VideoCipher® II descramblers feature custom very large scale (Fig. 7-2) integrated circuits (VLSI) K-bits/sec.—all being delivered within the standard 63.5 μsec horizontal line format authorized many useful in direct-to-home broadcast systems as well as CATV and SMATV, and have been in volume production since December 1984. When specifically authorized, consumer descramblers may receive all

programming going to cable and multiple system installations, and also feature an on-screen display, parental lockout capability, a financial register for credit recall, and text services for programs, messages, inquiries, or extra information. At home, these descramblers produce channel 3-4 remodulated AM video for rf and monophonic FM sound, as well as baseband video for monitors and dual audio outputs for stereo. There is also an auxiliary data output for software control at data rates up to 88

121

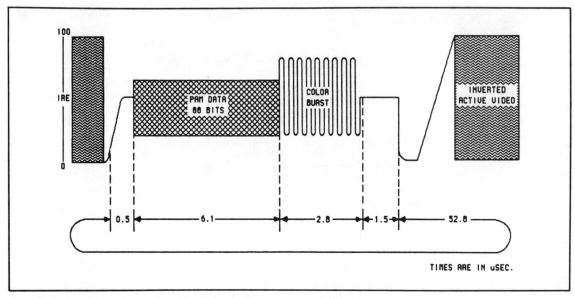

Fig. 7-2. Horizontal line format for VideoCipher® II (courtesy of M/A-COM).

years ago on December 17, 1953 by the Federal Communications Commission as NTSC.

Each descrambler has a special "public" address as well as a "number" of unique DES keys stored within its microprocessor. As the illustration shows, the *scrambler* must have inputs including descrambler attributes, the monthly key, program attributes and program key, as well as the descrambler key. All this information is dual-encrypted and transmitted over some satellite channel. With monthly keys and other appropriation stored in the descrambler's nonvolatile memory (and not subject to power outages) some 600,000 descramblers may be addressed per hour so that those having received the monthly key can decrypt both program keys and attributes for clear program sound and viewing.

Tiering instructions reach descramblers in individually addressed messages in addition to the monthly keys. This then is compared with the various program attributes accompanying each key to allow or disallow reception. Separate tiering for CATV and SMATV is also furnished so that programmers have independent control of the various affiliates. Central contols for consumers may be operated by as many as 24 individual businesses, with subscriber service based on XYZ zip code coordinates. In addition to advance telephone calls or presubscriptions, there is also an impulse pay-per-view facility in the VideoCipher® II descrambler built around a tamper-proof credit register and controlled by a user-defined password. Dual audio channels may function as either stereo pairs or for dual-language purposes.

VideoCipher® I's have been designed with discrete components and are primarily used in commercial applications. The Columbia Broadcasting System is said to be using this system on its news shows. In production since January 1984, this system time-shuffles video via a cryptographic keystream and hides the picture totally, while treating audio like that in VideoCipher® II just described (Fig. 7-3).

During scrambling, active video on each line is A/D converted at 4 × 3.58 MHz (color burst), then stored in multiline memory. Lines are then divided into various-length segments, which are read out in random order, reconverted to analog and then transmitted.

Descrambling actually reverses the process, with memory readouts reconstructed in reverse via A/D and D/A processing for complete video recovery. In the scrambler you will find buffers and clampers, the digitizing circuits, memory, multiplex

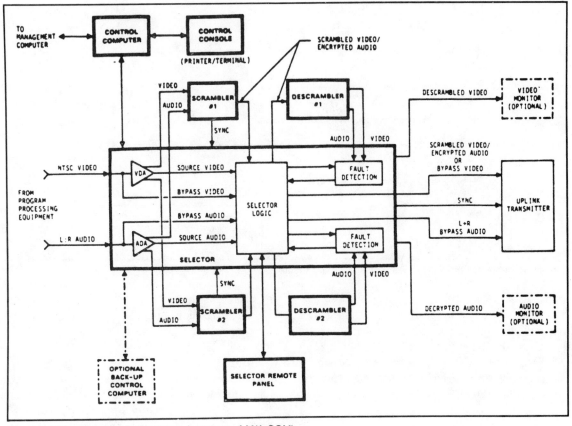

Fig. 7-3. VideoCipher® I Subsystems (courtesy of M/A-COM).

for sync addressing and control, along with the digital audio, and finally the D/A reconversion, all of which is passed through a low-pass filter and then transmitted. Audio, of course, is the same as that for VideoCipher® II, previously detailed.

Should the entire key list be stolen in the VideoCipher® I system, each uplink list has a single key generation number for the unit, and this very simply requires instituting a corresponding new key generation number. There is also an intermediate anti-theft mode called a "fixed key." Here a fixed test key becomes part of encryption and is particularly desirable during system startup or installation. In the event of message errors, a 16-bit redundancy check attaches to each message, and if this does not check correctly, the message is rejected. Further, any message having key information has to be received twice in precisely the same order to pass this

16-bit cyclic redundancy check. Accuracy also (Fig. 7-4) depends on accurate synchronization, and this is done by a system frame count and a 24-bit sync stream. Descramblers receive sync from the transmitter over their control channels. Key changes are then coordinated and the 24-bit sync sequence aligns both line and sample counters for common timing reference and appears in the first line of all VideoCipher® I frames.

Finally, control and management computers offer database management and message generation supervision. The control computer has a large reserve of unit and address keys with which it generates various random keys and formats, which are then mixed and routed to scramblers. At the same time, the tandem management computer supports system interfaces and authorizes or deauthorizes the many units involved, including the many identifica-

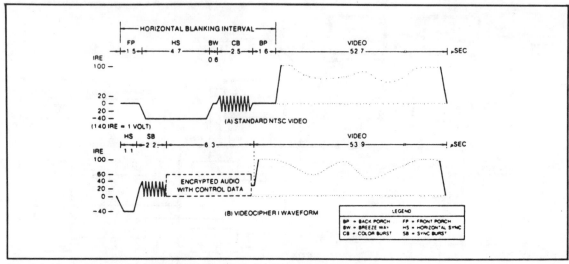

Fig. 7-4. Line waveforms for NTSC and VideoCipher® I (courtesy of M/A-COM).

tions. Financial and billing operations are also possible. And that about wraps up available information on the two VideoCipher® systems as they are presently constituted, with many thanks to Dr. Mark Medress of M/A-COM Video Products Group for sharing this good knowledge with us and our readers.

MULTIPLEXED ANALOG COMPONENT (MAC) SIGNALS

Shortened to a quickly identified *MAC*, this British-originated system is still undergoing study and refinement but shows every promise of becoming a significant factor in *commercial* satellite transmissions and reception, along with several other advantages such as bandwidth expansion, widescreen displays, and secure content containment.

Somewhat akin to the French SECAM color system, (translated into "sequential with memory") this is a multiplexing system designed to eliminate cross-color and cross-luminance (crosstalk), the high frequency color subcarrier and aliasing, which is baseband intermodulation with the sampling frequency.

Actually there are several versions of MAC, with possibly more forthcoming, as the full potential of the system becomes recognized. In the U.S.

and Canada, at the moment, Scientific Atlanta seems to be the major developer and is spending considerable time and energy toward that end. These versions (all FM) are:

A-MAC—Supports the idea of single /multiple FM on a digitally modulated subcarrier at 7 MHz, added to video before modulation.

B-MAC—The time-division multiplexing of sound into the line blanking space, with composite signals modulating the carrier.

C-MAC—Sound digitally modulating carrier during line blanking, and abaseband modulating carrier during line scan.

So far, it seems that C-MAC is at least the British favorite, while B-MAC appeals to North Americans (Fig. 7-5).

The British would time compress luma and chroma information during line scan by a ratio of 3:2 for luminance and 3:1 for chrominance by sampling the analog signal and reading it out at some adjusted rate. This would entail eight bits for digital sync, 186 bits for sound or data, and 1102 samples for analog video.

The mix, interestingly enough, would then offer as many as eight companded audio/data channels with luminance carried on each scan line and chroma sequentially with little pre-emphasis and no color subcarrier. Prefiltering, however, does limit verti-

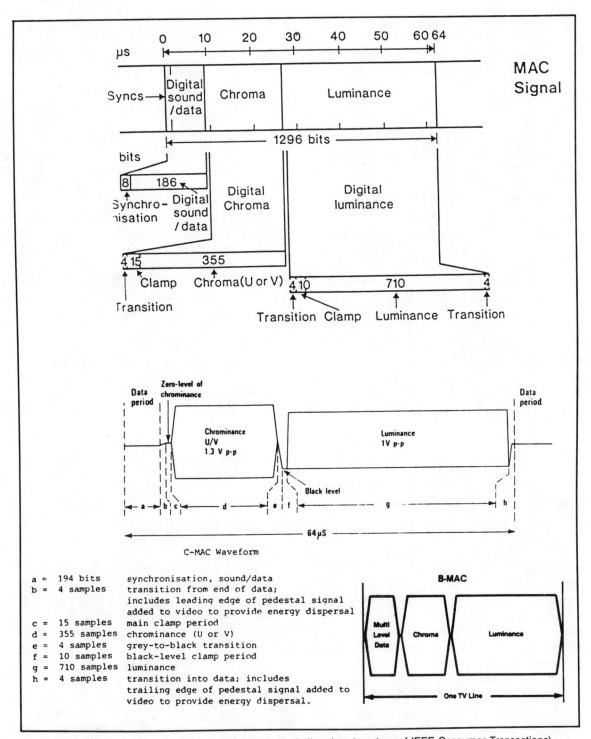

Fig. 7-5. The MAC signal and its B-MAC and C-MAC single line data (courtesy of IEEE Consumer Transactions).

cal resolution because of line averaging, but aliasing can be held below interlace flicker. C-MAC is also compatible with teletext which, the British say, can be transmitted during field blanking (vertical blanking) at a bit error rate of 10^{-3}, which corresponds to a C/N ratio of 4 dB.

Satellite downlink frequencies (for Europe) would be just above our Ku band at 11.7 to 12.5 GHz and could be received by a 0.9 meter reflector (2.95 ft.) and suitable electronics. According to W.G. Stallard on the U.K.'s Independent Broadcasting Authority, time multiplexing techniques are easily scrambled and there can also be additional development of high definition TV, especially for projection television. As shown in Fig. 7-5, time period a amounts to 194 bits; b to 4 samples; c to 15 samples; d to 355 samples; e and h to 4 samples each; f to 10 samples, and g to 710 samples. Notations U/V are the red/blue color difference signals—all courtesy of Mr. Stallard and the IEEE Transactions on Consumer Electronics from which the report was digested.

D-MAC would frequency multiplex data at rf, centering video at 70 MHz and data could then be added on some separate carrier at a higher frequency. Unfortunately, two receivers are required.

The North American choice seems to be B-MAC, which time division multiplexes audio and data in multilevel code within line blanking of 9 μsec. Video is much the same as C-MAC, although system bandwidth is constrained to just a little over 6 MHz. This dynamic range permits multilevel data in the video portion and is said to be "ideally" suited to cable, SMATV, UHF, or terrestrial microwave without any decoding at various intermediate distribution points. It is also compatible with video recorders (VCRs) and can be detected within regular inexpensive satellite receivers. Sync for this system operates on one line of the vertical blanking interval as a single digital word and permits receiver lockup at 0 dB C/N.

Audio for the system is designed as 4-channel digital with 31.4 or 31.2 kHz digital sampling. Delta modulation offers a dynamic range (at the descrambler) of more than 84 dB, when data is encrypted according to DES. We are told that 94 K bits is

standard, with any audio channel permitted data transmit and receive at 320 K bits/sec. Video scrambling can be done with simple inversion, more complex line reversal or rotation, line shuffling, and translation. Line shuffling and line translation scrambling seem to be the desirable methods of more secure encryption. The first uses field storage for line sequence reorganization, while line translation is subject to horizontal line time shifts with variable blanking times. Patterns are changed every frame. And for all this, 4×10^{12} (billion) addresses are possible at a rate of 1×10^6/hour.

The format, according to John Lowry of Scientific Atlanta, consists of time compressing the usual 52.5 μsec active scan line to 53 μsec, making 17.7 μsec available for R-Y, B-Y color difference information, and leaving the rest for B-MAC data, which is delivered at the rate of 1.86 megabits/sec. Six channels of adaptive Dolby delta-mod are included and the data channel is enciphered under complete control of the originator. Receiver screen format may be either standard 4×3 or 16×9 (aspect ratio), and the decoder is now available as a unit of custom-designed integrated circuits.

OAK'S ORION

Used by the Canadians for their satellite security systems, Oak Industries, Inc. has adopted the Orion technology, which may even allow partial studio and partial transmit earth station scrambling when studio and transmit earth stations are widely separated—a rare circumstance now, we're told.

At the studio, video may or may not be inverted on a line-by-line and/or frame-by-frame basis, all computer controlled, digitized, and encrypted. This is then transmitted over internal wiring or external microwave to the transmitter where audio is digitized, reformatted, and inserted in place of horizontal sync, maintaining these signals between the usual white and black levels, and moving the sync back-porch from 0 to 75 IRE. A decoder, meanwhile, has access to studio encryption via special signals inserted in the 1.33 msec vertical blanking interval. Video/audio signals may also be sent "plain language" through the microwave system (if used) then encoded at the transmitter and subsequently up-linked as secure communications. Receive decoders are remotely addressable by computer, which may be either an IBM PC system for small systems of less than 5,000 decoders, or an IBM Series I for larger systems.

A Sigma sound system has also been included except for two samples plus parity for each TV line, with 12-bit digitizing of each sample compressed to 8 bits. There is an optional 14-bit network-quality sound system available also, but will require a sub-carrier for sound transmission. In the encryption system there are periodic key changes provided, new keys delivered in the vertical blanking interval, while the master key is sent to each decoder en-crypted and uses the box (individual) key already stored in each decoder. Such preset keys may be customer-changed in the field with Oak's aid and blessing.

The overall system consists of a control com-puter, pre-encorder, post-encoder, and decoder (Fig. 7-6). The pre-encoder contains an input video processor to amplify and clamp video at 0 dB IRE blanking and also a 4.09 MHz clock for frame refer-ence and timing signals generated in the *timing generator*.

The *input audio processor* samples and digitizes audio and compresses it from 12 to 8 bits, which are then encrypted with a key from the address proces-sor and computer. *The output audio processor* con-verts parallel data bits to serial bits in sync with horizontal video scanning.

An inversion now produces a random sequence of inverted signals that alternate among field/field, line/line and invert/noninvert so the computer can insert scrambled information into these individual modes via the *address* and *output video processors*. At this point, the *address processor* originates com-

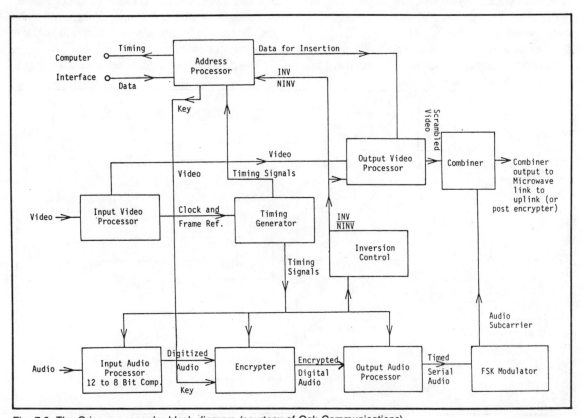

Fig. 7-6. The Orion pre-recorder block diagram (courtesy of Oak Communications).

127

mands resulting in computer-generated addresses and encryption keys while converting address and key data into serial intelligence for video output.

The *output video processor* then combines all address, key, and control data from the address processor for insertion into the vertical blanking interval. The *combiner* collects all encyphered audio and video into a single output for computer processing. (If studio and transmitter are separated, an FSK modulator may be used.)

Computer software will store all decoder addresses, generally block non-system decoders, permit temporary address of decoders in other systems, block unauthorized or stolen decoder operations, and generate encrypted keys by random pseudo-selection. A permanent list of subscriber addresses is maintained and the system will accept videotext or other suitable data for blanking interval insertion. The combined video, digitized and encrypted audio, as well as computer-generated data are all combined in the post encoder and sent as a single signal to the microwave transmitter.

The *post encoder* consists of a video-audio splitter and video attenuator, followed by video and au-

dio processors, a timing generator, digital processor, monitor, scrambling enhancer and output video processor (Fig. 7-7).

Input video processing generates timing clock and reference sync, in addition to amplifying and clamping video blanking, while the *audio processor* detects audio subcarrier(s) and reconverts from serial to parallel format.

The *timing generator* then develops clock and timing pulses for encoder audio/video control, and the *digital processor* stores audio that is delivered to the *output processor* (above) during horizontal sync/blanking times, as well as a digital reference for the decoder to detect scrambled signals and produce a frame reference. The output processor now combines audio and video, and advances the color burst level to 75 IRE units. Data swing potential and modulation are next created by the *scrambling enhancer,* at the same time a *monitor* circuit examines signal conditions, whether scrambled, nonscrambled, clock phase lock, and digital parity. If there are problems, external indicators advertise faults. Signals are now ready for transmit.

The *decoder* (Fig. 7-8) includes a clamping am-

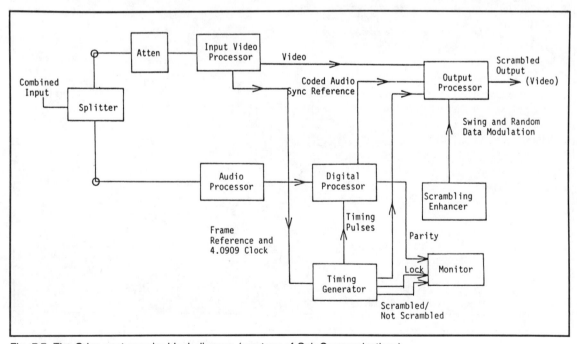

Fig. 7-7. The Orion post-encoder block diagram (courtesy of Oak Communications).

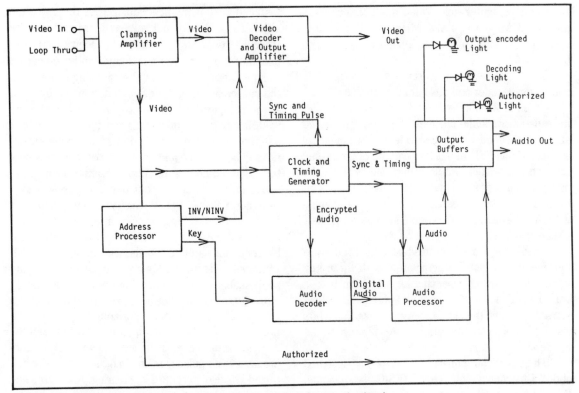

Fig. 7-8. The Orion Decoder block diagram (courtesy of Oak Communications).

plifier, address processor, video decoder, audio decoder and processor, a clock timing generator, and output buffers with lamp indicators showing outputs, decoding, and authorizations. According to Oak, they operate this way. The *clamping amplifier* clamps input signal color burst, the *address processor* looks at vertical blanking interval data and, if properly authorized, transmits the necessary "authorized" signal. Invert/noninvert status and decryption keys are also decoded. The key goes to the audio decoder, while invert or noninvert video instructions are routed to the video decoder.

From the input clamping amplifier, the *clock and timing generator* receives system sync and converts this to clock, sync and timing information for over-all decoder control. With sync and timing now transmitted to the audio processor, audio decoder, video decoder and output buffers, video and audio are now decoded in time sequence, and audio is returned to ordinary binary logic, which is then converted to ana-

log. *Output buffers* supply low impedance drives for audio, sync, and indicator lamps. System address rates are 3,600 messages/minute, address numbers 2,097,152, key lengths 32 bits, along with 49 program levels.

OAK'S CABLE SYSTEM

The company also has three cable scrambling systems, the first two for rf and the third for baseband with remote control, namely:

☐ TC 35 for 35 channels (rf)
☐ TC 56 for 56 channels (rf)
☐ Sigma for 83 channels (Baseband)

Encoding is accomplished with a Sigma encoder for enciphering one specific channel before system-wide distribution. Any one of 56-tiered levels may be assigned to any encoded channel by a tag word

129

through a computer link. Video and audio carriers are 45.75 MHz and 41.25 MHz NTSC-specified, respectively, with usual output impedances of 75 and 600 ohms.

The Sigma system operates with a 550 MHz converter/decoder and descrambler. In this Oak cable system, total horizontal and vertical sync are removed and two audio channels digitized, encrypted and "embedded" in the video. Two control channels—one FSK modulated and the other passed through the vertical interval blanking period—the first containing program authorization and control information, while the second has channel and tagging data, with separate encryption keys continuously varied and specified for each channel.

These keys are patented and guarded by a multi-level key distribution system with three key variables, including a specific key for each box, a variable second-level key common to all authorized subscribers, and the regular service keys. Each box also has a unique identification address known to the headend computer.

The 64-bit communications protocol is designed about a frequency-shift-keyed (FSK) data channel that delivers continuous information to the decoders, with special protective features against box exchanges and "spoofing."

The *decoder* uses any television receiver's tuner for channel selection in the EIA or IS-15 box, and only a single remote control is required for both TV and decoder, which deciphers all signals at baseband without remodulation accompanied by artifacts and bandpass reduction.

Remote controls have a 21-button keypad for channel selection, recall volume, and power on/off. An optional keypad also has parental control. An optional program timer is also available that can program 15 stored events for one month's advanced viewing.

ZENITH'S Z-TAC®

Used primarily in cable systems for both video/audio and pay-per-view operations, the Z-TAC® AND Z-VIEW® systems are important from a national "secure" traffic standpoint since they are installed in so many headends across the U.S. And although they may not appear in active satellite transmissions, such signals are received and encoded at the many cable headends and transmitted to subscribers via baseband scrambling rather than the customary rf methods currently in use by most of the competition. Therefore, the method and the system are both important from the standpoint of a different technique applied to secure communications. There is also a Phonevision pay-per-view system that combines telephone transmission from subscriber to headend, but this is a one-way system rather than Z-VIEW which is two way and does not involve the telephone. Our interest, therefore, involves Z-TAC® and Z-VIEW® as they relate to cable receiving satellite signals, with their claimed advantages of better signal security, in-band addressability, consumer product compatibility, more features, and future flexibility (Fig. 7-9).

Here, at baseband, horizontal sync is suppressed, controlled video inversion occurs, and the average picture level sustained below that of the suppressed sync pulses, maintaining a continually distorted image of perpetual line tearing. And every one or two seconds such sync pulses will *not* be depressed even without any transmitted timing or decoding information, along with random video inversion that is encrypted in digital data transmitted during the vertical blanking interval.

To decode, a proprietary LSI integrated circuit reinserts sync pulses *only* when suppressed by the encoder, and another IC deciphers instructions to return video to its normal state. But video decoding does not operate unless a program tag in the vertical blanking interval matches that already in the decoder's memory. Being in-band, a selected channel is always demodulated (detected). The decoder can always operate on any information in the vertical blanking interval. Thus there is no trapping out of the data channel, which could occur in out-of-band addressing systems, and a lost or stolen unit, or even an overdue account may be silenced by the headend, in addition to program authorizations being changed without home service. Each Z-TAC system controller can address and control up to 64

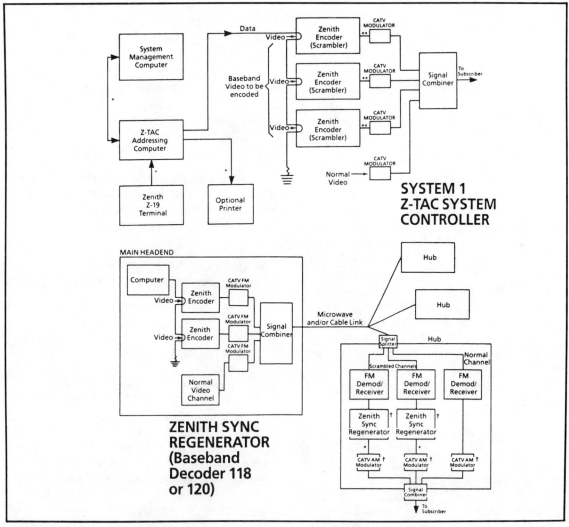

Fig. 7-9. The latest Z-TAC cable TV scrambler/descrambler system, including sync generation (courtesy of Zenith Electronics Corp.).

encoders, with converter/decoders authorized in tiers, of which there are 20. The box may not be used unless receiving data.

There are four channel banks in these series of tiers, each with five program categories and may be changed from the headend at will. Such tiering permits custom programming, with one tier designated for remote control, and lost or stolen remote units will no longer operate. There is also audio, since sound is muted at the decoder on unauthorized chan-

nels, but scrambled channels may also have audio in plain language as an attraction for curious subscribers.

Newest Z-TAC settop converter/decoders permit up to 74 channels with single cable and 148 with dual. The decoder automatically selects cable A or B. Bandwidth is 550 MHz and addressability can access 10,800 subscribers/minute. Should there be a power failure, a rechargeable battery in every decoder continues decoder program authorization for

24 hours and will resume operations at the last received authorization level. You will also find a new infrared Zenith remote control that can turn on/off the converter/decoder, has up/down channel and volume selection, mute, direct access, favorite channel, clear and data entries, plus parental control. There's also a dual control for those with Zenith remote-controlled television receivers. Audio/video outputs from Z-TAC® are also now installed in the newer units for TV monitors.

Z-VIEW

The newest Z-VIEW® system has been designed for two-way cable systems and operates as a real time impulse/system, in addition to status monitoring capability, channel monitoring and opinion polling. The unit is simply added to the Redi-Plug on the Z-TAC® decoder, with program requests transmitted directly to the headend via the remote keypad. Power levels for Z-VIEW installations and interrogations are automatically conducted by the headend computer and any problems immediately noted. Downstream signals are passed through Z-TAC®, and upstream signals through biphase PSK modulation.

For two-way cable systems, Zenith has also developed a unique method that is simply an extension of the usual one-way systems now in general use. In downstream, a computer system controller and data encoder are required for management, billing, addressing and control, in addition to a headend receiver for upstream returns. Software is written in Pascal, C, and macro-assembler, and all I/O (in/out) becomes direct memory access, with total memory, including database for 60,000 consumers being just 1.5 megabytes. Channel monitoring is also included but may be omitted if desired. Microwave downstream distribution, however, does require additonal equipment such as a frequency translator, and possibly a headend receiver at each hubsite.

The system operates with two simultaneous protocols: polling—used for all headend-initiated transactions—and contention, which becomes the subscriber originated actions. Although polling is somewhat slow, Slotted-Aloha contention protocol with a special backoff algorithm apparently is very

suitable for two-way operation. This, we are told, can operate in both polling and contention modes. Network nodes may be polled at the rate of 60/second. The backoff algorithm is used for retransmission of an upstream request until acknowledgement from the headend even under very noisy conditions. Upstream messages have a total of 480 slots/second and are synchronized.

TROUBLESHOOTING DESCRAMBLERS

There's only limited information available on this subject, as you might well expect, but this may help you over a few of the more obvious lumps and bumps—at least in the beginning.

THE M/A-COM VCIIC (NOW GENERAL INSTRUMENT) DESCRAMBLER

This is the industrial/commercial descrambler and *not* the consumer type for which we will have coverage next. Therefore be guided accordingly when using this material, which has been supplied directly from M/A-COM for our collective applications. Naturally, you're supposed to have an installation manual and this should be consulted for any wiring instructions and test point locations.

First, verify receiver compatibility. Then check specifications for any required modifications. Consult the list of compatible receivers in VCIIC user's guide; and any modification instructions that are available from the manufacturer or M/A-COM (800)845-2748 or (704)322-4220.

Next, confirm unit authorization with appropriate programmer; connect a voltmeter to pin 1 of terminal board 1 and ground. Adjust AGC potentiometer between J-1 and J-2 for + 4 Vdc, if required.

When receiving a scrambled signal, power, sync, and auth lights should light. If signal is unscrambled, power, sync, and bypass lamps are on.

Make sure the unit is properly interfaced with the receiver: J-1 for unclamped video from receiver; J-2 output to redundant descrambler, and if there isn't one, J-2 must be terminated in 75 ohms.

Clamped video (J-3) from receiver; J-4 video output to modulator. Also check TB2 pins 7 and 8 and 5 and 5, which are respective audio input from receiver and audio output to modulator. Clamped and unclamped outputs from receiver should be contained in manufacturer's specifications.

Check both clamped and unclamped video outputs from receiver and adjust for 1 Vp-p into 75 ohms, if needed. Either a waveform monitor or oscilloscope is required.

Check video output from Videocipher® at J-4, also for 1 Vp-p into 75 ohms. Any adjustment required is done with gain potentiometer between J-4 and TB1, using monitor or scope.

The audio output level should read 0 dBm with either an audio level meter or spectrum analyzer. If required, change audio adjust pots between TB1 and TB2, but *only* when the descrambler is authorized.

VIDEOCIPHER® II DESCRAMBLING CHECKS

There are actually four of these models in existence. M/A-COM, the developer, supplied the Series 2000E and 2000E/B, while Channel Master offers the same units with its own designations of 6400 and 6401. The difference is that the 2000E and 6400 work with 70 MHz i-fs from an LNC or LNA/downconverter *as well* as video/audio baseband adaptable to all systems if you have a monitor or TV/monitor receiver for video display. The 2000 E/B and 6401 operate *only* on baseband and are *not* adaptable to 70 MHz rf without a special modulator not offered as an option.

In perusing both M/A-COM and Channel Master Operator Manuals, the only difference seems to be a CM/paragraph on "purchasing a Program," which is the entire purpose of scrambling anyway. So we'll stick to M/A-COM's information derived from the manual and an interview that could not be extensive due to the very nature of the equipment and its obvious objective.

So let's begin with a double *warning!* Since video is lightly enciphered and audio hard enciphered to the point of registering nothing but noise, any tampering with internal electronics will cost you a bundle for repairs. For instance, monkeying with the CMOS (very touchy) large module, which has little or no device gate protection, will cost you $150; and

digging about with a soldering iron will raise the ante to $190, or more. In other words, if repairs are required, return the unit undamaged to its parent-originator for problem resolution. Any other route might turn out to be extremely expensive.

The operator manuals offer specific instructions for routine hookups, so we won't repeat what you should already know except to caution that all cabling and connectors *must be free of shorts,* opens, and leakage. We'd suggest at least an ohmmeter check before initial connection or labelling the unit defective. It will save a lot of headaches and needless downtimes. In addition, be sure such cabling is 75 ohms, well shielded, and securely mated to your F or BNC connectors, whichever is appropriate.

Setup procedures and information, however, are another matter entirely, and into this we can offer a little insight thanks to M/A-COM technician Edward Miller and chief, Tom Winslow.

On the front of these VideoCipher® descramblers are nine function keys and 10 numeric keys, in addition to ENTER and CANCEL. Nine on-screen displays (0-8) are available for SETUP, while 0-9 numeric keys may enter information such as passwords or page numbers. Then there are such plain language functions as *View, Help, Next Prg., Text, Message,* etc. The latter we'll not discuss since operator manuals cover them well. But let's work with the setup and other display instructions and see if those won't help.

1. When the Videocipher® light is on you are descrambled.
2. If the satellite light isn't lit, Videocipher® output is lost through the rf modulator but usable through baseband.
3. In the event of a blank screen and both lights are on, but you aren't authorized, go to setup O for on-screen instructions. Often you will see an SM, but this must be SA, meaning scrambled authorized. For setup No. 1 aid, you need an FF and your particular number.
4. In the fixed key mode, no authorization is required since you're in universal authorization. On a bottom line you'll see FA (authorized), SA (authorized) SM (scrambled awaiting message), or SB

(missing bits). Then on *the* bottom line you'll see something like this: 01 (sync), 00 (audio hold), SA 101065 (clock, with final numbers constantly changing). If the audio hold is incrementing there is probably a 2F (in hexadecimal), audio will fail.

If you're checking signal level in Setup 1, 50/50 would be perfect, but 45/50 is usually a reasonable approximation. Anything under 50/45, however, and you're probably in trouble and should try and upgrade reception one way or another.

5. Service Identification. If the reading is *none*, then you require authorization. Thereafter, proceed to setup 0 and set CBDO (1 or 000). Authorized service then becomes ID:AO

6. Next go to Service 0 and read 16AO or some increment thereof. The Service ID and final two units of 16AO should match. Here, the unit is actually your geographical location combined with zip code. And in the diagnostic data, the clock and frame counters should be incrementing at equal speeds.

7. In the 2000E (the 70 MHz i-f system) there are *no* user adjustments. And, above all, don't try and adjust the i-f demodulator. In the baseband receivers, AGC can be adjusted. But in the composite video, if i-fs are out of alignment, equipment won't authorize since the encryption module is affected. And on nonscrambled channels, both audio and video baseband adjustments are possible. You may increase or decrease amplitudes to suit your receiver/monitor.

There are, of course, additions that might be included involving extra programming, but what you have in the foregoing should be enough to indicate if your equipment is either in or out of order—and that's really what we would want you to know.

Chapter 8

Test Equipment and Applications

IN A PUBLICATION ON SATELLITE EARTH STATIONS, we're going to do something unusual. We're going to discuss bonafide system and circuit applications of digital voltmeters, power supplies, oscilloscopes, spectrum displays and spectrum analyzers to help you evaluate and troubleshoot their electronic parts. And we're going to include a brief description of what makes this equipment tick. In short, how it works and what it does. It would also be beneficial to talk about sweep-signal generators, but these must produce frequencies in excess of 12 GHz (10^9 Hz) to be useful, and they are extremely expensive plus being totally microprocessor controlled. The price, about $40,000, and the generators' complexity make any such description rather futile. In addition, we have yet to see a single one of these units that can be FM-modulated sufficiently to pass *either* gated rainbow or color bars, and until this occurs, we really don't have a rounded discussion available. We will state, however, that only a *signal* generator and not a sweep-signal generator is required to do both reflector and electronics analysis and

troubleshooting. Designers, of course, have different problems and probably need the sweep section, especially for feeds. In satellite receivers, output filters are clearly defined by a spectrum analyzer so the sweep portion is unnecessary from a service standpoint and any block downconverters *must* provide 500 MHz of spectrum which is easily defined by signal reproduction in either an analyzer or TV receiver. Therefore, we can conscientiously leave that portion of the discussion where it lies since there is little more to be said of any consequence.

Oscilloscopes, however, have a special position in *all* troubleshooting where there are waveforms, transients, oscillations, current flow, digital logic and electric-electronic signals of virtually any description. The only scope limitations are sensitivity, frequency, time duration, and signal amplitudes (magnitudes). Today, 100 MHz scopes are common instruments, and tomorrow 200 MHz units will become just as ordinary.

But where the regular oscilloscope can't compete, the spectrum analyzer takes over. These instruments usually record their vertical measurements in decibels and horizontal dimensions in frequency—totally different from the oscilloscope whose vertical ranges are in volts-per-division and horizontals in seconds, to microseconds, or nanoseconds. The analyzer, however, can handle spectrums into many gigahertz (GHz), and signals 100 MHz/div. wide or wider. It can also view very low frequency information from dc to a few MHz in detail that no oscilloscope could hope to tackle. And while we use oscilloscopes and analyzers for different purposes, they do complement one another and both are serious TVRO servicing necessities. Neither instrument, on the other hand, can measure ohms (only an E/I ratio), nor current flow, except with special current probes for the oscilloscope. Most spectrum analyzers won't even accommodate dc voltages or power beyond +30 dBm which is exactly 1 watt (dBW). So overloading the frontend will cost a pretty penny since analyzers are usually in the $25,000 to $50,000 categories and dc coupled at 50 ohms input impedance.

Granted, this is a very considerable amount of money—as much as private residences used to cost only a few years ago—but no other instrument can do what a spectrum analyzer can and display the results on a cathode-ray tube with all readouts alive and glowing in green, non-glare phosphors. Is such equipment durable? They better be or all of us owners are headed for the poorhouse. So far, my own personal preference has been Tektronix because of portability, serviceability, and price. Because they're good people with excellent service, we really don't expect to change. Many thousands of good products have originated in Beaverton, Oregon. May they continue!

Yes, some of TVRO test equipment is very simple, and no, not all of it is inexpensive. But whether or not you're servicing the equipment you sell, sooner or later you're going to need almost every piece we'll be discussing throughout this chapter. Can you get by with less? Possibly, if your service is limited; absolutely not should you intend to do the job correctly, including site surveys, receiver repairs, and an occasional antenna analysis (covered in another chapter of the book). What, therefore, we hope to do in this chapter is pretty much a dog and pony show with liberal applications to acquaint you with good, working equipment that is currently available and relatively new in the market. The newest will be a brand new spectrum analyzer just released by a very major manufacturer who has spent considerable time in tailoring this product both for field/lab use and instituting a sizeable price reduction for everyone's benefit. You should be agreeably surprised, and this particular manufacturer will sell literally thousands of this instrument which, as we begin the chapter, we are now using with excellent results.

All the new equipment in the world at rock bottom prices still won't do TVROers any good unless they can use it well. We therefore propose to load this chapter with both theory and direct applications in the hope that some of each will be absorbed and adapted as the number of satellite earth stations exhibit substantial increases in 1988 and 1989. With commercial and consumer reflectors dotting roofs and landscapes, these should be golden years for the entire industry—at least for the survivors from 1986 and 1987. This, by the way, may be the period of weeding out lesser manufacturers and distributors, leaving only the stronger elements in the marketplace.

AN ELECTRICAL INTRODUCTION

In the television business we normally think of ac (alternating current) variable (VARIAC) sources since receivers have their own ac to dc (direct current) conversions ranging from simple diodes and capacitor filters to rather complex switch-mode units usually triggered by pulses from the flyback transformer or horizontal output. Only when such ac/dc conversions fail completely are pure dc supplies required to "fire" the receiver for intense troubleshooting—and this doesn't happen often because many repair shops don't have the necessary equipment. Therefore, the common procedure is to repair or modular-replace the ac/dc translators first, and then continue on with the other troubles. Actually, a good deal may be learned from any receiver by monitoring current drawn from some variable ac source as it energizes any type of receiver. And if you want the results in watts, the simple power equation for ac rms or dc current becomes:

$$P = EI, \quad P = I^2R \quad \text{or} \quad P = E^2/R$$

These little equalities are handy since most equipment is rated in terms of power drawn rather than separate voltage and current specifications. Having two of the three terms, therefore, the third is easily found by simple substitution. E, of course, is voltage, and I is current. All rms (root mean square) values represent the same heating effect ac has passing through a resistance that's accorded to dc—nothing more weighty than that. In addition, the R term may also be some impedance Z at the specific frequency, usually either 60 Hz (for half-wave rectification) or 120 Hz (full-wave or bridge rectification). So Z, in terms of ohms would, of course, supplant pure resistance R in the three equalities should the occasion demand. The reason an impedance rather than resistance might be used would be the effect of capacitance and / or inductance in the power supply circuit. You should forever remember that capacitative reactance and inductive reactance are always factors in any active circuit, and are expressed as follows:

$$Xc =$$
$$\frac{1}{2\pi fC} \quad \text{with C in farads}$$
$$X_L =$$
$$2\pi fL \quad \text{and L in henrys}$$

while $\pi = 3.1416$
and f = frequency

And where *any* impedance determination is required:

$$\text{Impedance } Z = R + j\left(\omega L - 1/\omega C\right) \text{ or}$$
$$Z = \sqrt{R^2 + X^2}, \quad X \text{ being reactive}$$

for an *L* and *C series* circuit at resonance where current and voltage are in-phase and only resistance limits the current flow. The symbol ω (omega) means $2\pi f$, as given above.

In a parallel circuit at resonance:

$$\text{Impedance } Z = \frac{1/R - j\left(\omega c - 1/\omega L\right)}{(1/R)^2 + (\omega C - 1/\omega L)^2}$$

which is a rather hairy equality indeed, and should be handled somewhat more simply, if possible. So from the reactances, find the total impedance Z, the total current I through the parallel branches and do simple arithmetic:

$Z_t = E/I_t$ since voltage in any parallel circuit is always a constant.

Now you have a condition where impedances are lowest in series circuits and highest in parallel circuits at resonance. In a power supply, therefore, to attain the least ripple and most current, series impedances must be very low indeed, only on the order of a few ohms at most. Conversely, to prevent circuit loading when in shunt (parallel), voltmeter and oscilloscope impedances should be on the order of 10 megohms. So this short study in impedances does have its merits and you should remember them.

One more little tidbit that is always useful. If you want to know the impedance of some ac output, connect an oscilloscope probe to the arm of a suitable variable resistor—you should have a general idea of the impedance beforehand so the potentiometer won't be overly large or small—and connect the arm and one end of the pot across said output. *Decrease* the impedance until the waveform reduces to half value; you may then measure the ohms value remaining across the resistance for an approximate impedance. This, then, is a shunt impedance across the output that, upon reaching half value, approximates the peak (not peak-to-peak) of the waveform.

Meters, you may or may not know respond to some *average* value of the ac waveform, while oscilloscopes always reproduce such waveforms as peak-to-peak if "ground" or dc is in the middle—and this goes for sinewaves as well as those of the more complex variety. So you might as well learn that:

$$\text{E average} = \text{E peak} \times 0.636 \text{ and P-P}$$
$$= \text{rms} \times 2 \times 1.414$$

$$\text{E rms} = \text{E average}/0.899$$

$$\text{E peak} = \text{E average}/0.636$$

And always, peak voltage times peak current equals peak power. So whenever you can, try and procure a voltmeter that reads in rms instead of average and has a decibel (dB) scale to boot. We'll get to all this shortly; but initially, let's see how digital voltmeters operate since they're somewhat more sophisticated and considerably more accurate than analog (vane) meters even if these have so-called mirror-backed scales and super calibration. In digital meters, of course, readouts are in tenths or hundredths of volts, current, or ohms rather than 3 to 10 percent of the average analog type display. And now that their liquid crystal displays (LCDs) are considerably faster responding than previously, digital meters are a joy to operate and their accuracy, especially in assessing digital circuit responses is a joy to have and hold. Here, analog meters are just about useless. On the other hand, when glancing at some ac magnitude such as transformer tuning or slow switching voltages, some sort of analog readout is always helpful. So what we're really saying is that a combination of the two would be ideal—and that's just what we plan with the aid of John Fluke and company, which is recognized as a leading U.S. manufacturer of many varieties of precision test equipment.

To keep the discussion in perspective, however, let's start with variable power supplies and work up, since they, too, have meters, often for both voltage and current, and some even supply an average power that's fairly indicative but seldom accurate.

POWER SUPPLIES

Among this tribe there are two varieties: ac and dc, each being useful in both laboratory and field analysis of TVRO systems. But neither of which has a great deal of utility without both I/E ranges and relative accuracy. Fortunately, better things are coming in smaller packages and, therefore, what we'll discuss in the following paragraphs may be easily "toted" around for either inside or outside service. Can you survive without one or the other? Possibly the ac source, but certainly not the dc supply, since LNA/LNB/C source operating voltages are essential, and you may also want to substitute some dc in the actuator drive if that's the way its particular circuit operates. In this respect, however, make

sure there's enough current to move or impel the actuator without blowing fuses first, last, and always. For such occasions, of course, always carry an appropriate fuse along, or better yet, replace said fuse with an equivalent value circuit breaker. In the long run it costs much less and is many times more convenient to push a button than replace a fuse. Three chassis holes and a pair of suitable wires does all of this nicely.

AC POWER

For our purposes, such ac power consists of a passive variable-inductance isolation transformer that will reduce the value or ordinary house or shop voltage from 360 Vac peak-to-peak (or 120 V rms) to some small value approaching zero. If the equipment you're servicing is not isolated from the ac line (or *mains* as our British cousins are fond of saying) then a variable isolation transformer is an absolute *must*. And even if said receiver or (whatever) does have some sort of electro-optical or transformer isolation, any leakage to the line will also be averted by the VARIAC, as well as protecting whatever other test gear you might be using. Nothing destroys an oscilloscope faster than a non-isolated hot chassis and a dozen or so amperes of current. And if this is a spectrum analyzer and you blow the first mixer, your bill could easily amount to $700. Having been this route, sad to relate, your author knows only too well.

For our basic example, we'll use a simple B&K Precision unit that's double fused and 2-ampere isolated, whose single meter registers both voltage and current (Fig. 8-1).

As you can see it's a bare bones arrangement with an initial F1 ac fuse, an on-off power switch and neon lamp indicator. The transformer is tapped down twice, the second time for its variable voltage control. You then see a second (F2) fuse, and then the primary of an iron-core isolation and coupling transformer, the 3-wire J1 output/outlet, more lamps, followed by the amps/volts switch and the diode-rectified calibration portion.

With the ac output adjustable from 0 to 150 Vac, the unit supplies some 2 amperes of current, very sufficient to power equipment at its usual 115-120

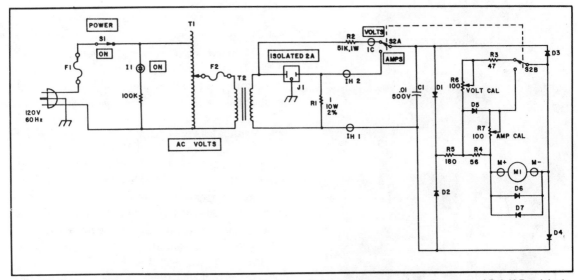

Fig. 8-1. A simple ac variac and isolation power supply for modest current requirements (courtesy of B & K-Precision).

Vac rating, but not enough to operate electronic gear requiring heavy amperage. Supplies costing many times more are required for large current outputs.

Across the secondary of T2 and in parallel with R1 is a 0.01-μF, 500-V capacitor, also in parallel with diodes D1 and D2. These diodes are shunted across the network of resistors supplying voltage and current to the voltage and amperage calibrating potentiometers as well as the M1 meter. Diodes D3 and D4 are also in shunt with these networks, and all rectify ac voltage from switch S2A to the calibrator. Diodes D6 and D7 are shunts across M1 for meter protection, with rectified dc on either side of the meter face. Calibration networks permit larger or lesser potentials to deflect the meter for relatively accurate scale readings. Meter full scale accuracy is $\pm 5\%$. It's up to the calibrationist and his 6-ohm, 240 W load (can be light bulbs) to do the rest for current, or open circuit adjustments for volts. Some power supplies also have a leakage circuit that will be useful in evaluating the isolation of hot chassis. That's really all you need to know about basic ac power supplies up to several amperes. Above that range, the costs increase almost vertically if there is any voltage range at all.

When troubleshooting, watch for both high current flow (low voltage) and little current flow (higher than normal voltage). If a short is suspected, increase voltage levels slowly while watching current drain. You'd be surprised how quickly this approach and a little analytical cranial application will solve your problem. But with zero current flow, all voltages present will probably be high.

DC POWER

Now we substantially depart the world of electricity and enter the fascinating galaxy of electronics, where there *are* several light years of difference (Fig. 8-2). Here, we'll work with another B&K Precision supply that just reached the market in late 1986. Here, also you will find a highly developed dc source supplying 30 volts at up to 3 amperes, with load and line voltage regulations of 0.02% and rms ripple of no more than 1 mV. All these excellent specifications, of course, require considerable electronic circuits and engineering, including parallel pass transistors, two bridge rectifiers, several integrated circuits (UA741s and LM301), in addition to 10 transistors, four zener reference diodes and 11 other diodes as blocking and temperature-compensating semiconductors. Do recall that zeners usually clamp voltages but pass varying currents, while blocking diodes must be forward biased by at least 0.7 V to

Fig. 8-2. A new 30 V/3-A current/voltage limiting, highly regulated power supply with automatic V/A crossover (courtesy of B & K-Precision).

conduct; otherwise, they are nonconducting and block either current or voltage from passing through.

This particular supply operates either in the constant current or constant voltage mode and is current or voltage limiting. Further, when either E or I setting has been exceeded, the supply automatically switches over, allowing effective transition between the two. For more power, two of these Model 1630 supplies may be connected in series for 60 V outputs, or in parallel, doubling the maximum load current. When doubling current, however, do increase the size of your leads to prevent overheating and burnup. Smoking power supplies usually don't have many minutes of longevity. Fortunately, however, you may "float" this supply above ground, if necessary, by unblocking the metal short across the common or return terminal and ground where actual grounds are impractical.

Two voltage sources supply ± 15 volts and + 24 volts for both parallel pass transistors Q108 and Q109, as well as the other integrated and discrete semiconductors in the equipment. VR101 and VR102 are the fine and coarse voltage potentiometer con-

trols receiving drive from one of the uA741 amplifiers, with VR104 and VR105 setting the 0 to 30 V limits by dc biasing this IC and its companion amplifier LM301, which form an output for the base of Darlington Q103 and Q104, the Q108-Q109 pass transistors and current/voltage outputs. A limiting feedback also occurs via the base and collector of Q107 and diode D11 from a sample of Q108's output. Another bias IC, a second uA741 also joins the other two sources at the base of Q103, which is clamped at maximum by 12-volt zener D107. Connected to the output of U105 appears to be a temperature compensating network of D103, zener D104 and transistors Q105 and Q106. These ICs and their transistors are also acting as constant voltage regulators, maintaining the VR101/102 settings as determined by the operator (Fig. 8-3).

The current adjustment occurs with coarse and fine voltage controls in their center positions, the HI-LO switch on HI, and trimmer potentiometer VR106 set for 3.2 amperes at the power supply output terminals. This, by the way, is a trimmer control in series with the X and Y terminals and also in series with VR103, a bias for the same U105 just discussed. Trimmer VR108 subsequently calibrates the high current and VR109 the low current. For voltage, VR107 trims this meter also. CR201 and CR202 are probably the voltage-current switchover relays, activated when needed by voltage and current settings and transformer tapdown requirements.

As you can readily observe, dc supplies with their various control settings, in addition to careful filtering following their bridge rectifiers are a hundred times more complex than simple ac equipment. But if adjusted occasionally and not deliberately overloaded, they can give excellent service over long periods if properly designed.

OSCILLOSCOPES

Unfortunately, most manufacturers are forgetting analog equipment (such as television receivers) and concentrate on digital apparatus. This is very convenient for wide bandpasses and low vertical deflection factors, but not at all suitable for electronics with considerable voltage swings and large IR drops. Too bad we had to "lose" Tektronix' Eu-

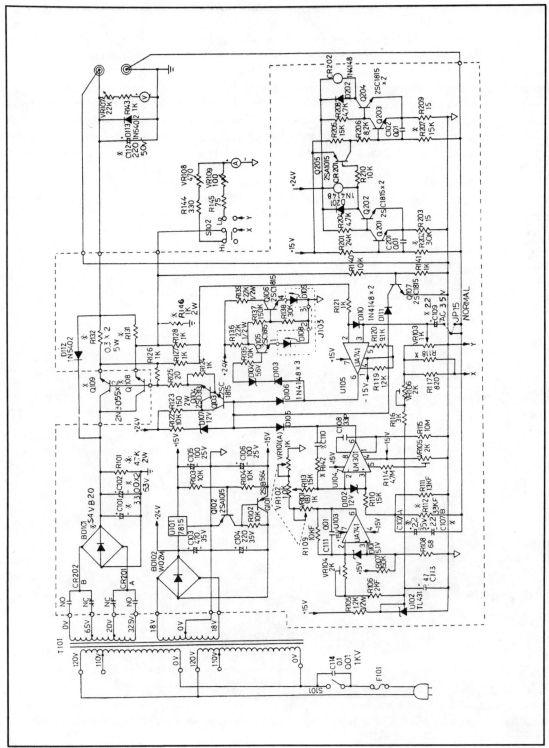

Fig. 8-3. A considerably more complex dc source, schematically showing difference between the Model 1630 and the Model 1653 (courtesy of B & K-Precision).

ropean Telequipment and some of the others with voltage-responding frontends of from 20 to 50 volts per division and well defined, lighted graticules. Most all U.S.A. oscilloscopes today have only 5 V/div. vertical displays, but do concentrate on digital displays, nanosecond (10^9) super timebases, and special trace effects. Otherwise, Hameg (West Germany) is still producing at least a 60 MHz, 3% accurate oscilloscope, with a time base in low microseconds and even nanoseconds, and vertical deflection on the top end of 20V/div (Fig. 8-4).

If, however, you want all the other goodies and don't plan to display voltages in excess of 400 volts with a 10:1 probe, then one of the super scopes at several thousand dollars will certainly do. Conversely, if you plan to use your equipment for TV and any high voltage work, better think twice and procure an instrument with not less than a 1,000-volt vertical deflection ability and, preferably, 1,600 volts,

since vertical output *tubes* in the old receivers actually produced that much swing. However, you'll have to carefully survey the market for both good construction and suitable specifications; unfortunately, the duo are now hard to come by. We'll investigate desirable vertical and horizontal parameters in detail a little later following some basic theory of operation plus 10:1 probe explanations and tuning, which all needs to be understood when working with visual display equipment. We might add, that the newer scopes with many integrated circuits and flat ribbon-connector wiring are decidely more reproducible than those with discrete transistors and single-lead wiring. Why? Masks, metallization, and transistor doping in ICs are much better controlled than for separate transistors, even though discretes will usually handle considerably more voltage and current than monolithics. Longevity should increase also, because currents and more uniform circuits are

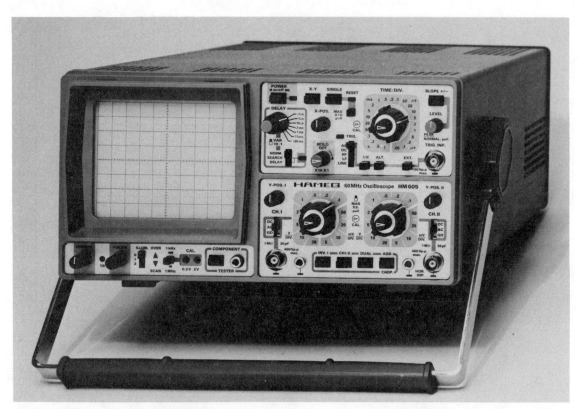

Fig. 8-4. Hameg's reasonably priced 60-MHz dual-trace oscilloscope with wide-ranging vertical amplifiers and time base settings to 50 nanoseconds (courtesy of Hameg, W. Germany).

better controlled with tighter designs and highly regulated power supplies. Even cathode ray tubes have been upgraded in the newer, superior models.

CONTROLS AND DISPLAYS

With an all-metal case and locking carrying handle, the Hameg HM-605 is neither fancy nor unusually attractive, but functionally you'll find it outstanding in both price and performance. It possesses many attributes of very expensive instruments with some advantages, but is not difficult to operate even with Channel 1-2 triggering, Channel 1 inverse, hold off, delayed sweep, a component tester, X-Y display, 10× trace magnification, in addition to a time base that switches to 0.05 microseconds, and to 5 nanoseconds in the 10× position. Time base triggering also includes ac, dc, HF (high frequency), LF (low frequency), and the usual line sync. There's also a single-shot available for those requiring readings of single, aperiodic traces. A 1% calibrator supplies a squarewave at 0.2 V and 2 V, respectively, and vertical settings also include dc/ac and ground. Separate time base triggering is also available as an auxiliary input. Above this are ± slope and a variable level control for both peak and "normal" corrections.

An 8 × 10 division vertical-horizontal semilighted graticule is also included for the instrument's 5-inch diagonally measured, flat faced cathode ray tube. A switch connects either the 1 MHz or 1 kHz calibrating frequency next to the component tester, which can check capacitors, diodes, transistors, or inductors by showing lines or circles, along with vertical lines for shorts or horizontal lines for opens. While semi-effective for obvious faults, we would certainly recommend standard transistor checkers or curve tracers for any device that may either be intermittent, have dubious gain, or subject to undesirable oscillations. In-circuit open or shorted capacitors and inductors are usually obvious either from distorted waveforms or low voltage displays. So while a component tester is handy, definitive evaluations out-of-circuit are often required for anything but catastrophic failures in either passive or active components.

Bandwidth for both vertical channels is spec'd at 60 MHz, with 12 calibrated attenuator positions evident between 5 millivolts and 20 volts-per-division. A variable attenuator will increase sensitivity to 2 mV/div. For the two trace-alternating vertical amplifiers, a three position switch may select ac, dc, or ground, and either one or both channels may be used, along with appropriate triggering in either the chopped (fixed at low frequencies) or alternating (standard) modes as one trace is seen and then the other.

A very nice pair of miniature 1:1 and 10:1 (low capacitance) probes are supplied with the instrument, which require virtually no recalibration after initial setup. Optional are test cables and 100× probes, in addition to a 4-channel amplifier, if needed. And when making measurements, any vertical over-scan causes yellow LEDs to light indicating too much vertical deflection, and in which direction, either up or down.

A time-selectable sweep delay between 100 nanoseconds and 1 second with 10× magnification allows sweep starts from almost any portion of the waveform and has the effect of substituting a second time base used in delayed sweeps. You will also find a holdoff control that varies the time between two successive sweeps. It is especially useful for aperiodic signals and burst, but can reduce signal brightness at advanced settings.

ADJUSTMENTS

Potentiometer adjustments include: Ch.1,2, external X, and Y1, Y2 gains, the usual dc levels, +140 V power supply, ×1, ×10 magnification; astigmatism, final amplifier current adjust, CT gain and centering, calibrator voltage adjust, Ch 1, Ch 2 ac symmetry and Y input balance, overscan, squarewave response Y amp., and external X centering, in addition to sweep amplitude, high voltage, sweep calibration and peak trigger adjust plus intensity set. This list should satisfy anyone that the equipment is fully adjustable (Fig. 8-5).

CIRCUIT DESIGN

Except for the negative 1250 V, half wave rectified and zener-shunted supply (−1250 and −1217

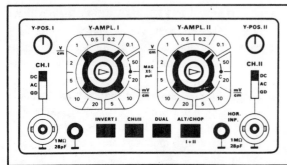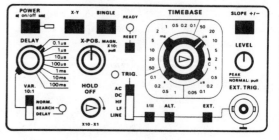

Fig. 8-5. Drawings of vertical amplifier and time base controls for the HM605 (courtesy of Hameg).

with a 33 V zener in between), the rest of the seven supplies for this oscilloscope are highly controlled, with most regulated by ICs and heavily filtered against ripple. Iron core losses in the power transformer are approximately 3 watts (Fig. 8-6).

Inputs for both Y (vertical) amplifiers are both series and shunt capacitance adjustable, along with a three-position switch for ac, dc, and ground. As usual, the Y preamplifiers are single-gate JFETS, with balance controls in shunt. Additional bipolar amplifiers follow in dual high-gain stages for the cathode-ray tube, and a special circuit provides pick-off trigger processing for Ch. 1/2 trigger amplifiers. The final two bipolar stages deliver a hefty drive to vertical plates of the cathode-ray tube, since their collectors are energized by the larger $+140$ V potential in the power supply. A polarity reversal switch in Channel 1 inverts any incoming signal, while Channel 2 and Channel 1 deliver triggering for the gate driver stage channel flip flop as well as the chopper generator—the stages which determine alternating (normal) or fixed oscillator (low frequency) trace displays. Separate switches at these outputs determine whether the displays are single or dual and alternating or chopped.

The 12-pin D14-370 P31/113R medium-phosphor cathode-ray tube is served by a pair of push-pull amplifiers for unblanking, turning its cathode on and off as signals arrive at its plates, and intensity, focus, and astigmatism potentiometers are set for the various dc potentials among the appropriate grids.

Sets of driver amplifiers now receive trigger $1/11$ pulses from the aforementioned pickoffs and the

operator selects whichever he desires, locking incoming traces to specific waveforms.

The time base, adjustable in 23 discrete, detented steps between 1 second and 0.05 microseconds (plus a $10 \times$ extender), consists of discrete and integrated circuit subsystems forming gates, flip-flops, an X (external) amplifier, and an RC time base switch and oscillator, accurate within better than 3%. Here an unblanking (removes blanking) pulse permitting trace display is generated, as well as sweep amplification and oscillator/X-amplifier amplification. And if incoming signals are non-recurrent or marred by excessive transients or noise, the time base may be externally triggered from the same source if suitable. Comparators, sensors, sweep and hold off flip-flops, resets and sweep control logic are all involved, primarily as integrated circuits.

The calibrator board has at least one NAND IC and several discrete transistors that can be made to operate at dual frequencies for both Y amplifier and 10:1 LC probe compensation. You may, however, want to use very fast rise time generators to check the instrument's Y amplifiers because of its 60 MHz bandpass and the various trimmer adjustments. For time base settings, insert timing "spike" voltages through the vertical terminals, and use an accurate counter at 1 kHz, 10 kHz, 50 kHz, 1 MHz, 20 MHz, and 50 MHz for maximum calibrations. They should all be within $\pm 3\%$ or better.

In time base language, these frequencies turn out to be: $T = 1/F = 1$ millisecond, 0.1 millisecond, 20 microseconds, 1 microsecond, etc. At 50 nanoseconds, of course, $F = 1/50 \times 10^{-9}$, or $.02 \times 10^{9}$, which is a rather high frequency, indeed, since it's

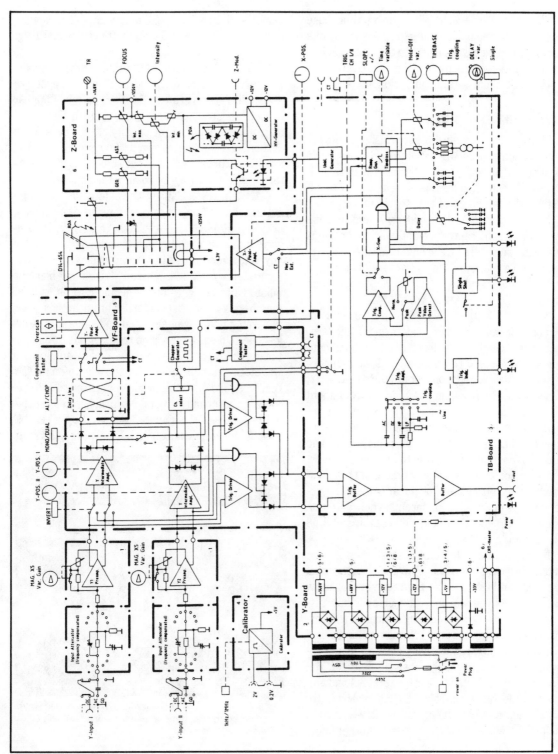

Fig. 8-6. The HM605 Hameg oscilloscope block diagram used throughout the scope discription (courtesy of Hameg).

20 MHz, to be specific. When doing time base calibrations, put no more than two cycles in any one centimeter and then work between the first and ninth graticule lines for maximum accuracy. Graticule 0 and 10 don't count in the calibration scheme.

WAVEFORM EXAMPLES

Since we're working almost exclusively with audio/video and processing satellite receivers, let's look at some "example" waveforms to analyze their shapes and content, since this is the best way to understand the workings of any servicing scope.

Naturally, we'll use test patterns, and all these waveforms will be reproduced at baseband since rf in satellite receivers are frequencies best investigated with a spectrum analyzer—a joyful task we'll delightedly commence once the oscilloscope portion is complete.

Now even though satellite transmissions for audio and video are in FM, video and audio are, nonetheless, detected just like any other rf demodulation and presented to speakers and the cathoderay tube as plain sound from about 60 Hz to 15 kHz, and pictures with frequency responses from about 30 Hz to 4.2 MHz. Color sidebands, as you may recall, are centered about the 3.579545 MHz suppressed subcarrier that must be regenerated and frequency coordinated in the television receiver. Therefore for chroma (large detail color) and luminance (fine detail video) to appear in their respective portions of the screen, careful synchronization among line (15,734 Hz), field (59.94 Hz), and 3.58 MHz chroma must be attained.

In consequence, the transmitter—whether it be standard broadcast or satellite uplink—has to transmit synchronizing pulses so the receiver will know what to do. As you will see, all such sync information arrives at the receiver during horizontal and vertical blanking intervals of 11.1 microseconds and 13.33 milliseconds, respectively. The horizontal interval, however, has only a single line for the horizontal sync pulse and color burst (sync) and amplitude, while the vertical blanking interval has a total of 21 lines available not only for the slower vertical sync pulses, but also for a great deal of other infor-

mation such as VITS/VIRS test information, captioning for the deaf, and Teletext transmissions (Fig. 8-7).

We won't go into all of the above, but you should see several test patterns that are equally applicable to satellite receivers and do most certainly appear on selected transponders from time to time. You may ultimately find them almost indispensable when evaluating a satellite receiver following repairs. And for this purpose, we'll look at several of these patterns, along with appropriate explanations.

Multiburst. Usually consists of a flag (large pulse) followed by six bursts of discrete oscillation between 500 kHz and 4.2 MHz (Fig. 8-8). It is always a measure of the high frequency response of any video receiver. Almost two cycles are shown, separated by a single horizontal sync and blanking pulse. Note the very clean fall and rise times of all members of the display, illustrating both a good generator and a well-serviced and calibrated oscilloscope. Unless a television receiver has a comb filter, by the way, *full* reproduction of this multiburst waveform is hopeless. This is why monitor/TV receivers are desirable when connected to satellite receiver baseband outputs. Normally, you'll receive full response if the monitor is issued by a reliable manufacturer and has enough bandwidth of its own.

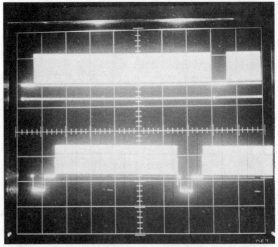

Fig. 8-7. Vertical (top) and horizontal (bottom) video waveform displays appear somewhat similar but have totally different video/sync content.

146

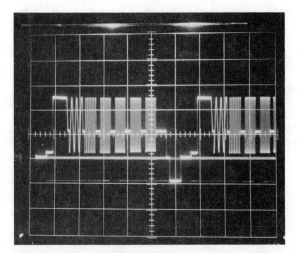

Fig. 8-8. Multiburst determines video horizontal (high frequency) resolution between 0.5 and 4.2 MHz.

A Linear Staircase. Most staircases are shown with color burst modulation, as in the lower portion of the double exposure picture (Fig. 8-9). But the upper staircase without modulation offers the best possibility of judging a receiver's linearity, which is the ability to process information without high frequency bends or low frequency rolloff. In other words, each staircase must have a similar amplitude and be square on top. Note that the lower

trace also has 3.58 MHz chroma multiburst following the horizontal blanking pulse.

Color Bars. These are intended to indicate good chroma processing through any receiver, at least through the video detector (Fig. 8-10). Both their amplitudes and positions are relevant and they consist of the usual red, blue, and green, plus their complements of yellow, magenta, and cyan. One white and one black bar enclose the six colors at the top and bottom ends, respectively. Compression or oscillations in these color bars point to a poorly designed or defective receiver, whether satellite or TV. These are generated only by NTSC equipment as compared to gated rainbow generators, whose 10 bars are chopped segments of broad red, blue, and green chroma with the usual yellow-to-cyan phase changes. Either display, however, will indicate relative color saturation and tint (hue) phase when viewed on any TV's cathode-ray tube since both are crystal controlled. But only the NTSC signal signifies precise chroma amplitudes and 75% saturated colors.

VITS and VIRS. As previously stated, these can be transmitted on lines 17 through 19 of the vertical blanking interval (Fig. 8-11). Although no longer required, VITS (vertical interval test signal) and VIRS (vertical color reference signal) appear occa-

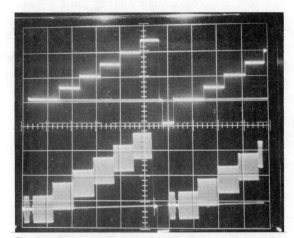

Fig. 8-9. A linear staircase (top) through any receiver confirms good amplification, linear amplifiers, and satisfactory signal processing. A modulated staircase (bottom) supports all of the above.

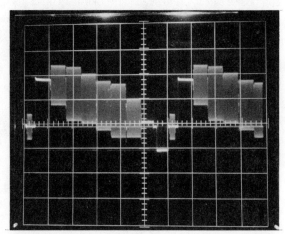

Fig. 8-10. Color bars indicate good chroma processing for both amplitude and IRE levels at least through the receiver's video detector.

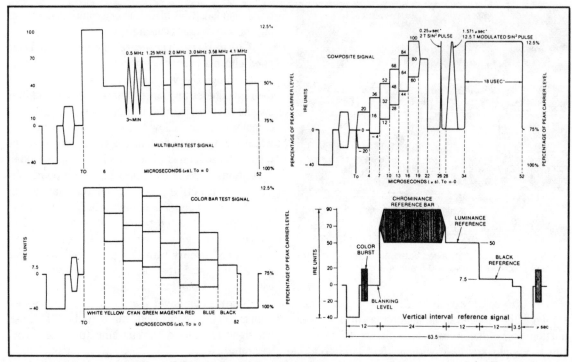

Fig. 8-11. VITS and VIRS signals are normally broadcast on lines 17 through 19 of the *vertical* blanking interval, although only line 19 is now set aside for VIRS, with no provision for VITS.

sionally and are still highly useful when they do. Therefore, a brief explanation is in order since the composite signal, often seen with color bars on fields one and two of line 18, is an *excellent* analyzing means of accurately evaluating *any* video receiver.

There are also occasions when this same composite waveform has been broadcast during the video scan interval and, therefore, is easily visible without superior equipment as opposed to those signals in the blanking interval which ordinary oscilloscopes can't sync satisfactorily. The pattern appears in the upper right of the VITS-VIRS family.

As you can see, the sync pulse occupies −40 to 0 IRE units on the left, followed by approximately 8 cycles of burst and then six modulated staircase steps. After that are the 2 T and 12.5 T sine squared pulses and the 18 microsecond window. Both pulses should reach 100 IRE units, as should the window. In using these for receiver characteristic evaluations, any loss of pulse amplitude means luma or chroma gain distortion, baseline curvature of the 12.5 T

pulse indicates both chroma-luma gain *and* delay distortion, while baseline contraction or expansion shows low or excess chroma content. The 2 T pulse represents luminance content only, while the 12.5 T has both.

The 18-microsecond window discloses ringing, high frequency (sides) or low frequency (top) distortion, in addition to line and field (time) distortion, which cause trace thickenings at top and bottom. Differential phase, we might add, may only be measured with a vectorscope connected to red and blue outputs. This is true for either gated rainbow or NTSC vectors, except that the rainbow vector is easily displayed at the R and B inputs to a TV receiver's cathode-ray tube. However, *both* oscilloscope channels must be inverted to show proper pattern polarity. Inverting channel 1, however, will rotate the pattern 90° and avoid some confusion while channel 2 rotation alone won't help. In addition to a composite signal as shown, the 18 μsec window is sometimes substituted by a modulated pedestal signal in the form of a stepped red hammerhead that will further pinpoint chroma/luma distortion and phase nonlinearities.

The VIRS color signal (lower right) is good for chroma/burst phase comparison and white/black reference levels—and that's about all.

Oscilloscope operating controls may be gleaned from any worthwhile scope manual, including the important use of dc amplifiers as voltage level measuring means. We could easily continue this dissertation on oscilloscopes for another ten pages and not miss a timing pulse, but the foregoing are prime topics with which you should be familiar, and the remainder would only clutter up more space without adding immediately applicable knowledge; so we'll turn to a vastly more complex but enormously useful topic, that of spectrum analyzers.

Before leaving this subject, however, we would *stress* the use of dc amplifiers for general non-ac voltage assessments, and delayed time bases for minute examinations of special portions of waveforms. The remainder of most applications we have already covered in some detail and will probably have more to say in the troubleshooting chapter on receivers. There, the various measurement techniques should speak for themselves and bring you up to speed in a hurry. This portion has been a rather basic introduction.

SPECTRUM ANALYZERS

The domain of spectrum analyzers is often considered either forbidden fruit or alien territory. Granted they are highly complex, do certain things that many don't understand but, in the final analysis, are one of the most useful instruments ever invented. Our job, then, is to interpret what they do, show how they do it, and illustrate helpful applications that will aid you in your work. In so doing, we will touch on video, audio, and satellite concerns directly related to what you may be or possibly are doing. That's probably the best way we know to offer useful instruction along with relevant backup theory of operation. The newsman's "who, what, why, where, and how" are totally applicable here because of the dearth of general knowledge.

Essentially, spectrum analyzers are divided into three main categories: swept-tuned, real-time, and those that process fast Fourier transforms. The first are tuned/filter heterodyne receivers; the second produce all frequency components within range and consist of a series of filters whose display is the product of such filters times their bandwidths; and the third category resolves complex waveshapes into frequencies by computing fast Fourier transforms.

Fortunately, microprocessors have now solved many formerly insurmountable complexities, substantially broadened the range of these analyzers, and placed in the hands of technicians and engineers a masterful means for both system/circuit design as well as investigative troubleshooting. Analyzer ranges used to be confined separately to kilohertz, megahertz, and low gigahertz, but the better instruments now have spectrums that begin in the kilohertz and extend far into the gigahertz. Our 7L5 Tektronix, for instance, processes input frequencies between 10 Hz and 5 MHz with resolution accuracies as low as 10 Hz—excellent for low audio and video analyses within NTSC parameters. Our 7L12 displays signal spectra from 100 kHz to 1.8 GHz and can easily resolve both video and block downconverted satellite signals in sufficient detail for most applications. Both, by the way, are swept frontend analyzers, neither of which is microprocessor controlled. This, of course, dates their origins to the later 1970s, but also maintains costs within reason since both are plug-ins that require a mainframe for power and CRT display. Many of the 1980s models (Fig. 8-12) are *not* of the plug-in variety since they have extended ranges and are reasonably portable even though carrying weights are often a problem. A few of the very recent instruments also feature both 50- and 75-ohm switchable impedances, the latter up to 1.8 GHz—an advantage that is thoroughly useful in the satellite earth station business since downconversions are ordinarily between 70 MHz (LNAs) and 950 to 1450 MHz (LNBs) with the latter midpoint usually appearing at approximately 1.2 GHz. There are some in-between blocks but they are now the exception rather than the rule and could eventually die on the vine, if for no other reason than being incompatible with the rest of the industry.

Whether microprocessor-controlled or not,

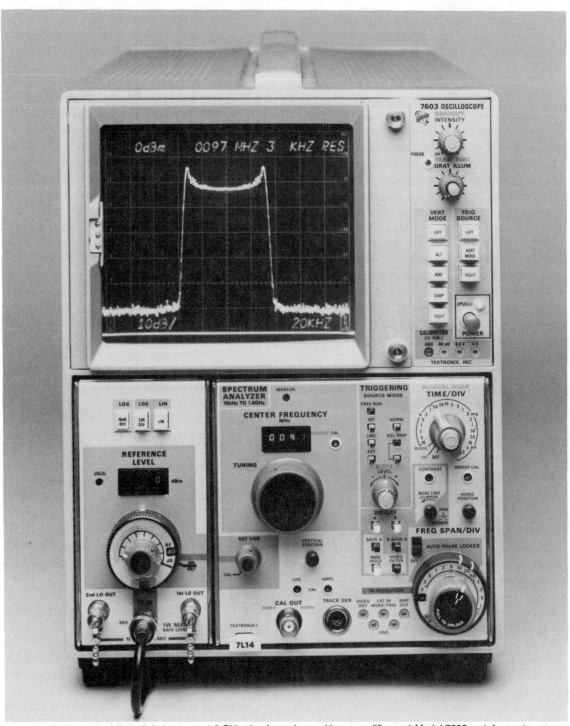

Fig. 8-12. Photograph of 7L14 digital storage, 1.8 GHz plug-in analyzer with preamplifier and Model 7603 mainframe (courtesy of Tektronix).

however, the basic spectrum analyzer functions remain as conceived and only their tightened electrical specifications and more flexible applications have changed. For instance, the introduction of markers and visible parameter readouts have helped considerably in more accurate signal evaluations. Consequently what we propose for now is a description of some of these continuing functions for your familiarity and then the description of an entirely new breed of instruments just making their appearance in the U.S. market, along with appropriate basic applications. Thereafter, you should be reasonably familiar with various other measurement conditions materializing in the applied troubleshooting and analytical chapters. Once you're used to working with this equipment, you'll find it impossible to operate without one. For TVRO they are absolutely essential!

For an example, we'll use the 7L12 (the non-digital forerunner of the 7L14) and its block diagram, followed by control descriptions and fundamental applications. That should be enough to get you started before embarking on added complexities, which must be noted before ending the discussion (Fig. 8-13).

With a dynamic range of 70 dB and sensitivities of −100 dBm to +30 dBm, this swept frontend spectrum analyzer may have its input signals attenuated from 0 to 60 dB by a ±0.2% dB accurate step-adjustable attenuator. A 1.8 GHz low-pass filter attenuates higher frequencies to prevent spurs in the first mixer, followed by a 3 dB padder isolator and then the first mixer. Here, the incoming signal is mixed with tuned voltage from the 1st YIG local oscillator isolated by a dc block swept and tuned to frequencies between 2.095 and 3.9 GHz. Below 100 kHz spans the second local oscillator (LO) is now swept and the first is phase-locked to its reference, a 2.21 MHz oscillator and pulse driver. This output enters a sampling gate along with voltage from the directional coupler, and any phase shift is discovered in the error amplifier. With phase lock ON, phase differences are filtered and amplified and routed back to the 1st LO as its control.

Sweeping for the 1st LO and 2nd LO originates from a special sweep generator developing a 10 V ramp and timed by capacitors switched in sequence by the TIME/DIV. operator-controlled selector, or automatically in the SPECTRUM position at better than 100× control range. Such timed sweeps are then amplified and applied to the YIG coil driver, establishing current for the tuning coil and, of course, the YIG LO. If or when the frequency SPAN/DIV is placed in MAX SPAN, coarse center frequency tuning is remoted and the YIG is swept its complete span, generating a marker coincident with the COARSE frequency setting.

At low frequencies, a summing amplifier receives information from the buffer amplifier as to the 1st LO frequency lock and transmits it to a digital voltage memory and thence to a summing amplifier. Here, inputs are also received from the frequency SPAN/DIV selector and fine CF control. A ramp is generated so that the 2nd LO's center frequency can shift equally but opposite to that of the 1st LO, offsetting the center frequency change. The 2nd LO now maintains the signal in its original position prior to phase lock of the 1st LO.

A traveling wave damper accepts these 2.095 1st i-f signals and isolates mixer output from 2nd LO reflections which continue through a 2.2 GHz low-pass filter, and then the 2.095 GHz bandpass filter where they finally arrive at the 2nd mixer. Here the 10 MHz bandpass 1st i-f is down-mixed to a frequency of 105 MHz with an i-f bandwidth of 3 MHz established by cascaded helical resonators, amplified and then filtered for the 3rd mixer.

Local oscillator for mixer No. 3 is set at 95 MHz, which now reduces the 105 MHz 2nd i-f to 10 MHz and is then preamplified for 0-70 dB gains in 10 dB steps and also for the bandpass resolution filters that extend from 300 Hz to 3 MHz. All information within this passband is subsequently amplified in a post resolution and function i-f amplifier for both variable gain and gain-slope compensation, offsetting increased microwave sensitivity loss at higher frequencies. A 2 dB/div. amplifier is also included but not illustrated since it is used for small, incremental displays rather than broad or high amplitude information. Signals are now detected.

A video amplifier then takes over and is controlled by frequency filters, stretch fall times, and baseline brightness suppression. It then enters the

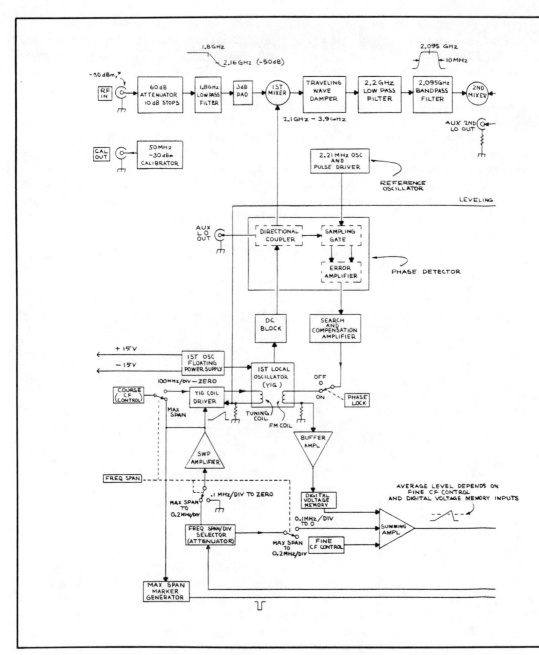

Fig. 8-13. Block diagram of the 100 kHz to 1.8 GHz 7L12 spectrum analyzer (courtesy of Tektronix).

vertical amplifier to be displayed on the CRT along with horizontal ramps and sweep gates that drive horizontal plates of the CRT. Not shown, also, is marker injection into the video at a summing ampli-fier driving the vertical output. And that concludes our rather intensive but, we hope, illuminating description of Tektronix' old but very good 7L12 module.

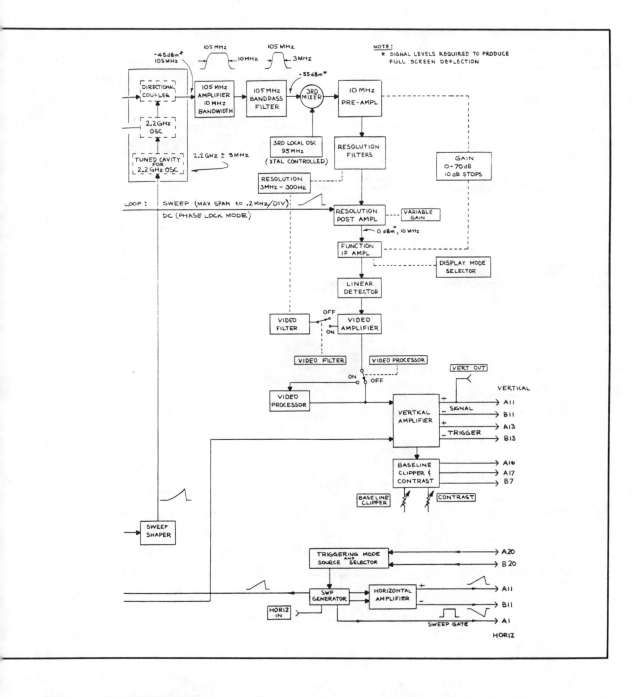

ANALYZER CONTROLS

Now that you know how the analyzer operates, it's time to understand operational controls, connect all this with internal electronics, and develop a solid basis for *any* spectrum analyzer application. We'll try and help by using Tektronix' own well-thought out drawings and callouts (functional descriptions). Inputs, attenuation, frequency selection and modes

153

of operation are initial targets, followed by time base, triggering, spans, filters, and resolution. At first this may sound somewhat difficult, but you can't operate an analyzer and derive worthwhile benefits unless you are familiar with the way it works. We'll start with the top left portion and work down. See Fig. 8-14.

First you see termination caps for the 1st and 2nd local oscillator outputs or test points used also for a tracking generator accessory—an auxiliary unit

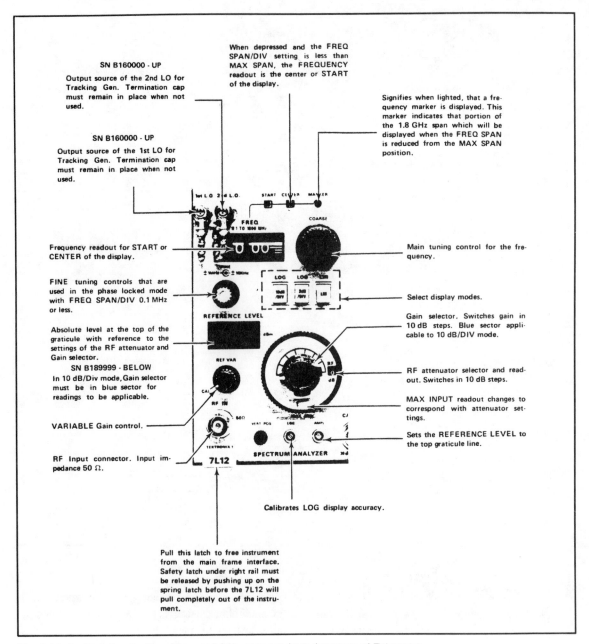

Fig. 8-14. Analyzer input, attenuation, and frequency readouts (courtesy of Tektronix).

we're not concerned with here. Next is the manually tuned *center frequency* readout that is normally calibrated to 1% and is usually accurate to within less than 10 MHz over the 1.8 GHz instrument range. If you want additional accuracy, the 50 MHz calibrator (Fig. 8-15) should be connected to the rf input and differences added or subtracted from the dial readings to obtain an absolute accuracy (including parallax) of 2%. The analyzer display and center frequency may be centered, or moved to the extreme left if you wish to see only the information to the right of reference.

Log/log and linear mode select buttons do exactly as they're marked and provide vertical scale

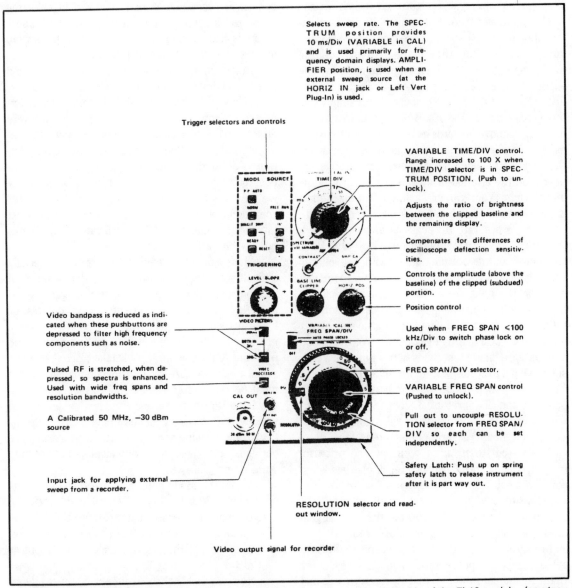

Selects sweep rate. The SPECTRUM position provides 10 ms/Div (VARIABLE in CAL) and is used primarily for frequency domain displays. AMPLIFIER position, is used when an external sweep source (at the HORIZ IN jack or Left Vert Plug-In) is used.

Trigger selectors and controls

VARIABLE TIME/DIV control. Range increased to 100 X when TIME/DIV selector is in SPECTRUM POSITION. (Push to unlock).

Adjusts the ratio of brightness between the clipped baseline and the remaining display.

Compensates for differences of oscilloscope deflection sensitivities.

Controls the amplitude (above the baseline) of the clipped (subdued) portion.

Position control

Video bandpass is reduced as indicated when these pushbuttons are depressed to filter high frequency components such as noise.

Used when FREQ SPAN <100 kHz/Div to switch phase lock on or off.

FREQ SPAN/DIV selector.

Pulsed RF is stretched, when depressed, so spectra is enhanced. Used with wide freq spans and resolution bandwidths.

VARIABLE FREQ SPAN control (Pushed to unlock).

A Calibrated 50 MHz, −30 dBm source

Pull out to uncouple RESOLUTION selector from FREQ SPAN/DIV so each can be set independently.

Safety Latch: Push up on spring safety latch to release instrument after it is part way out.

Input jack for applying external sweep from a recorder.

RESOLUTION selector and readout window.

Video output signal for recorder

Fig. 8-15. Time/division frequency spans, filters, and triggering appear on the right side of the 7L12 module (courtesy of Tektronix).

readings of 10 dB/division, 2 db/division, or linear—the latter being read from the left side of the graticule markings, while 10 dB and 2 dB log readings are simply per division, reading from either top or bottom.

The frontend gain selector (attenuator) is next, and you will note two controls, one for gain and the other for rf. Both switch in 10 dB steps. Gain is connected to the final 10 MHz i-f and has only four positions, after which gain is electrically locked out and readings are *not* true. But gain (0-70 dB) *and* attenuation (0-60 dB) together produce a dynamic window display of −130 dBm. In the 2 dB position, the max. amplitude of 14 dB may now be added to the −100 dBm reference for a dynamic range of -114 dBm. Most of the time, of course, you simply use the 60 dB attenuator at 10 dB/div., otherwise reference levels move upwards as the gain selector is engaged. Total reference levels are then read out in the darkened window above, while rf settings appear atop the attenuator switch in a small window on the right. Your variable gain control on the left is seldom used and should be kept in the calibrate position for accurate dB scale readings.

Analyzer signal input is through a 50-ohm BNC connector at the bottom, along with the plug-in safety latch and vertical (baseline) position controls. Then on the right are a pair of log and amplitude potentiometer adjustments for LOG calibration and total amplitude used in simple operator-setting for accurate vertical display evaluations. We might add that fairly frequent calibrations of this type are a considerable aid to accuracy both for dB and frequency. They aren't difficult once you've been through the process, and all operator cal. control sets are conveniently on the front. In later spectrum analyzer-controlled units, calibration is often done automatically—but then, again, you pay the price for modern conveniences, and also repair charges when some fiendish microprocessor breaks down.

Timing and frequency portions of the 7L12 plug-in are just about as complex as the vertical/gain group, although calibration is considerably simpler and really involves but a single control, that of the sweep calibrator potentiometer just above center right. In addition, the external sweep recorder and 50 mV/div. video signal output jacks for recorders require no further explanation since they're simply recorder plug-ins. The time/div. and trigger selector controls, however, are something else, as are the span and resolution detented tuners (Fig. 8-15).

The TIME/DIV may be automatic, as in the Spectrum, position delivering a 10 msec/div sweep rate, allowing the variable control to expand 100 times, permitting a time increase to about 1 sec./div. for special analyses. Or it may be used in selecting calibrated sweep rates from 0.5 msec to 1 μsec. There is also an amplifier setting for *external* sweep in special applications when required.

Below the time division control are contrast and sweep calibration potentiometers to adjust baseline/display brightness ratios and to contract or expand horizontal timing markers for accurate dispersion. The baseline clipper may be used to "remove" extended "noise" while the horizontal positioner determines the placing of all 10 marker positions following sweep calibration. Occasionally we have also used this control to produce center coincidence with the frequency readout dial—at least for one particular 50 MHz (calibrator output) frequency and a few harmonics.

Mode sources, fortunately, are not especially difficult since they're nothing more than a series of pushbuttons denoting P-P Auto triggering at slope/level settings of the Level/Slope controls, or free-runs with no signal. Normal trigger requires a minimum amplitude of 0.3 division and there is no free run. And single sweep will take place only when signal amplitudes are 1.5 divisions in magnitude and must be reset after each signal passes.

Free Run, Internal and Ext. modes denote the various sweep circuit modes for internal, external triggering, or none at all. Free Run and Normal are our usual settings for spectrum displays but not time domain analysis.

Below the mode source(s) are three pushbutton filters of 30 kHz, 300 Hz, (combined 3 Hz), and video, a video processor that stretches the fall time of pulsed signals to make them more visible. Following these are the 50 MHz calibrator output at −30 dBm.

Now we tackle the *Frequency Span per Division* and Variable Frequency Span selectors, along with the phase-locked loop switch used when the frequency span is less than 100 kHz/division. Since this is automatic, we usually just leave this switch on all the time. The Freq/Span selects horizontal frequencies between 0.5 kHz to 100 MHz per division. But in the Max Span position the full 1.8 GHz analyzer range is permitted plus a notch marker for frequency identification and display reduction identification. In the zero (0) position, the analyzer converts to a tuned receiver for time domain inspection of signal characteristics. There is also a variable frequency span control available when released from its detented Cal position.

In Cal, the Freq Span/Div and Resolution knob controls are locked to provide frequency related displays that remain in calibration. Resolution settings vary from 300 Hz to 3 MHz and determine widths of specific signals (such as transponders or video) under investigation. Seldom do we unlock these two unless an unusual resolution setting is required and then special care is taken not to exceed the instrument's calibration range. When a frequency marker is displayed, a lamp on the vertical portion of the plug-in lights, and some 7L12's also have out-of-calibration lamps as well. With the foregoing thoroughly digested, you're now ready for a few demonstration measurements and a word or two of further explanation.

LIVE EXAMPLES

But just to keep your feet on familiar territory, we'll be different (as usual) and show a double-exposure of an oscilloscope display even though it's not in precisely the same time relationship because of graticule differences. This will, however, demonstrate both the differences and utilities of the two instruments graphically.

We'll begin with a simple 1 MHz sinewave (Fig. 8-16). In the top trace the scope duly records the phenomenon, and then below you see the traditional double sidebands of the fundamental sinewave, each at 40 dB below reference, with the reference, itself, having an *amplitude* of 70 dB and measuring 22 dBm, just below the 30 dB reference. Resolution here is 30 kHz and each division is 500 kHz, proving the frequency accuracy of the analyzer. The

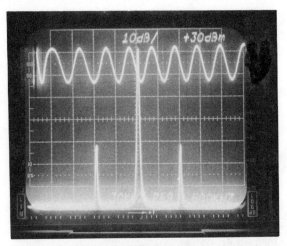

Fig. 8-16. Oscilloscope and spectrum analyzer displays of a 1 MHz sinewave. Note what pass for upper and lower sidebands.

scope also calibrated accurately, by the way.

Were these sidebands only 6 dB down from the carrier this would represent 100% modulation. As stated, they're 40 dB down so you have only 2% modulation. As sideband amplitudes increase they should be inspected for harmonics, and any less than 26 dB down represent more than 5% distortion and must be removed either by repair or replacing the equipment. Harmonic distortion and power level measurements are also fairly simple and accurate with an analyzer. If the second harmonic, for instance, was 35 dB down, there would be only 1.78% distortion. And signal-to-noise of the fundamental here would measure 70 dB from peak tip to noise floor. In AM, the sidebands and *not* the carrier contain all the power. But in FM, the carrier and multiple sidebands combine in transmissions with a resultant called the modulation index.

$$\text{Modulation Index} = \text{Frequency Deviation/Modulating Frequency}$$

So the higher the modulation the greater the number of sidebands and the wider their occupied bandwidth, making a deviation ratio equal to:

$$\text{Deviation Ratio} = \text{Max. Deviation/Highest Modulating Frequency}$$

And the greater FM frequency deviation for some audio bandwidth, the better interference and noise rejection becomes.

Our second example appears as nothing more or less than an old-fashioned square wave that has pretty good rise and fall times and no low frequency droop or distressing overshoot. Analyzer frequency is 200 kHz per division, making it easy to interpret the harmonics, since that's what a square wave consists of. After the initial harmonic to the right of line 1, the remainder are lined up nicely at 200 kHz intervals just as they should be. Blips in between you may ascribe to voltage transitions, while resolution for each is 30 kHz. As you can see, all are better than 35 dB down from the reference, and recede as frequency measurements increase (Fig. 8-17).

In the third example, we become somewhat more sophisticated with an L – R (left channel minus right channel) waveform directly out of a stereo FM generator. The scope shows this as a balanced demodulator stereo output consisting of 38 kHz modulating sidebands, which the spectrum analyzer faithfully reproduces below. If you want to know channel separation between the Left and Right channels, take scope or wideband ac voltmeter readings and calculate the following:

$$\text{dB separation} = \frac{\text{Right channel audio}}{\text{Left channel audio}} \text{ (Fig. 8-18)}$$

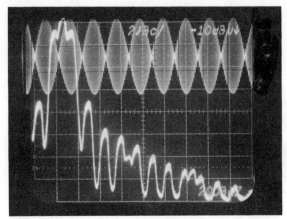

Fig. 8-18. Typical stereo L-R FM waveform with spectrum display below.

Or simply measure the two with a low frequency spectrum analyzer and *subtract*. The difference is your channel separation, and it better be 25 dB or more for good results.

If you're planning spectrum analyzer displays for FM modulation at microwave frequencies, say C band, the results at 3.9 GHz and 2 MHz/division look like that in Fig. 8-19. Note the bandspread is 10 MHz and the level 0 dBm. There are many components in this one resulting from complex modulation—actually a color bar signal generator.

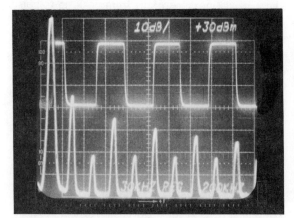

Fig. 8-17. A simple square wave displayed on scope (top) and analyzer (bottom).

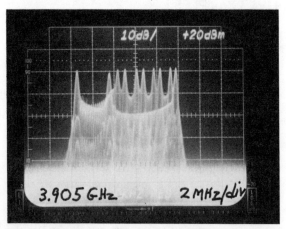

Fig. 8-19. At 3.9 GHz, FM video modulation on the spectrum analyzer appears 10 MHz wide at 0 dBm and looks almost three dimensional due to the slow sweep effect and phase swings.

As you can see a spectrum analyzer is something more than just a useful instrument, it's really your right eye and arm combined.

Bandwidths at least double that of signal frequencies are sufficient to transmit FM intelligence, and because transmitted energy divides between carrier and sidebands, the average unmodulated power output is the same as any modulated constant output. FM power, however, is a function of rf excitation, amplifier efficiency, and output stage biasing.

Since both video and audio are FM signals in satcasting, we thought you'd like to know some of the more intimate details gleaned throughout the years.

DIGITAL VOLTMETERS

Different from analog meters as night and day, these "logic masters" are infinitely more accurate—at least the better ones—do a few more things, and often have an auto-range function that is a blessing to many who have repeated difficulty in finding the proper voltage or current setting. On ohms measurements, however, beginning and ending ranges are often limited, and dB readouts may not respond to even the higher kilohertz frequencies. So there's good and bad in the DVM selections, but accuracy and auto-ranging do make them convenient for most users.

Usually, 3 or 3½ digits are sufficient for dc accuracies of 0.5%, but 4½ digits are preferable for another factor of 10 (0.05%), if the cost differential isn't prohibitive. Ac and ohms accuracies increase with the added digit proportionally, and a separate dB range becomes very handy when evaluating audio. For video, it's usually easier and more practical to work with scopes and spectrum analyzers, because most of these measurements involve ac waveforms and relatively little ohms or dc voltages other than various levels emanating from integrated circuits. And if you don't need more than 3% accuracies, the scope will do this for you also. Just don't try dc measurements with an unguarded (dc block) input spectrum analyzer. The results can be disastrous and extremely expensive.

CONVERSIONS

There are probably a dozen ways to convert ac measurements into dc, the first being an ac/dc converter. We'll resist the temptation of doing a survey exposition, however, and concentrate on one or two types of operational characteristics you may find interesting since they're in considerable use throughout this country and others.

Dual slope integration, Tri-Phasic™ A/D converters and an Iso-Polar™ reference circuit is the system with which we're most familiar, and many instruments under the name Data Precision are still operating with it. We don't intend to scrutinize all the ramifications of this useful system, but certainly certain phases of it are instructive and applicable to other equipment scattered about.

When input signals enter, the multimeter begins a three-phase measurement period. The analog integrator loop is first servoed to ensure zero offset corrections. Selected inputs and ranges then establish whether ac/dc/ohms are being measured and are then placed in series with zero offset compensation and the A/D converter. The signal is now integrated for 100 msec. The input is then disconnected from the A/D converter and replaced with a reference signal in opposing polarity and fixed magnitude, being integrated in the second ramp until the output is zero. This level is sensed and becomes the conversion's end if occurring within 200 msec. If there is an overload and no reading, the meter then reduces all integrator output voltage and begins the initial phase to recommence the conversion cycle. Such meters usually can withstand a 100% overload without harmful effects. Many others only offer 50% overload specifications, and cheap DMMs just blow.

For dBm measurements, an input attenuator is set to a 100:1 initially for the −20 to +20 dB range, and a 1:1 attenuation for the −60 to −20 dB range. Inputs are then scaled and registered as a voltage for the A/D converter at 100 microvolts/count. For ranges 5 dB beyond the scale, a blanking signal cancels the display. Some of these meters even have outputs for digital printers of one description or another. If you're doing any considerable ohms measuring, however, you should look for high and low ohms availability, and readouts that cause considerably less confusion when displayed directly rather than in terms of decimal kilohms. Otherwise, such meters—and they aren't exactly inexpensive—perform admirably over a number of years with occasional rechargeable battery replacements, especially when left unused on the shelf.

FLUKE'S MODEL 77 DMM

The 77 and its several brethren are 3½ digit, 3200 count display digital multimeters with fast analog bargraphs and a battery life of 2,000 hours. It is only necessary to choose any function such as volts, ohms, or amperes and the meter automatically switches to whatever range has the best accuracy and resolution. Then if the range-hold button is engaged, the meter retains its setting until said button is released (Fig. 8-20). But that's not all. An audible tone identifies current flow in impedances of 150 ohms or less, and a short tone indicates drops of some 0.6 volt, which are usual forward bias voltages for semiconductors in basic transistor categories. See Fig. 8-21.

Dc voltages through this meter are accurate to within 0.3% + 1 digit, ac voltage measurements are spec'd at 2% + 2 digits; ohms at 0.5% + 1 digit; dc current at 1.5% + 2 digits, and ac current at 3% + 2 digits. Readouts are liquid crystal (LCD). Max rms voltages ranges are 750 ac, 1,000 Vdc; max. resistance 32 megohms, and max. ac/dc amperes are 10. This particular multimeter (because of its low cost) does not have a dBm function. Dimensions are 1.12″ high, 2.95″ wide, and 6.55 inches long and weight 12 ounces. Case is said to be "virtually" drop proof.

The three DMMs in this series resulted from a John Fluke development of its own AP75 analog digital (multimeter) chip (ADC) coupled with a Sharp SM-5 microcomputer IC still in many hand-held calculators. This latter integrated circuit permits inclusion of a rapidly responding horizontal bargraph allowing quick and accurate adjustments of peaking and dipping (nulling) circuits or subsystems. It also allows sample and hold measurements (Fig. 8-21). If you really think you need the dBm function, Fluke does publish a convenient microvolt/millivolt/dBm table for 50/75/600-ohm impedances, which you may find useful. But do use a straight edge rather than trying to look crosseyed at the numbers—it's easier.

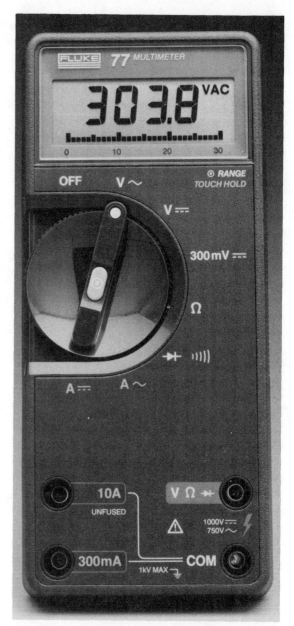

Fig. 8-20. The model 77 autoranging multimeter with both analog and digital functions (courtesy of John Fluke Mfg., Inc.).

How the 77 operates can be described fairly easily with the aid of the 70-series multimeter service manual. But since it contains little more than a switch and a pair of large-scale integrated circuits and a crystal readout, the schematic is of little value ex-

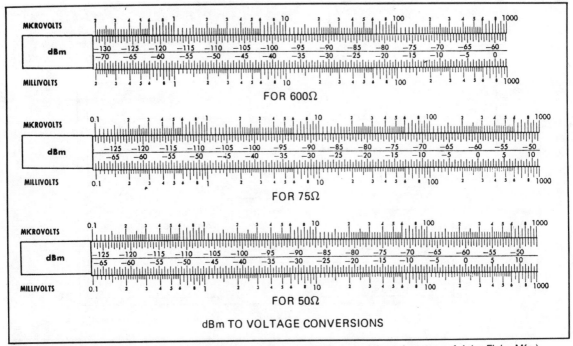

Fig. 8-21. Chart of voltage-to-dBm conversions for the three separate impedances (courtesy of John Fluke Mfg.).

cept for servicing, although no voltages or waveforms are given. Reference oscillator frequency for the AP75, however, is noted at 32.768 kHz.

This meter also uses (you might have guessed) dual-slope integration, with two voltages, one the input, and the other a reference, required for any measurement cycle. Inputs are integrated in the U1 analog (Fig. 8-22) IC and A/D converted, clocked by the Y1 crystal-controlled counter. Range and function controls are then sent to the U2 microcomputer, along with A/D samples as U2 drives the LCD digital display as well as the analog bargraph. Overvoltage protection derives from both voltage levels and resistive shunts, while current conditioning originates from other resistors developing the input voltage. Spark gaps also fire at voltages between 1200-1800 V, while two fuses protect the mA ranges, and a wirewound opens with excessive inputs. The ohms ranges are protected by back-to-back zener diodes. Product Manager Dr. Tak Tsang observes that 14 of 51 components in the Model 77 are "used only for protection." He adds that an "acceptable DMM must be simple to use and must

tolerate all conceivable errors." That's a good reason, perhaps, we choose a Fluke digital multimeter. With its many features and acceptable price we're sure you'll like it. During 1986 it sold for only $139—and that's pretty inexpensive considering the dc accuracy, auto ranging, the analog-digital functions, and a special diode test we almost failed to mention.

Supplied with a rugged, shock absorbing halfcover that doubles for either a bench stand or belt holster, we suggest this is the prime voltmeter for both satellite and TV servicing for ac rms voltages not exceeding 750 and dc voltages up to 1,000. Lowest range is 3.2 volts with a resolution of 0.001-volt.

For satellite earth station measurements it is highly appropriate because of auto ranging, display holding ability, self test, 10-ampere current ranges, and input impedances of 10 megohms or greater, with everything protected by three fuses except the 10-A extended scale. The self-test, all segment meter display is also handy, especially with weak batteries.

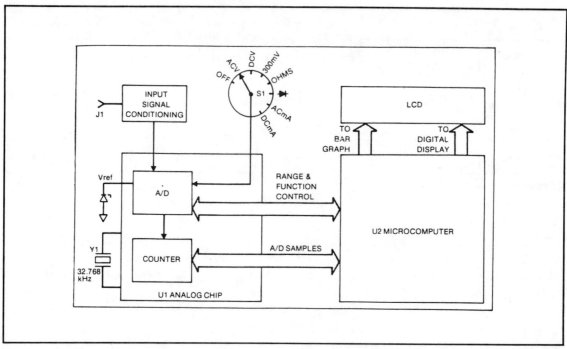

Fig. 8-22. General block diagram of the Model 77 (courtesy of John Fluke Mfg.).

DMM APPLICATIONS

When the meter selects ranges, the digital portion updates at 2.5 times/second while the bargraph analog portion strobes at 25 times per second. An OL appears when there's an overload. Keep all this in mind as we proceed to *external* tests of both positioner and receiver with their covers on. In other words, here's what you can do quickly and accurately in the field without exposing internal electronics. In this way, if either receiver or positioner actually requires a shop job, then substitute equipment or some other alternative can carry on while repairs are completed. Unless your mobile van has sophisticated electronics, parts, and adequate service literature, only basic field repairs or investigations are possible.

Figure 8-23 shows both a T-1 M/A-COM receiver and positioner as two separate entities, which they are, as well as wire sizes for the polarizers. Such 22 AWG sizes, however, decidedly do not apply to actuator drive voltages, which require considerable current and AWG 14 wire. Otherwise, all

else is 22 AWG, including actuator control voltages and pulses. These same wire ratings should be true for other receiver/positioners as well, but you'd better check to be sure. Actuator control wires also require shielding to prevent either radiation or pickup to/from ancillary sources.

Obviously, if the actuator doesn't operate you measure these outputs. If the receiver is apparently defective, check ac and LNB fuses first. Check (ac) if the receiver doesn't light. If the receiver produces the usual no-signal noise, check the LNB fuse. But do *not* depend on eyesight alone. Do a continuity check on both fuses to be sure with the ohms portion of the meter. Open fuses with no apparent symptoms have fooled many an eyeball, including our own. Operating voltages to the LNA/LNB are sometimes very touchy and just a little extra current will take their fuse protection out every time (Fig. 8-24). With the fuse replaced, you may also measure the dc voltage and dc current to the LNB by simply using a barrel connector, two pieces of 22 AWG wire and a ground strap. Current, of course must flow *through* the meter, while voltage is measured in

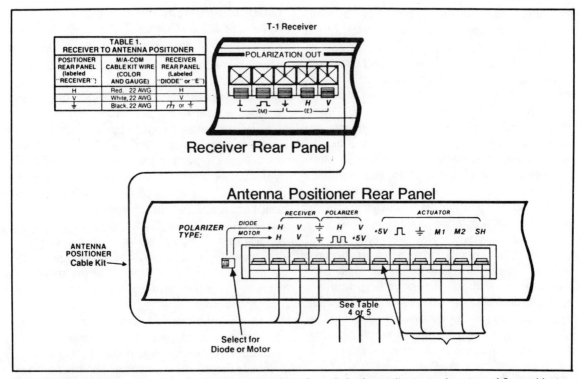

Fig. 8-23. M/A-COM's positioner/receiver back panel hookups for polarization and actuator (courtesy of General Instrument /A-COM).

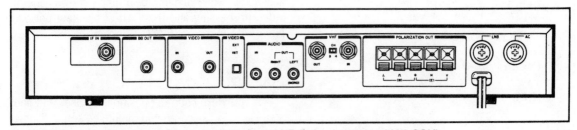

Fig. 8-24. Signal inputs and outputs connections. Note LNB fusing (courtesy of M/A-COM).

shunt with the equipment. For a T-2 receiver and a Panasonic Ku-band LNB, the measurements were 121.5 mA and 17.68 V—all dc. Unfortunately, not many LNA/Bs give current drains, only voltages. This is another reason to install *only* matched components, then you'll know you're making the proper connections. Understand now, how important auto ranging for both current and voltage can be? On manual meters you can overrange in a second and blow precision resistors right and left. Many LNA/Bs, however, will work between +15 and +24 V with-

out a whimper, although gain can be reduced toward the lower end. If you're operating two LNBs in orthogonal (90°) positions, current drain, as you might expect, will just about double because both are supplied by the same source.

Polarization excitations, including the pulses, may also be measured fairly readily with a voltmeter that has both dc and analog functions. Beginning at the right, with either H (horizontal) or V (vertical) ON, the dc measurement is 11.06 volts, and when OFF, 9.01 volts. Similarly, the pulse portion in M measures 1.25 Vac when ON and 0.804 Vac when off (or when the pulse completes its cycle). At the extreme left, the operating voltage is 5.14 volts dc for each polarity switch. The only other metered measurement possible with the receiver is to measure its current drain (here 1 ampere) if you want to put the meter in series with the ac line. Otherwise, the remaining receiver measurements are those originating from signals and must be evaluated by either a spectrum analyzer or oscilloscope, since this meter has no dB function that accommodates either audio or video. These we will undertake later.

The antenna positioner is something else again, and it, too, has a polarizer in addition to drive for the reflector's actuator. This time, however, because of the 12 terminals, two of which are grounds, we'll list the readings in order. In this listing, OL stands for overload, which means a large transient upon turn on. We might add that all readings for the positioner are ac except the two +5 Vdc terminals. We'll work from right to left, with each measurement taken as the positioner commands the actuator to go to another satellite.

SH		0	(drain wire)
M2	OL	3.18 Vac	
M1	OL	3.4 Vac	
Pulse		1.97 Vac	
+5		5.04 dc	
Pulse (double)		1.84 Vac	
VV		1.952 Vac	
HH		2.067 Vac	

Grounds, of course, are zero volts and should be zero ohms, too, when referenced to chassis.

This, then, is a good indication of what can be done with initial checks either in the shop or outside. Using orthogonal LNBs with no skew involved, we, did, however *not* connect the five polarity terminals to the left of the actuator. All voltages on the left were taken on bare terminals connected to *nothing* but the positioner. With current flow, some of these readings may change.

Next, we'll work with oscilloscope readouts at baseband, followed by spectrum analyzer displays at rf.

TROUBLESHOOTING WITH OSCILLOSCOPES

After our initial and somewhat exhaustive explanation, we hardly need to belabor the whys and wherefores of oscilloscopes. Sufficient it is to say they have dc and ac vertical amplifiers and time bases that may be inverted (mathematically) and converted to frequency, although not to the accuracy of even a modest digital counter. Your oscilloscope is a signal seeking device that tells you in terms of voltage, and seconds to nanoseconds, if a signal is present, what its magnitude is, and its total duration. For instance, should your time base be set to 2 milliseconds/division, then a single field of video and blanking should appear for 16.68 milliseconds, or just over eight divisions. And should your vertical dividers detent to 1 V/div., and the signal appears to cover five divisions, then its amplitude is exactly five volts.

On the other hand, a single line of video only appears for 63.5 microseconds, including blanking, so there is a considerable difference between 2 milliseconds and 10 microseconds when timing video waveforms. But you can readily distinguish between the two since only a single line produces recognizable detail, while an entire field simply shows general video processing and the vertical blanking period. Now let's work on TVRO.

PULSES

If you were counting positioner pulses and had a storage oscilloscope, you might see some display such as this: a short off time and a long on time, since the nature of the beast is rather slow and methodical. But do note the different levels. Pretend that the off pulses—those that are negative going—start from 0 reference and go positive during the pulse interval. Even if you don't have a storage (very expensive) instrument, you can still see rises and falls in levels at slow sweep speeds, and you know the unit is working, especially if you use dc amplifiers. Ac inputs will not register true values, only the charge and discharge of the input capacitor. Time durations, here, are only important if the actuator is consistently misbehaving, not dead or self-

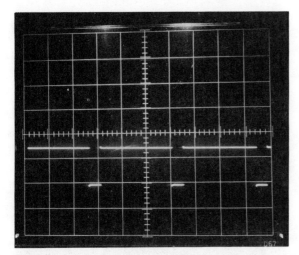

Fig. 8-25. Pulse types common to TVRO positioners.

destructing. The same can be said of 0 and +5-volt terminals. When on they will show "high" and in the off state, "low" (Fig. 8-25). Remember, too, that oscilloscopes display peak-to-peak voltages. If you want an rms reading, you'll have to divide by 2.828 if you're dealing with sinewaves.

Pulses, on the other hand, are a different story entirely, and their calculations involve width, cyclic rate, and amplitude. Stated in unvarnished English, the rms value of any pulse is its maximum voltage multiplied by the square root of its width divided by the duration of one cycle.

$$E_{rms} = E_{max} \sqrt{t_d/T}$$

Where t_d is the pulse width and T the time of one cycle.

In our initial pulse example, if each division amounted to 1 volt or 1 millisecond, then,
$E_{rms} = 1.6 \sqrt{0.5/3.5} = 1.6 \times 0.378 = 0.605$ volt

The milliseconds for pulse width and time duration, of course cancel since 10^{-3} and 10^{+3} subtract out. This, then, is the *effective* value of any pulse of equal width and period.

LINEAR DISPLAYS

In ordinary signal processing, receiver signals are usually linear—where their characteristics are plainly visible—as opposed to digital, which must be D/A converted before reaching any viewable cathode-ray tube. You must use test patterns, of course, since the image will often move rapidly in motion scenes and make evaluation impossible (Fig. 8-26).

Here, the usual 6-color bar display in almost two cycles, intermixed with I and Q chroma information at the base (above blanking) and at the top of each waveform. This is a normal pattern in all respects, and only shows a little low frequency rolloff with horizontal sync pulse slant. Time base set for 10 μsec/division and 0.2 V/div.

But look at what's happening in the next example (Fig. 8-27). You have the horizontal sync pulse, then color burst, the 12.5 T and 2 T spikes, followed by a 25 μsec window showing abnormal thickness. That window should (and does) appear at 100 IRE and is suffering from line and/or field distortion, as well as reduced amplitude of the 12.5 T (color) and 2 T (luminance) pulses. This means there are either transmission problems or reception is poor; and it's probably the latter. Check this one out, beginning with reflector orientation and then skew. This is decidedly *not* a good picture!

If you're addicted to scrambling, the HBO on F3, channel 13 is distinctly for you. As you can see, it's a miserably mish-mashed signal that will take dollars and special equipment such as VideoCipher® II

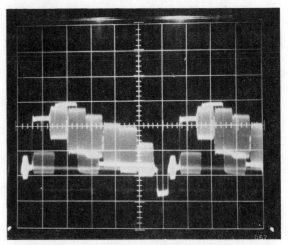

Fig. 8-26. An ordinary color bar pattern viewed from transponder 7 on SATCOM F3 following video detection.

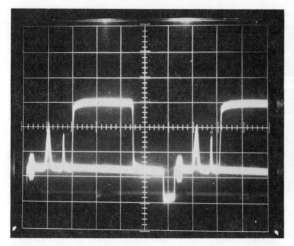

Fig. 8-27. Line or field distortion thickens the 25 μsec window and both luma-chroma 2T pulses are way down in amplitude.

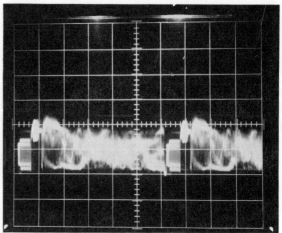

Fig. 8-29. The Orion system on Canada's Anik Dog 1 also shows polarity inversion.

to decode if you really want to spend that kind of money (Fig. 8-28).

More scrambling in this next waveform. But this time it's the Orion system adopted by Canada. Note signal inversion and horizontal pulse filling. But at least you can separate color burst loud and clear (Fig. 8-29).

The last of these oscilloscope pictures shows another color bar display, but there are lots of sparklies showing (tops of the color bars) and heavy center steps down the staircase. Definitely, your an-

tenna orientation is off on this one. We would suggest you try both azimuth and elevation changes immediately here, then check other satellites to be sure extra problems haven't surfaced, too. The photo is of Westar V, transponder 18 (Fig. 8-30). But after you position for Westar, be certain some of the other satellites haven't been slighted. Occasionally some transponder may be pointed to another area than the one where you're located. Then, there's little you can do except deliver a few censored expletives and move on. Unfortunately, that

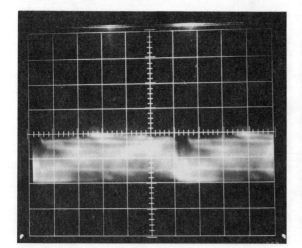

Fig. 8-28. No, not a defective receiver, just HBO scrambling.

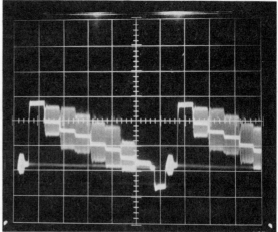

Fig. 8-30. Westar V shows color bars, but channel 18 needs a good touchup—lots of sparklies here.

particular frequency translator and amplifier didn't have you expressly in mind. He/she/it is booked for bucks not free interlopers.

TROUBLESHOOTING WITH SPECTRUM ANALYZERS

We've already said about as much on the subject of spectrum analyzers as we should, but an additional word or two about the "beast" won't hurt, especially if you (and many others) have little or no familiarity with it. Decibel (dB) scales at low frequencies may appear in terms of dBmV dBm, or dBμV at varying impedances between 50 and 600 ohms, depending on the analyzer and its applications. As an example, audio measurements are often or usually made at 600 ohms, microwave frequencies at 50 ohms, and video at 75 ohms. Some low-frequency analyzers like Tektronix' 7L5 have switchable impedance inputs, and these can come in very handy when making precision measurements. Otherwise, switching around at will can result in losses that may even amount to as much as 6-10 dB. A few relationships and Fig. 8-31 should aid you if impedance translations are necessary.

dBm   (75 ohms) =   dBm (50 ohms) + 5.72
dBmV (75 ohms) =   54.5 + dBm (50 ohms)
dBμV (50 ohms) =   (50 ohms) dBm + 107 dB

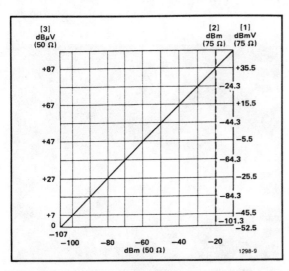

Fig. 8-31. Impedance-matching graph illustrating the 50/75-ohm dBm/V/μV relationship (courtesy of Tektronix).

Remember to treat minus (−) signs algebraically. For instance, −20 dB + 30 dB = 10 dB every time. But 30 dB − (−20 dB) = 50 dB, also every time. Remember that decibels may only be added and substracted, not multiplied or divided! And here, two negatives always make a positive, while two positives remain plus.

While the resolution bandwidth of any spectrum analyzer remains a function of the analyzer, it depends on sweep speed, frequency span, and incidental FM, with measurements taken at the 6 dB down points. At higher frequencies, a video filter can be used to reduce noise and MHz/GHz spectral components, in addition to modulation spread between closely spaced information displays. But you must understand that frequency span changes do affect both resolution bandwidth and sensitivity so that frequency span increases require sweep speed decreases. The remainder of analyzer instructions should be contained in your (or someone else's) operator's manual supplied with each instrument. And if the analyzer you're using has no auto-calibration, you should take a few minutes to calibrate both frequency and dB responses before measurements commence. You'd be amazed how often this simple procedure is deliberately neglected by both engineers and technicians. Shame!

GOOD/POOR SPECTRAL SIGNALS

Sometimes when you're working Satcom F1 you'll find a number of channels don't seem to be operating. But this isn't necessarily true, since they may be transpondering data and/or voice rather than video. Then there may be unmodulated carriers here and there that supply only a blank (black) raster for those television receivers with good dc restoration. Remember, too, that at C band channels are 36 MHz wide and separated by 40 MHz each, with stagger tuning for V/H offsets. In the F1 photo (Fig. 8-32) you're viewing eight transponders in one polarity, with several others "peeping" in between from the other (polarity). The carrier-to-noise level, however, isn't much better than 12 dB, so some of these channels won't appear quite as bright and crisp as they should. Towards the right side of the photograph you will see rather high crosspole (less than 10 dB) which

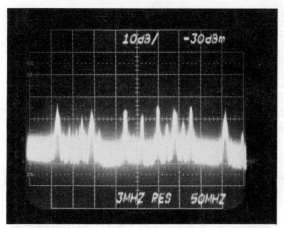

Fig. 8-32. Satcom F1-R's signal is only fair on this particular installation.

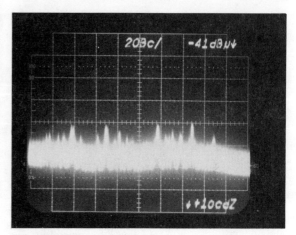

Fig. 8-33. (Telstar 301). Not only is there poor C/N ratio, but a great deal of interference, too.

is always a problem because of V/H interference. This may be the result of pointing error and it may also originate from a V/H switch such as we are using that fails to have enough built-in isolation between the switching series of diodes. If such is the case, low-value signals with excess signal-to-noise ratios may well exhibit undesirable crosspole such as this one.

These switches accept orthogonal inputs and convert to a single vertical or horizontal polarity input for the *average* receiver. If such switching did not take place outside the receiver, it would have to occur within. But if we had our druthers, internal receiver switching would probably be preferable to a relatively inexpensive diode array operating outboard and having an additional set of connections. You can, however, hook up two or four receivers to such arrangements and still obtain pretty good reception. For single TVRO receivers, however, orthogonal leads from the reflector directly to the receiver would be preferable. Conversely, it's been very handy to connect a spectrum analyzer to one of the switch's outputs and pretend it's another receiver. And that may be something you just might like to remember. Check analyzer responses against a color monitor's pictures and you can learn a great deal.

If you think F1 looked a little rough, take a look at Telstar 301 (Fig. 8-33). Not only is it *loaded* with unacceptable noise but signals are low, interference

high, and you'll immediately find all sorts of troubles. In addition, the signal is way down in the "mud" and nothing but a real miracle can pull it out. Would you use an amplifier here? Don't forget that amplifiers don't know the difference between noise and good video—they'll simply amplify both unless you spend a considerable amount of money for special electronic processing and noise clipping.

The fundamental answer is, of course, "no." Just try and juggle a little better signal input. T301 should look better than this on even a mediocre system, let alone a good one. Where you will have the most trouble is with low elevation satellites from ex-

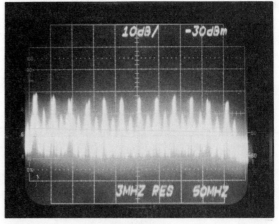

Fig. 8-34. If all your satellite signals are this good, you can sell your system to the world!

treme northern/western locations; and these you may not access at all. Much will depend on the satellite's footprint and obvious signal strength at *your* location.

Just to show you that all is not lost, however, the final photo is of Galaxy 1's even numbered transponders showing some crosspole but a fairly clean pattern and plenty of C/N (Fig. 8-34). Here, crosspole will *not* interfere with the operating and viewed transponders since it is relatively small in comparison to both amplitude and modulation.

And that should just about wrap up the spectrum portion of this chapter. When analyzing receivers, we'll look at some FM and audio, too. But here we're dealing mainly with signals directly off the satellite, and *before* i-f and detector processing.

You will also observe that only actual satellite transponder radiation was used rather than that generated by signal generators. This was done deliberately so you would be able to apply all of them to actual field and laboratory conditions—although sometimes fact is stranger than fiction. We hope they are thoroughly useful.

Chapter 9

Troubleshooting Problems and Solutions

AFTER ALL THE *"HOW TO"* TALK THAT PRECEDED this chapter, we'll now get right down to the nitty gritty of actual problems and their solutions. We'll use both our own information and that obtained from the manufacturers. While we can't tackle every single possibility, coverage should include most of the common situations and a number of special circumstances. Because we have already given a rather thorough explanation of test equipment and its uses in Chapter 8, the contents here will amount to more of a listing with explanations rather than particular waveforms or dc/ac voltage measurements. Several of the better manufacturers, fortunately, were willing to cooperate and so we have a reasonable number of additions to what has already been described. Principally, however, we would like to stress common failures rather than exceptions, but authentic "fixes" are always welcome from any source.

Fortunately, TVRO receivers have no high voltage, high-powered vertical and horizontal drive circuits, nor cathode-ray tube amplifiers, tuners, and V/H blanking such as television receivers. They do possess local oscillators, mixers, filters, baseband video and audio outputs, modulators and demodulators, and highly regulated power supplies. In addition, all incoming signals are frequency modulated rather than FM (sound) and AM (video) as in TV. Videocassette recorders, on the other hand, convert to FM video because of color processing, then reconvert to AM for standard video, thereby limiting luma/chroma bandwidths accordingly. In satellite receivers, normal video/audio composite bandwidths approach 8 MHz, including lots of subcarriers for audio. But because of NTSC limitations, video remains a maximum of 4.2 MHz at its best, and audio, even in multichannel sound, has a bandwidth of only 50 kHz.

At baseband these outputs are usually available on rear satellite receiver terminals at 75 ohms and 600 ohms, respectively, adhering to our U.S. industry standard. Don't attempt to measure such outputs with low impedance test gear. For oscilloscopes use a 10:1 probe (10 megohms), and for meters, anything between 10 and 16 megohms is acceptable. Stuffing the probe of a 20,000 ohms/volt meter on the 20-volt range to measure an output of 1 volt means you have a full scale sensitivity of 400,000 ohms shunted across either 75 or 600 ohms. But on ac, the meter's sensitivity is only 10,000 ohms/volt, so this means only 200,000 ohms maximum, and that is hardly enough. Were equipment shunt resistances higher, the 200 kilohms would decidedly become a load. Furthermore, ordinary meters have a definite frequency limitation and only special (and expensive) multimeters have ac responses exceeding some 10 kilohertz. This especially applies to dB scales, which decidedly leads to measurement errors. Now you can see why lower frequency spectrum analyzers should have switchable impedances to cover such eventualities and produce accurate readings remembering that a 75 to 50 ohms match costs a 5.7 dB loss if an analyzer is not so equipped.

TROUBLESHOOTING PROCEDURES

Unless this is an initial issue (and then anything can happen and usually does) most types of equipment has a service history. Specific breakdowns occur because of certain component failures, poor solder joints, mechanical stress, or hot/cold complications. Block downconverters and the old LNAs should be affected much more by freezing temperatures rather than heat. Reflector-antennas, on the other hand, will deteriorate faster under hot sun and drenching rains. Logic circuits in antenna positioners are likely to miss a few counts now and then, especially after several years of aging and overloads. Batteries eventually lose current in remote controls, and oscillators in such handheld units are prone to die quickly with mishandling or a good water bath.

All this is why you must be perceptive in first analyzing the failure and then attacking it logically and with accurate test gear. If you spend a lot of time guessing you don't belong in the business. TVRO should be considerably easier to diagnose and repair than television. Actually, we don't really think there's any comparison since there are so many fewer circuits and challenges. I-f frequencies are considerably higher, however, and local oscillators

and mixers can become a problem without good voltage regulation and stable components. In time, too, remote and on-board switching components will become failures, and power supplies are always susceptible to power surges and transients, especially during lightning storms. Sticking relays may also become bothersome, and indicator lamps on the front panel do have finite lives.

Fortunately, the mechanical and indicator problems are often visible, but pure electronics are not. Therefore, to really service TVRO equipment, you'll have to have scopes, meters, spectrum analyzers, and signal generators. There's no other way to do the job properly and establish a reputable operation. But once a worthy reputation is attained, TVRO servicing should become a good, long range business with adequate profits and steady clientele. Equipment sales, too, can become just as important as service, especially if the two are recognized for value and quality. Both, however, require intelligent training from industry leaders who have both product and ability—unfortunately there are not too many of these. At the moment, the need for *national* training in electronics as well as reflector/mount mechanics is a considerable necessity. We're not speaking of a few hours, but days of intensive classroom and hands-on instruction so that the better technicians can absorb enough overall information to do a creditable job in the shop or outside. As in television servicing, the customer must be served!

TECH TIPS

We'll begin this portion of the chapter with R.L. Drake, then Satellite Technology Services, M/A-COM, and any others who have so kindly permitted their service information to be printed. Some of the contents may be reworded but all basic information is there for you to use in the event of modifications or troubleshooting. We sincerely hope it's helpful when you do have a problem. But since this is *not* a book of complete schematics, you'll have to use your own because several manufacturers do not permit us to publish them in full. All *routine* service adjustments that haven't been changed or modified, continue to appear in your owner manuals, and will not be included.

ESR-24

Modulators are not factory-installed on all units. Remove receiver cover, place modulator switch in the channel 3 position and adjust the channel 3 oscillator coil (Fig. 9-1) to video carrier frequency of 61.25 MHz using a good frequency counter, which may require amplification. Do the same for the channel 4 position, which is adjusted for an oscillator coil frequency of 67.25 MHz. The final step is tuning of the audio carrier on the modulator board for a zero beat of about ±1 kHz with the receiver loosely coupled to the modulator board and "set to 4.5 MHz."

The modulator should now be ready to operate according to specifications, and should be as accurate as your digital counter. A spectrum analyzer examination may not hurt if you want to check relative amplitudes of the video and audio carriers and any possible spurs.

ESR-24 receivers with serial numbers *below* 4138: there are only a few mA of current from the odd/even terminals, and an external transistor is needed to energize a 12-V, 180-ohm resistance relay for H/V polarities. A 2N3904 transistor is suggested (Fig. 9-2) from the odd terminal with two

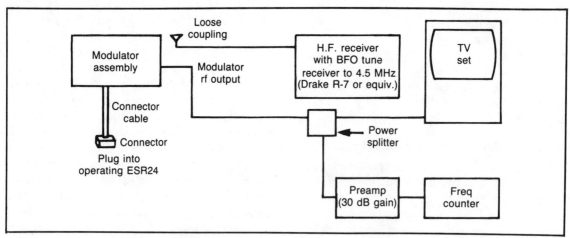

Fig. 9-1. Initially, TV modulators were not installed on all ESR-24 receivers (courtesy of R.L. Drake).

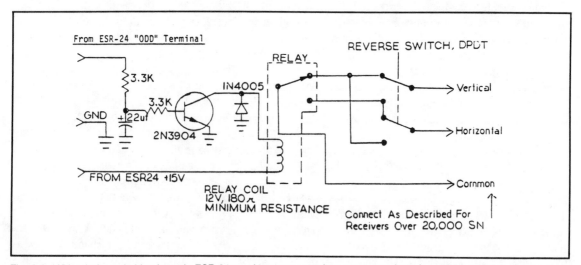

Fig. 9-2. H/V polarity switching in early ESR-24 receivers may need an extra transistor for 180-ohm relays (courtesy of R.L. Drake).

172

3.3-k resistors in series and a 22-μF capacitor in shunt to ground between the two before turn-on current reaches the 2N3904's base. In its collector, a 1N4005 diode, anode to ground, is required to absorb chattering relay spurs and current-induced voltage transients. For ESR-24 receivers with serial numbers between 4138 and 19,999, the even terminal has a +12-V swing, and also 80-mA of current to handle the relay. Therefore, a relay connected between the +15-V supply and the even terminal *will* operate on the odd channels.

For Orthomode feeds and dual LNA/Bs, connect a SPDT relay with 12-Vdc coil (less than 180-ohms resistance) between even and +15 Vdc terminals to serve as a polarity reversal switch, with

connections to the coax relay at the antenna, and one lead to the coax relay power supply (Fig. 9-3).

Polarotor™ feeds may require an additional transistor and a couple of resistors, one a 10-kilohm from base to ground of a 2N2222 transistor and a 10-k potentiometer across its collector to emitter terminals. Later Polarotor I units already have these components installed.

You may occasionally run into power supply problems with the ESR-24/ESR 2220. Positive 15-V, 12-V and negative 15-V sources are a set of four full wave (or bridge) rectifier diodes with 2100 μF filters and three voltage regulators, one fused on the rear panel (Fig. 9-4). If there's trouble, dc voltage checks or, better, oscilloscope waveform

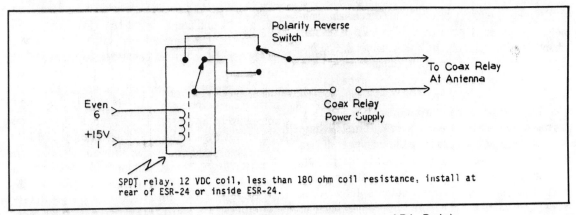

Fig. 9-3. Coaxial relay control used with orthomode (dual) LNA feeds (courtesy of R.L. Drake).

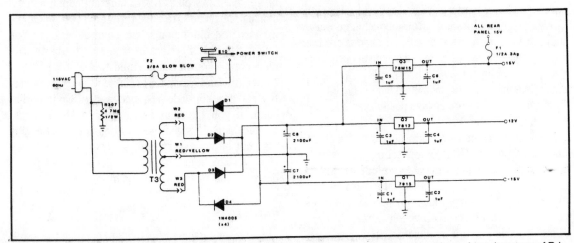

Fig. 9-4. Typical full-wave rectification, filtering and voltage regulation appearing in many such receivers (courtesy of R.L. Drake).

checks could spot it because the outputs should measure specified parameters and dc ripple should be in the low millivolts. Also look for hum bars if one diode quits. Regulation efficiency may also be established by variacing the power supply between 90 and 130 Vac. Faulty 1N4005 diodes here should be replaced in pairs, not singly.

Tuning voltage IC U7 may also give trouble once in a while and should be immediately recognized since there's no tuning output. If only a single channel is affected, any of the 13 diodes in the tuning section, or even processor U1 may be affected.

If you have no channel changes with the up/down buttons, then replace U-12. But if channels will not change with skip/tune switch, replace U-10 and U-12.

If there are jittery pictures only on certain channels, then increase the video level to 1 Vp-p on some channels with high output (often channel 7, ESPN). But be certain other channels remain usable.

Audio buzz or hum may result from bad power supply diodes, a modulator defect, regulator Q3, or low line voltage. Current from the external +15-V terminal should *not* exceed 300 mA. If the 3/8-amp fuse blows, you normally have either power diodes or regulator problems. Using a dc voltmeter and variac, bring up ac slowly to and above 100 Vac, while measuring the three regulator outputs. If the 1/2-A fuse blows there are cable or LNA problems and an obvious leakage or short. Simple resistance checks should tell here, but forward and reverse resistance *diode* measurements are often inconclusive unless there are absolute opens or shorts. Diodes are best checked with ac pulses in forward and reverse directions, monitoring outputs with an oscilloscope. Some digital multimeters have simplified diode checks, too. Remember: anodes are always positive with respect to cathodes.

A dark screen with wide horizontal bars and hum/buzz on TV CRT (if operating normally on broadcast channels) can also result from the ESR-24's power supply. Horizontal bars, on the other hand, are often produced by poor grounds, especially the receiver or downconverter. A *single* common connection is sufficient.

Channels drift or display reads incorrectly. Re-

align channel potentiometers and/or replace U4 or U6 (MC14510). The power supply regulation, here, is often a common fault in any multi-tuned frontend.

ESR-224

Drake lists no special problems with this receiver other than careful channel and audio tuning. Do remember, however, that one tuning potentiometer affects at least two channels, except pots for channels 1 and 24. Satcom F1-R appears to be the preferred signal source if it has a number of transponders in operation. We might also suggest F3 and F4; but then switch to some of the weaker satellites and see if your channel tunings are accurate there also. You must also adjust your AFC for zero volts on vertical polarization, cable compensation at one o'clock and fine tuning at 12 o'clock. Each channel must be tuned and checked, horizontally and vertically using a voltmeter connected to the main AFC test point.

You might also measure the +5-, −15-, +12- and +15-V outputs of regulators U-14 through U-17, respectively, for required dc potentials. In tuning audio, do recognize the red, blue, orange, black, or white colors of the ceramic filter and set audio for 1.7, 10.670, 10.730, 10.640, or 10.760 MHz accordingly (center-tuned, of course). Modulate your signal generator with 1 kHz 10mV, and deviate 10 kHz. The 6.8 MHz, 5.4 MHz and 8 MHz frequencies must be set also, as well as L8 for quieting with low-level signal input. The Q18 base through a 100-pF capacitor are the input points for your generator. You might also check generator frequency outputs with an accurate counter connected to a signal splitter. An RCA AH047 may do because it has some isolation and a rather wide frequency range. On the other hand, if you have an expensive, highly accurate "professional" signal generator, double checking may not be necessary. But unless you have precision, variable markers, such accuracy is not possible with the ordinary spectrum analyzer.

ESR-240

The tuning adjust for the 240 is much the same as the 224, although some steps in audio alignment are changed, including a preset 6.2 MHz and 6.8 MHz selection. You will find an i-f gain potentiometer adjustment in the frontend, with input generator set to 70 MHz at −25 dBm. There is also a video rear panel "invert" switch adjustment with R45 set to 0.9 Vp-p at the video output into a 75-ohm load. Then check clamp circuit by switching EDS switch on GSB-2000 on and off. Return video switch to its normal position.

The 70 MHz i-f alignment requires a tracking generator and spectrum analyzer with 3 dB point at 25 MHz and top ripple less than 0.5 dB. If you have such equipment refer to Drake's precise directions before undertaking this procedure. Like television receivers, this is no "eyeball" adjustment and needs even higher accuracy rather than simple 60-Hz sweep and basic markers (Fig. 9-5).

Finally, a remote control check might be in order with the REM switch set to *on*. An oscilloscope connected to pin 4 of the S2601 IC through a low capacitance probe will do the job. A 100-mV potential should be observed. Adjust T.R. oscillator R349 pot for a period of 1.7 μsec, equalling 590 kHz $\pm$20 kHz. Thereafter, check out with a known good remote control for the usual audio lamp lightings and mute positions. In the DEF position, the remote is defeated.

Channels in this receiver are still potentiometer-tuned but the diodes have disappeared, power supplies are much the same as before with some modifications including an overvoltage protect zener-transistor combination in the +15 volt source to the rear panel that "fires" above 18 volts.

You will also find a procedure for testing the remote control, which includes checking for bad solder joints, pc board breaks, bad batteries and connecting a scope to a control test point and adjusting *any* keyed waveform for 27 microseconds, the time taken to complete one full cycle at an amplitude between 1-2 volts p-p. If all's well, the receiver should respond accordingly. If not, troubleshoot and repair.

Where there is *no audio or video* in the 240 or 240A, check the +15-V supply, then the regulators, U1, and/or remove C9, a 22-μF 16-V filter if there is no tuning voltage at the i-f jack. Presumably, this is replaced with a known good unit since it is the cable compensating filter shunting CR1.

Hum or buzz in audio can be caused by: video termination plug misplaced (missing); audio adjust modulator needs realignment; video level too high. If the latter, however, your TV picture should appear somewhat dark also.

Channel change jumps or *won't change channels*. Replace U-14 and U-15, an MC 14538.

Scan doesn't operate. Replace U-309 and U-310, an MC 14511.

Scan stops as program button pressed. Replace U-12 (MC 14016) or U-24 (MC 14027).

Scan doesn't operate at all. Replace U-24 (MC 14027 or U-301 (MC 14584).

Both channel change controls result in up channels. Change U-305 (MC 14001)

Audio LEDs light simultaneously and won't switch. Replace U-305.

Format causes audio to cycle. Replace U-301 (MC 14584) or U-304 (MC 14027).

Polarotor doesn't operate. Check V/H controls

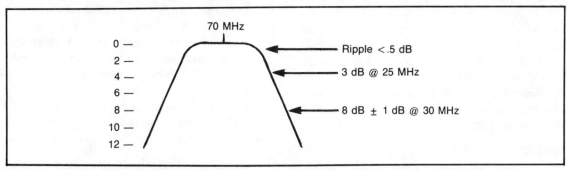

Fig. 9-5. All five coils in the ESR-240 passband should be adjusted for this response (courtesy of R.L. Drake).

and preset horizontal at 3 O'clock and vertical at 12 O'clock (from front). If no + 6 V at rear, replace U-3 (MC 7805). Pulse should read 6 Vp-p on scope.

Half amp. fuse blows with *open* circuit. Replace Q-21.

No tuning voltage at i-f jack. Disconnect i-f cable and measure −5 to −10 Vdc. If none, replace U-17 (MC 1458 or LM 359). There may also be leakage through C-9. If so, remove.

Infrared doesn't operate except with another receiver. Check rear defeat switch, replace U-307 (TDA 4040), or frequency cycle should extend 1.7 µsec and is adjustable with R349.

Program feature won't switch satisfactorily. Check IS-2168, diodes CR-26 through CR-31, and then C-91, 92, 94 for shorts (0.0047 µF).

Receiver won't turn on. Disconnect +15 Vdc terminal from downconverter and try once more. Should unit function, you have a cable, downconverter, or connector short or leakage. If not, check the fuse and replace, if necessary, but then change Q-21 (Tip-31). If the receiver still is dead, check U-27 (MC 78M15) or disconnect polarotor leads. Power supply faults, of course, can cause the same problem.

ESR-324

Many of the service notes for this receiver are concerned principally with tuning and i-f alignments. There is a quick AFC check, however, that makes a lot of sense. Detune one channel slightly and then short the AFC test point to ground with a clip lead. When this occurs, the particular channel should detune at once. Short removal should recover satisfactory tuning. Alternate fine tuning extremes will usually produce an AFC variation of ±0.6 volt. The i-f −3dB bandwidth on this receiver is 25 MHz, and spreads to 30 MHz at 8 dB down on the response curve. Audio ceramic color codes remain the same with identical frequencies as those referenced for the ESR-224, as do the audio tuneup instructions, with the generator signal going to the base of Q22 via a 100-pF capacitor.

ESR-424

This is a very popular microprocessor-controlled receiver and close attention has been paid to its performance. Therefore, we have a fair number of tech tips available from R.L. Drake.

Receiver won't turn on. Unplug line cord and wait for 10 seconds, then try once more. If no response, remove IR module and make another attempt. Should these two fail, check power diodes in the secondary of T3 and the two IC voltage regulators following if a dc problem such as low voltage and high or low current is indicated. Recall that another part of the receiver can be drawing current entirely independent of problems in the power supply. And remember, high current, low voltage denotes a leakage or short, while high voltage, low current usually means an open in normally designed circuits. In a totally open circuit, current does *not* flow.

Receiver turns on but with odd readouts. Find RESET pins near receiver's front and short these together. Should problems clear, replace C87, a 1 µF capacitor.

No video. Go to U5 and check dc on pins 1 and 14; both should register between 5.5 and 6.5 Vdc. If these values are not present, replace C82 and C81 with same value but 25-50 V working capacitors. Next, change modulator or connect video output to an oscilloscope or VCR. Bouncy video on *some* transponders can be "cured" by adjusting video level potentiometer on main receiver board; or find yellow trimmer in rf modulator and adjust for best picture; or locate Q-10, and if generic type (KN3904), replace with *Motorola* 2N3904.

No audio. Change modulator or check audio output with an oscilloscope with the receiver tuned to a normally operating transponder. If the transponder (or others) have audio tone and test pattern, check for a sine wave on pin 6 or U-7 and continue tracing. If no sine wave is present at pin 6, check Q11 and Q7, the local oscillator and mixer.

Low audio. Check operation of audio modulator coil. The same is true for audio buzz, and you may also reduce modulator video level (yellow adj.) or retard video level control on main receiver board. If audio "wanders" in the auto mode, change C91, a 10 µF cap.

Polarotor not operating satisfactorily. Control

board must be securely seated in socket (identical to the one in APS-424); or check out by substituting APS-242 board. Disconnect ac line cord and try again.

The +5-V regulator (MC7805) should have this output; if not, see that a +15-V input is present. If there is an input and no output, change MC7805 (U503) on Polarotor control board.

The pulse output may next be measured with a digital voltmeter and should read between 0.2 and 0.8 Vdc, varying when changing format. If it does not, and won't respond to Polarotor programming, change U502, an MC1455.

If the ESR-424 and APS-424 don't interface (mate) properly when changing channels or from one satellite to another, try these checks:

On back of receiver, there should be 0 Vdc on all *odd* channels and +5-Vdc on all *even* channels—no change with format. In early models, check 2N3904 and MC14011 on small circuit board to the right of power transformer. On later production units, all logic is built into the microprocessor, and the 2N3904 is located on the front panel and identified as Q701. Logic levels may also be lost if the SCAN switch on the receiver's bottom is partially set between NORMAL and SCAN.

No Audio or Video. Single conversion (LNA) units must have +16 V at the 16-V F output, and if not check Q28 and/or CR30. For block downconversions, make sure 16-Vdc switch is on and the jumper cable is connected between the 70-MHz input and output jacks.

Transistors Q1 through Q3 may also bear checking and dc voltages on base and collectors is said to measure 0.8 and 3-3.5 volts, respectively.

You might also check for 70 MHz tuning voltages at the F connector output. They should be about −4 V on Ch 24 and −10 V on Ch 1. If not, U-1 and U-4 are probable suspects.

U15 is also a possibility; input should be −20 to −25 Vdc. If not, change CR36, CR37. If output isn't about −15 Vdc, change regulator.

We won't print the ESR-424 alignment instructions, but do understand that you are dealing almost always in *negative* dB or dBm numbers; dBm being a precise decibel measure relative to one milliwatt.

When signal generator or spectrum analyzer values are *increased,* this simply means a *lesser* negative number. As an example −20 dBm to −10 dBm is an *increase* of 10 dB. Here, dB is simply a change in value and is relative rather than absolute.

APS-424

This is another high volume unit marketed by R.L. Drake, and internal adjustments as well as tech tips are supplied. It's advanced equipment that has a logic-operated microprocessor, usually quite reliable, but will decidedly balk if given the wrong instructions. We note the admonitions initially applied to contemporary receivers: unplug the ac line cord and wait 10 seconds, and/or remove IR modula and try again, are repeated here, indicating common microprocessor and remote control sensitivities that decidedly bear watching. Pushbutton switches should also operate freely.

All the above applies if the APS-424 won't turn *on.* It's also suggested that you check for 6 MHz at pin 12 of U11.

If there's *no display,* you should measure the emitter of Q12 for −24 Vdc at its base, and/or CR26. If this voltage does appear, replace U301 and U302.

When east or west positioner is depressed and the unit continues to move in either direction, check CR10 and CR11. If either or both are faulty, replace and check U9 for +5 V when east or west is activated, pins 10 and 5, respectively. If there is east or west movement immediately after ac is connected, replace U9 and check CR10-11.

Should log numbers have a diminished range or scan continuously, unplug ac and wait 10 seconds before reconnection; check U16 for +5 Vdc output, measure blue terminal on rear for +5 Vdc as well as R50 and L1. Resistor R7 should also be examined for adequate value resistance.

The remaining steps in this trouble section require the connection of a 10-kilohm potentiometer connected across the positioner's rear terminals to simulate an actuator. Then do the following:

Rotate the potentiometer and measure green terminal output on rear of unit for 0 to 5 Vdc. Pin 3 of U1 should also vary from 0 to 5 Vdc as the pot is rotated. If not, check R8-R9, and CE, C4 and C7. If pin 1 of U1 doesn't respond between 0 and 5 Vdc with pot rotation, replace U1. If all else operates, replace U3.

Should the polarity or format fail to operate: check board seating; unplug power cord for 10 seconds then reconnect; measure MC7805 regulator inputs and output (15 V versus 5 V), and if there are problems, replace. Pulse outputs should measure between 0.2 and 0.8 Vdc and vary when changing format. Also check Polarotor programming, or change U502, a MC1455.

If the Polarotor won't work, log numbers jitter, and east or west lamps light but relays don't operate, take out control board, then try east and west controls. If they and GOTO work satisfactorily, check C503 a 10 μF capacitor on the Polarotor control board.

SATELLITE TECHNOLOGY SERVICES

Another leader in the TVRO consumer home market, this company also publishes good technical information that merits worthwhile dissemination to the general service market. Furthermore, they are most cooperative and helpful in detailing possible problems that should apply not only to their equipment but others as well. Consequently, we hope contents from their service literature will prove useful to everyone.

LSR RECEIVERS

These receivers are shipped prealigned and should require no further adjustments other than those necessitating special attention during initial setup for optimum performance. As you should be well aware, those receivers with AFC, video level, and i-f gain adjustments usually need slight touchups for each less-than-routine installation when new, and possibly additional attention after an initial year's service. For the LSR receivers, here's what STS suggests:

1. Set video level control (RV102) for the usual 1 Vp-p measured at the video output jack. This will fully accommodate the 140 IRE unit measurement common to the industry.

2. With AFC *on*, adjust AFC balance for equal black and white sparklies on some *weak* transponder, and be sure picture quality is "equal or better" when the AFC is *off*.

3. I-f RV 502 should be set for meter deflection on *all* channels—in other words, sufficient signal strength, but not overload, much like a TV rf adjustment.

4. The RV501 AGC level control is next set for best picture quality on all channels. If set too high, the picture looks grainy; if too low, there will be streaking.

Receiver memory clearing sometimes may be required and is easily accomplished by desoldering the anode of D809 next to the battery, and then shorting its connected cathode end to ground, discharging all memory charge. The anode of D809 is then resoldered to the printed wiring board. In later models, STS says a master switch will be installed to accommodate this task without having to undertake the soldering-desoldering procedure.

Production runs with serial numbers 504 occasionally experienced microprocessor lockup when the polarizer is connected to the receiver. If there is a 100-ohm resistor in series with the output pulse terminal, cut the lead from pin 1 of CN302 to the pulse output, then add jump wire from pin 1 to the anode of D307.

MBS-AA RECEIVERS

Noticeable noise patterns may appear on CRTs of some television sets when power is applied to the actuator. To control this problem, go to the main board and solder a short piece of 18 AWG wire from pin 1 of U911 to the *main* case (Fig. 9-6). Then solder another AWG 18 wire from the ground side of C908 to the metal transformer case, making sure that all connections are short and securely fastened. Thereafter, remove the faceplate of the front PC board and solder another piece of the same type wire from pin 8 of U1001 to the top of the front panel's metal chassis. Then solder a wire between pin 8 of J1002 and the chassis. Finally, when using an MBS-AA, having a store defeat switch, solder another AWG 18 wire from pin 1 of U909 to the transformer

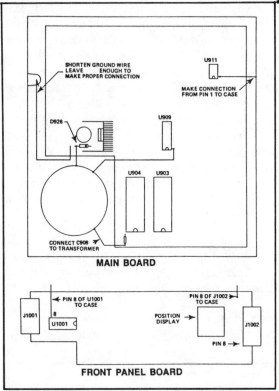

MAIN BOARD

FRONT PANEL BOARD

Fig. 9-6. An MBS-AA receiver noise pattern removal procedure (courtesy of STS).

case, and this completes the grounding modification.

In certain abnormal ac power conditions, the MBS-AA antenna actuator control may flash 00 and clear its memory. Switch the MBS-AA on and off rapidly with the polarization probe connected. Should memory clear, and flash 00, change R965 from 220 ohms to 1.2 kilohms so that the CPU may complete its normal run before reset.

Reed switch failures usually result from criscrossed wire connections. If a 36-V wire connects across the 5-V switch, the sensor is usually damaged as soon as motor voltage and current flows. Lower limits following 10 on the position display will then not change to 11- 13, etc., with arm movement from west to east. To be sure of the proper connections, program lower limit 10 into the actuator control, plug the molex connector into the rear of the control box, then go to the actuator and momentarily connect the two sensor wires from 15-20 times. If the actuator display goes either up or down from 10, all's well. But if there is no change, wiring is not correct and you'll have to start over *before* any motor voltage is applied.

Controller and actuator must operate together to accurately position the reflector, and this is accomplished by a counting arrangement between jack and controller. The controller furnishes 5 volts operating voltage to the two sensor wires across the reed switch. Normally open, said reed switch closes until a magnet connected to the jack's shaft crosses over and closes the switch. Pulses then travel down (Fig. 9-7) the sensor wire for the controller to count. When the magnet reverses position, the reed switch opens. Here, 12 pulses are required from the jack to change the display by one digit. When the antenna reaches a certain satellite position, this is stored digitally in memory, and the controller remembers the

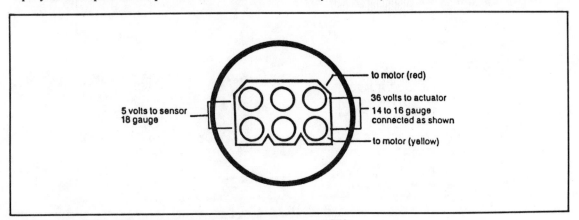

Fig. 9-7. Don't "kill" sensors with faulty wire hookups (courtesy of STS).

precise location. A reed switch sensor diagram supplied by STS is shown with all wire connections.

The RCS-1 timing modification is to work as an RCS-2 (which is then called an RCS-1 modified). Resistor R103 is removed and discarded, C106 is removed but saved. A 1N4148 diode is inserted in place of C106, and C106 is then connected between the junction of R106, the base of Q101, and the anode of 1N4148 to the ground side of C105. As Fig. 9-8 shows, the data stream has been modified substantially. You may now reassemble the shields and housing that were removed to make the modification. If more than one remote sensor is used with each receiver, sensor resistor R207 on the far side and lower left corner of the SR block should be changed from 56 to 22 ohms, apparently for additional current flow.

SR BLOCK

For ESP filter connection, unplug 134 MHz i-f line from second converter, plug filter input into second converter output, and then the 134 MHz lead into the filter's output. Filter power input must originate from 18-V source pin on the second converter: use No 22 AWG wire. You will also need i-f-to-female and i-f-to-male RCA connectors to complete the modification. For multiplex audio modification, simply clip pin 2 of U112 and solder a 47-k 1/8-W resistor between pins 1 and 2.

VideoCipher® compatibility on this chassis is accomplished by merely changing the value of the chip resistor soldered to the "negative" lead of C1G7 (182) from 1.8 k to 1 k. A carbon replacement is sufficient. Afterwards, reinstall the circuit board in position.

MBS-SR BLOCK

VideoCipher® may also be made compatible with this chassis by shorting resistor R1016—that's all.

M/A-COM T1

While the name has changed substantially (Gen-

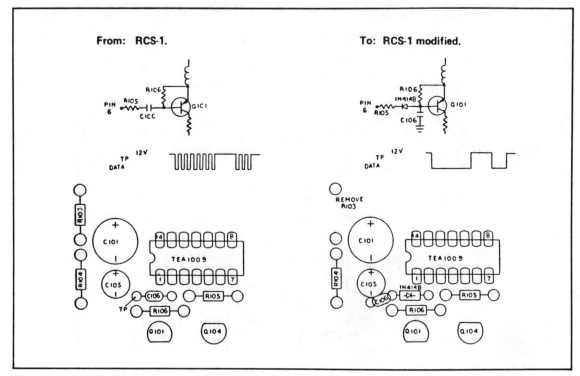

Fig. 9-8. With these modifications, an RCS1 will operate as an RCS2 (courtesy of STS).

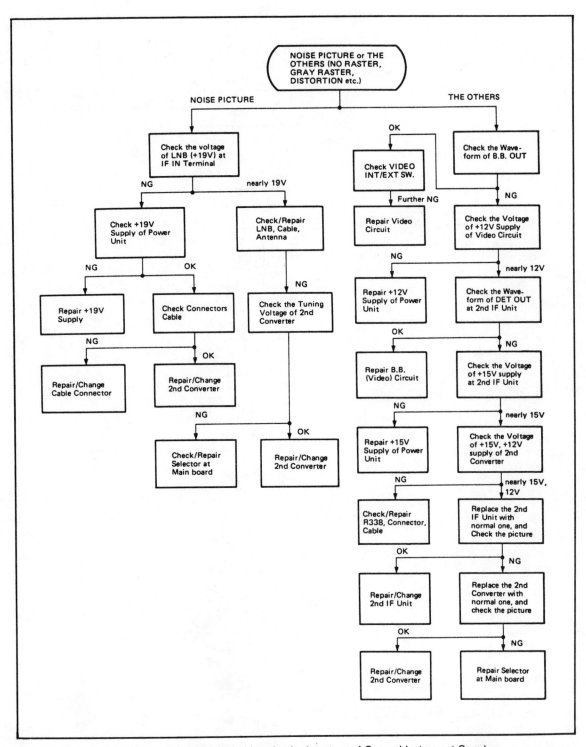

Fig. 9-9. T-I second converter, second i-f, and video circuits (courtesy of General Instrument Corp.).

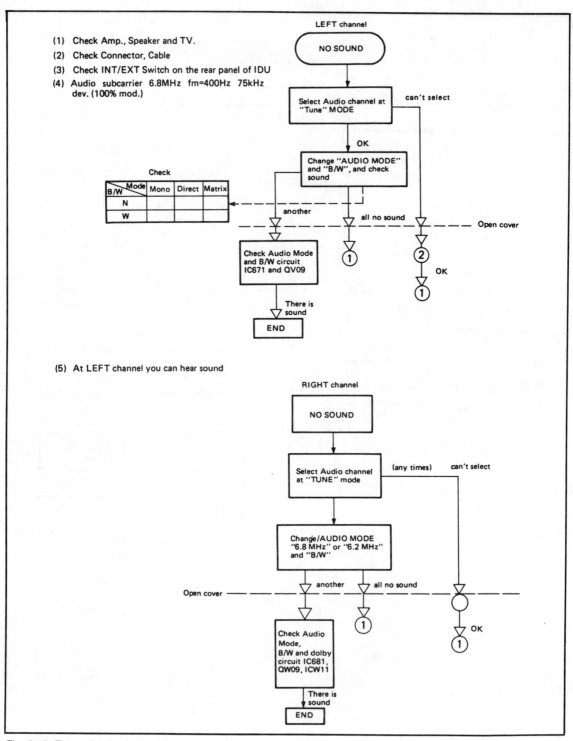

(1) Check Amp., Speaker and TV.

(2) Check Connector, Cable

(3) Check INT/EXT Switch on the rear panel of IDU

(4) Audio subcarrier 6.8MHz fm=400Hz 75kHz dev. (100% mod.)

LEFT channel

NO SOUND

Select Audio channel at "Tune" MODE → can't select

OK

Change "AUDIO MODE" and "B/W", and check sound

Check

B/W \ Mode	Mono	Direct	Matrix
N			
W			

another / all no sound / Open cover

Check Audio Mode and B/W circuit IC671 and QV09

① ② OK ①

There is sound

END

(5) At LEFT channel you can hear sound

RIGHT channel

NO SOUND

Select Audio channel at "TUNE" mode — (any times) / can't select

Change/AUDIO MODE "6.8 MHz" or "6.2 MHz" and "B/W"

Open cover — another / all no sound

Check Audio Mode, B/W and dolby circuit IC681, QW09, ICW11

① OK ①

There is sound

END

Fig. 9-10. T-1 audio circuit (partial) (courtesy of General Instrument Corp.).

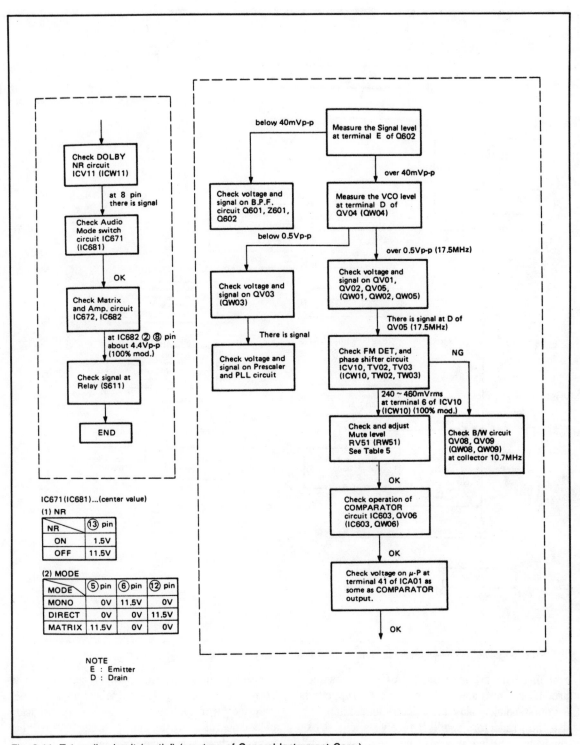

Check DOLBY
NR circuit
ICV11 (ICW11)

at 8 pin
there is signal

Check Audio
Mode switch
circuit IC671
(IC681)

OK

Check Matrix
and Amp. circuit
IC672, IC682

at IC682 ② ⑧ pin
about 4.4Vp-p
(100% mod.)

Check signal at
Relay (S611)

END

below 40mVp-p

Measure the Signal level
at terminal E of Q602

over 40mVp-p

Check voltage and
signal on B.P.F.
circuit Q601, Z601,
Q602

Measure the VCO level
at terminal D of
QV04 (QW04)

below 0.5Vp-p

over 0.5Vp-p (17.5MHz)

Check voltage and
signal on QV03
(QW03)

Check voltage and
signal on QV01,
QV02, QV05,
(QW01, QW02, QW05)

There is signal

There is signal at D of
QV05 (17.5MHz)

Check voltage and
signal on Prescaler
and PLL circuit

Check FM DET, and
phase shifter circuit
ICV10, TV02, TV03
(ICW10, TW02, TW03)

NG

240 ~ 460mVrms
at terminal 6 of ICV10
(ICW10) (100% mod.)

Check and adjust
Mute level
RV51 (RW51)
See Table 5

Check B/W circuit
QV08, QV09
(QW08, QW09)
at collector 10.7MHz

OK

Check operation of
COMPARATOR
circuit IC603, QV06
(IC603, QW06)

OK

Check voltage on μ-P at
terminal 41 of ICA01 as
some as COMPARATOR
output.

OK

IC671(IC681)...(center value)

(1) NR

NR	⑬ pin
ON	1.5V
OFF	11.5V

(2) MODE

MODE	⑤ pin	⑥ pin	⑫ pin
MONO	0V	11.5V	0V
DIRECT	0V	0V	11.5V
MATRIX	11.5V	0V	0V

NOTE
E : Emitter
D : Drain

Fig. 9-11. T-1 audio circuit (partial) (courtesy of General Instrument Corp.).

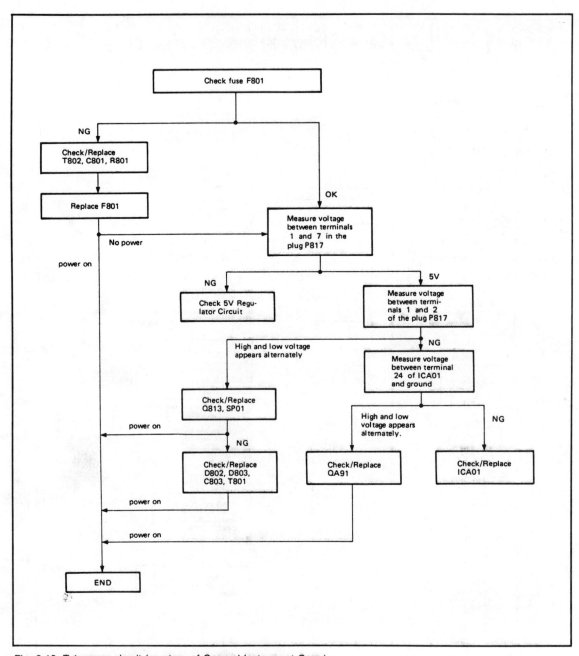

Fig. 9-12. T-1 power circuit (courtesy of General Instrument Corp.).

eral Instrument Corp.) the M/A-COM consumer product has not, and it still maintains a reputation for outstanding quality and industry leadership. We use their reflectors and T/H receivers almost exclusively and have always found them reliable and satisfactory in snow, ice, rain, or sunshine. The North Carolina-manufactured reflectors are especially noteworthy, being made of compression molded fiberglass, resin, and reflecting material that seems to hold shape and cope with the elements

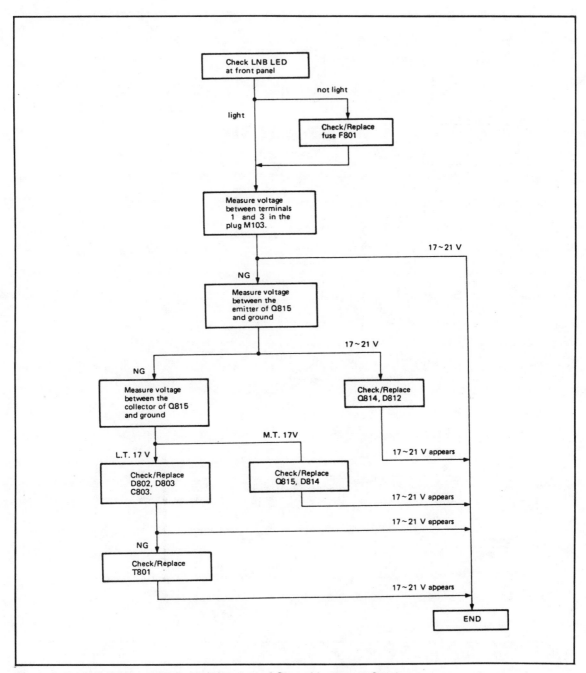

Fig. 9-13. T-1 LNB (19-V) regulator circuit (courtesy of General Instrument Corp.).

nicely. At C band, we access 15 satellites with relative ease using only a less-than-90° linear actuator. A horizon-to-horizon mount—to be installed later— should accommodate several more. At Ku, the T-2

receiver was immediately adaptable to the old USCI (the one that broadcast over ANIK C2 and failed) without modification and channel access time of usually less than two seconds. The T-2, however,

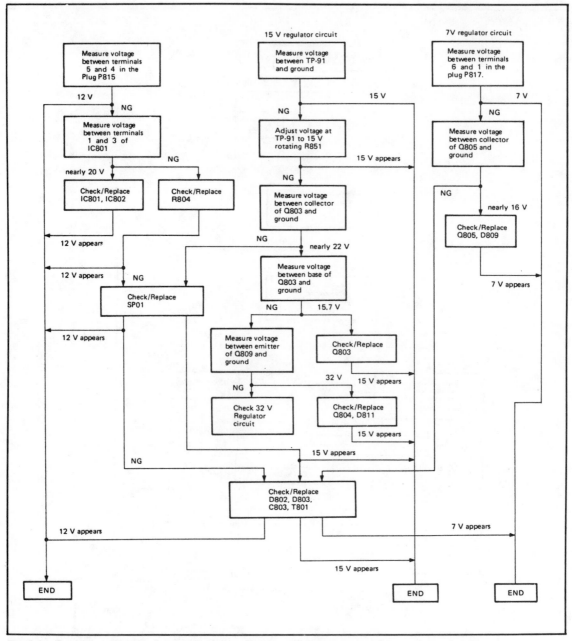

Fig. 9-14. T-1 (video), 12-V (audio), 15-V and 7-V regulator circuit (courtesy of General Instrument Corp.).

doesn't have stereo, and so we'll use several troubleshooting diagrams from T-1 to bolster the M/A-COM/ General Instrument cause. There is also some information available on the H-1. The general video portion of the T-1, T-2 receivers is similar and so one set of diagrams will be used here for both. Power supplies are equivalent also.

These units have now been on the market for

186

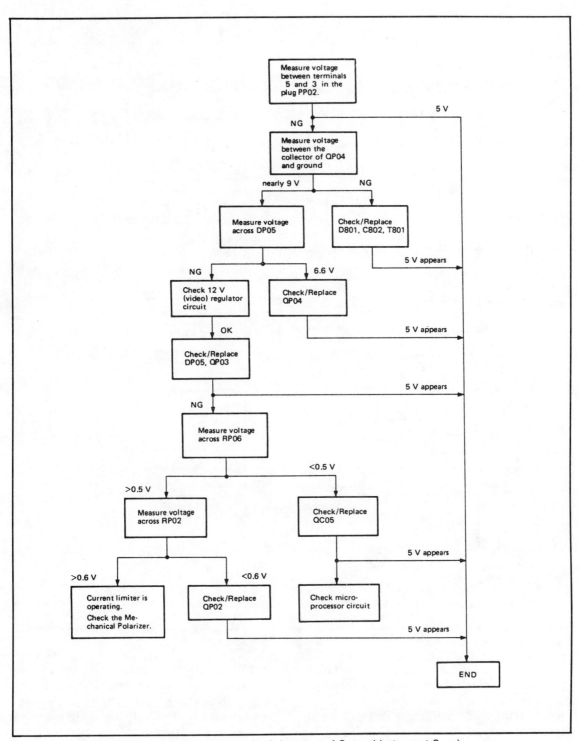

Fig. 9-15. T-1 mechanical polarizer 5-V regulator circuit (courtesy of General Instrument Corp.).

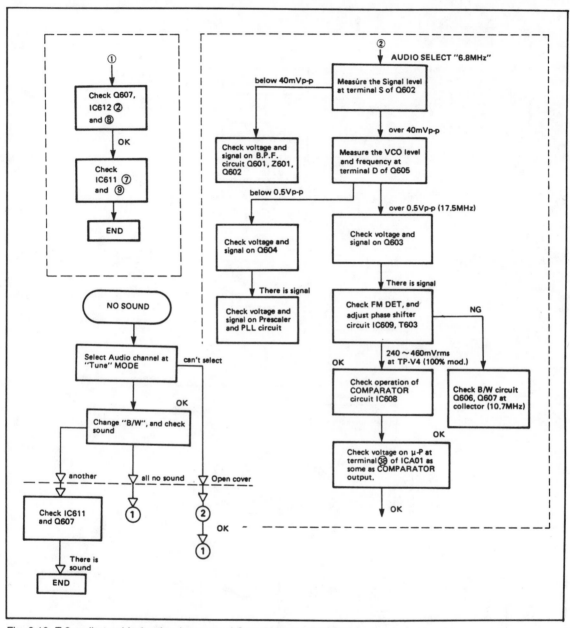

Fig. 9-16. T-2 audio troubleshooting (courtesy of General Instrument Corp.).

several years and a few of their troubleshooting procedures (supplied by M/A-COM) should come in handy. See Figs. 9-9 through 9-20.

Combining all this considerable information dealing with specific approaches to troubleshooting for a number of popular receivers and positioners, you should be able to apply equal or equivalent methods to almost any of the better receivers on the market, even though the circuitry may not be identical. This is certainly true for the Toshiba group marketed by Channel Master, Norsat, R.L.Drake, Zenith, and M/A-COM, etc.

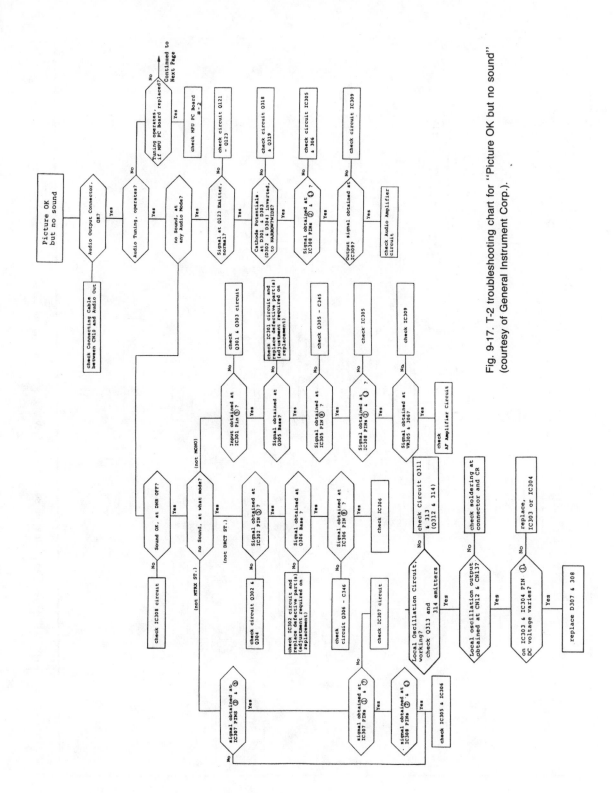

Fig. 9-17. T-2 troubleshooting chart for "Picture OK but no sound" (courtesy of General Instrument Corp.).

189

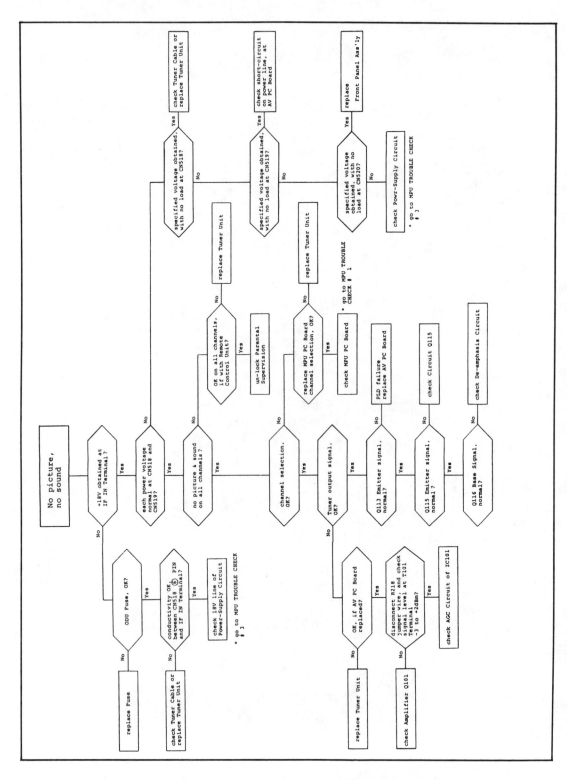

Fig. 9-18. T-2 troubleshooting chart for "No picture, no sound" (courtesy of General Instrument Corp.).

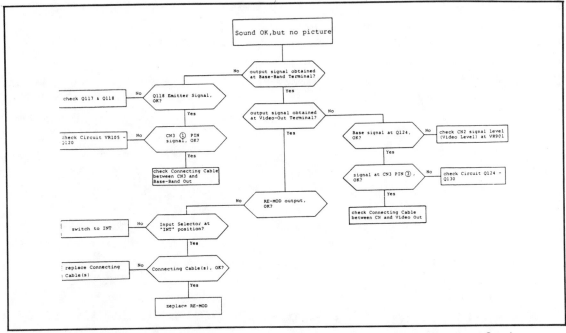

Fig. 9-19. H-1 troubleshooting chart for "Sound OK, but no picture" (courtesy of General Instrument Corp.).

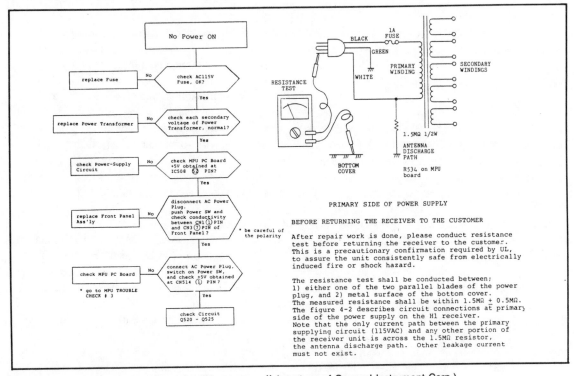

Fig. 9-20. H-1 troubleshooting chart for "No power on" (courtesy of General Instrument Corp.).

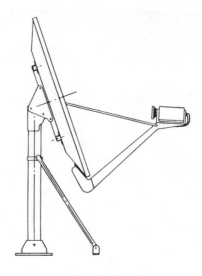

Chapter 10

Terrestrial EMI/RFI Interference and Solutions

THE WARNING THAT STRIKES SHUDDERS INTO THE being of anyone who is unfamiliar with its various problems; but to dedicated souls in the industry, T.I. is simply another challenge that must be overcome. Of course, if you're sitting on top of one of Ma Bell's or Sprint's transmitters, the economical thing to do would be *move*! But, thank heavens, such is seldom the situation, and a great deal of T.I. can be handled with some considerable degree of success, especially with newly engineered and even less costly equipment appearing first in 1986 and further improved ever since. Two prime movers—or filter factories we should say—appear to be Microwave Filter Co. of New York and Phantom Engineering of California. Each of course has its specialties that we'll revue in considerable detail. In the meantime, a good, healthy discussion of terrestrial interference causes would certainly be in order, followed by available minimizations and outright cures.

Terrestrial interference (Fig. 10-1) unfortunately, can only increase with additional microwave activity on earth for *both* C and Ku bands, making *all* satellite downlinks subject to difficulties ranging from just a few light sparklies to absolute picture blackouts. In addition, audio may eventually be marginally affected plus heavy black and white sparklies, color scintillations, and bandpass constrictions —sometimes all rolled into one. Fortunately, many symptoms are recognizable and may be approached immediately with some distinct possibility of affecting a reasonable, if not complete cure. Further, new trap units are now appearing that will work on a single channel only, if required, and have been simplified so that the consumer can operate them. Consequently, many families near the larger cities who would, under no circumstances, have enjoyed reasonable reception in the past are now able to compensate T.I. sufficiently to access not only most satellites but the majority of their transponders as well.

So the use of single and multi-purpose traps and filters has done much to clear the air of many difficulties heretofore considered impossible. As time progresses, such trapping and exclusion techniques,

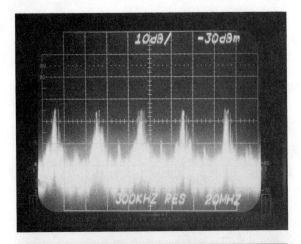

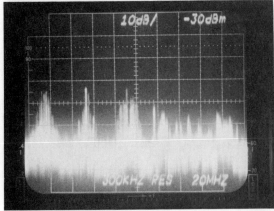

Fig. 10-1. Satellite channels can look like the noisy ones on the left or clean ones on the right. Reflector pointing must be accurate as well as *skew*.

undoubtedly, will undergo further improvement relative to both effectiveness and cost. As of now, $200 to $500 is not an excessive dealer cost for many of these more complex and specialized units. With mass production, such prices may, eventually, be cut in half, much like those for television. Although when dealing with microwaves, frequencies are many times higher and there's seldom such a thing as a simple filter, whether notch or passband. So don't expect too much too fast, but eventually, microwaves as we know them now will become an everyday technology, very similar to television. Some day hundreds of gigahertz will present their own challenges, much akin to our own today. Even as we write, 30 GHz and higher frequencies are being

proposed as the next spectrum bands to be occupied by government, military, and commercial enterprises. It's therefore important that those who intend to make a career of satellite station design, operations, and servicing follow developments closely, and remain thoroughly informed and substantially prepared. A good challenge builds both intellect and progress.

IN-BAND AND
OUT-OF-BAND INTERFERENCE

There are two distinct types of terrestrial interference prevalent in TVRO operations. One occurs *within* the usual transponder passband and the other *without*. Since terrestrial microwave shares (in an offset way) at least the C-band downlink frequencies between 3.7 and 4.2 GHz, whatever occurs on either side of transponder carriers (and sometimes in the middle) is termed in-band disturbance, whereas problems outside normal transponder range are identified as out-of-band (Fig. 10-2).

Actually, there's very little mystery detecting either type, provided you have plenty of amplification and a good spectrum analyzer. Unfortunately most service types don't have such necessary but exotic equipment, and therefore we'll try and work

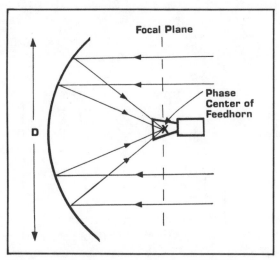

Fig. 10-2. Terrestrial interference may originate anywhere, but it must enter a TVRO feed to be seen and felt.

193

with both the expensive and low cost to instill most general appearances, causes, and practical cures. Esoteric approaches involving high-priced engineers and large R and D laboratories will be left to the convention paper readers to profoundly resolve. We'll take the low road and offer state-of-the-art solutions. The ensuing discussion, then, dwells upon the set of "real" numbers rather than non-reals often described as the square root of minus 1 (−1) and complex impedances and phase rotations such as 10 + 5j, although such are very much a part of all electronics, they can be made into very real numbers by just a little algebraic manipulation. Similarly, "imaginary" numbers may become positive numbers by multiplying them by the square root of minus 1 (−1).

If you haven't guessed by now, $\sqrt{-1}$ and operator "J" are one and the same. We're simply dealing with a convenient mathematical notation. Fortunately, j^4 becomes a positive "1" following its final 90° counterclockwise quadrant rotation. Therefore, whatever you call the j operator, there are methods of making him exit the complex number category into the real world—a subject you should surely remember from basic electronics and ac theory.

In-band and out-of-band trap and/or filter solutions are, fortunately, usually both distinct and different and are treated separately since one involves largely source-identifiable interference (Fig. 10-3) while the other could come from any direction, in-

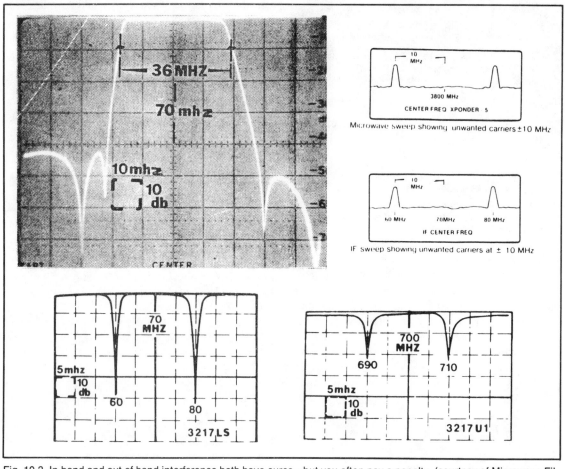

Fig. 10-3. In-band and out-of-band interference both have cures—but you often pay a penalty (courtesy of Microwave Filter Co.).

cluding secondary images if the original signals are in the *plus* dB categories. Interference more than 15 dB down from the initial transponder carrier usually presents small problems, or none at all. It's really the tall fellows that make all the trouble.

IN-BAND SOLUTIONS

Because in-band problems constitute better than 90 percent of all TVRO interference difficulties, these will be considered first, followed by out-of-band faults and what to do about them (Fig. 10-4). Usually, most in-banders fall at 10 MHz on either side of the transponder's rf carrier. When downconversion is completed, you'll find this same 10 MHz astride your final intermediate frequency passband (i-f) in the identical position. Therefore, before the FM signal is detected, you'll want to either suppress or completely remove said T.I. and keep it from appearing in the picture (usually) and sound (seldom). When you trap, therefore, instead of the usual 25-27 MHz i-f bandpass of your receiver, you reduce or slice your bandwidth to 20 MHz, because the upper and lower traps are now often designed to operate collectively (Fig. 10-4).

When bandwidth reduction occurs, of course, both broad color and fine detail are affected as well, perhaps, as already untrapped channels. Consequently, very careful trapping is required to prevent the introduction of additional problems that may turn out to be worse than the original. This is normally done with 3 MHz-wide notch filters extending some 15-20 dB into the modulation in reverse polarity (Fig.

10-5) cancelling Ma Bell, or whatever. In other words, if the interference is positive-going, then a negative spike of *voltage* can cancel the undesirable effect. This, however, blocks part of the picture, thus narrowing the bandwidth. The moral of the story, of course, is *not to trap* unless absolutely necessary; and certainly not before trying locally available shielding to achieve the same purpose but with considerably better results. As for the various ways and means of shielding, we'll describe some of the possibilities following trapping and other mechanical constraints. Meanwhile, let's continue with applications of these LC or LCR networks as applied to the various intermediate frequency amplifiers.

As you are probably aware, final i-f amplifiers may have midpoints of from 70 MHz to 500 MHz plus, depending on both initial design and eventual application. Usually 140 to about 250 MHz is to be found in the later model receivers, while some oddballs crop up here and there. The 70 MHz i-fs were easy to trap, but they belonged primarily to single-conversion LNAs plus converter systems where only one channel was tuned at a time. Block downconversions permitting two frequency reductions have worked much better, and the usual image frequencies and spurs wandering about have just about vanished. This is because the first heterodyning action is fixed and the tunable second heterodyne is

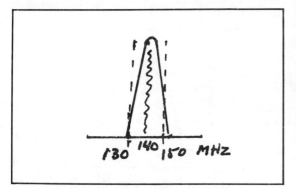

Fig. 10-4. Ma Bell interference usually arrives as 10 MHz on either side of the satellite carrier.

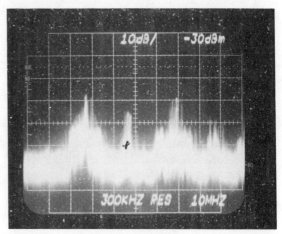

Fig. 10-5. A pair of fully modulated transponders on Galaxy-1. Center response identifies opposite polarity transponder.

within the shielded receiver itself, thereby eliminating a number of problems, but increasing costs and elevating i-f frequencies and passbands. Now, however, the entire 500 MHz C or even Ku band set of frequencies is received, as well as all the usual 24 transponders (at C band, fewer at Ku).

This is precisely why we would like as little filtering as possible: the normal C band channel bandwidth amounts to 36 MHz; Ku band varies all over the place from 36 MHz to at least 54 MHz and, we're told, even 120 MHz. Now, unless deliberately constricted channels are used for select transmissions, a narrowband 23 to 25 MHz receiver won't work. So the nearer your receiver approaches 30 MHz, the better off you are in any reasonable signal area. Such i-f bandwidths appear *only* in the best receivers and are filtered and compensated accordingly. A wide bandwidth—one at or closely approaching 30 MHz—offers relatively little additional interference pickup and always makes a world of difference in the picture, and, if stereo equipped, in the sound also, especially if the television receiver is also a baseband monitor. The best pictures in the world for consumer and probably commercial viewing come directly off the satellites. With the advent of 1125-line high definition television (HDTV), images and sound will be advanced over what we usually see today.

Spread out, a modulated carrier appears much as it does in Fig. 10-5. When T.I. occurs in any strength—say 10-12 dB *below* the 0 dB carrier, all but 20 MHz of picture and sound disappears and considerable interference is noted. At +10 dB, with interference rising, your TV screen goes black from overload, knocking out the picture entirely since this signal is stronger than even the original and the receiver tunes directly to it (Fig. 10-6).

Weak satellite signals look like salt and pepper, whereas microwaves on the prowl have a streaky effect and are pure audio. There can also be motorboating in the sound since these carriers are usually narrowband and affect audio first.

When some powerful commercial signals are received they can mix channels together, other signals may cause a fluctuation much like that of a weakly-braced reflector in high winds. This means

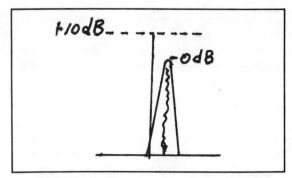

Fig. 10-6. If interference rises 10 dB above carrier (O dB), then you're wiped out!

there are bursts of heavy traffic, usually between the hours of 1700 and 1900 hrs., when the phone networks are extremely busy. In wideband T.I. you may have the same image over a number of incoming transponders and, on narrow bandwidth receivers, there may also be color noise. This can affect as many as six transponders in the reception area, and all on a *single* polarity—by all means look for such an inconsistency. All of which brings us to the subject of out-of-band T.I., which, fortunately, is not usually the offender, but needs to be handled as firmly as if it is.

OUT-OF-BAND SOLUTIONS

This can be either wideband or narrowband interference, and may be dealt with if recognized and confronted accordingly (Fig. 10-7). In effect, this is outside interference that's creeping in close to the carrier and generating either a direct or delayed effect, producing sparklies or other interference in the

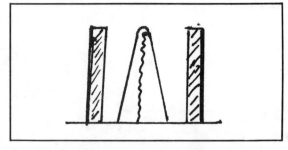

Fig. 10-7. Out-of-band interference is always seen on the outside of a normally modulated carrier. A bandpass filter usually becomes necessary.

picture. You may even have sparklies in specific colors occasionally.

Here, there are two main remedies: either fine tune your receiver, if that's possible, away from the interference; or reduce or reshape the receiver's bandpass to avoid the problem. If the interference is only mild, bandpass reshaping should work; but if strong, a surface-wave acoustical filter (SAW) may have to be used. Such SAW filters operate with *fixed*-tuned i-fs and one or several may have to be tried to minimize this wideband or bandspreading interference that's creeping in from the *sides*. It may also be possible to change your reflector from a shallow unit to one with deeper focal point and a narrower beamwidth. Sometimes, more than one cure is needed.

There could also be trees about that will shield you during the spring and summer. But by late fall most leaves have fallen, and you are in trouble again. There are also various buildings that might be used, as well as a low-lying area that might be beneath the various interference streams. Finally, fine copper or aluminum screening between your reflector and the interfering source may save the day. Unfortunately, a good deal of T.I. "trap" shooting becomes somewhat experimental after initial sure-fire attempts have obviously failed. If this is the resulting condition, then a block downconverter, feed, and spectrum analyzer may be your only salvation. You must know precisely the problem, and then understand how to deal with it. Fortunately, sharp bandpass skirts and minor bandpass reduction usually does the trick, but do check the other satellites and their various transponders to see if this procedure produces any adverse effects. Simultaneously, note picture resolution, definition and any "gargly" sound that might occur because of bandwidth reduction. Sorry to relate, you can never tell in microwaves until deliberate action is taken.

MICROWAVE FILTERS FOR TVRO

Similar to water purification filters, electronic filters actually remove various electrical impurities and deliver cleaner signals to any viewer with (hoped for) minor audio/video content losses. Naturally this is not always possible but the effects are usually bet-

ter than nothing. Nonetheless, filters do require judicious selection and application or they may not be effective at all. And we will *always insist* that interference reduction by means other than filtering is more desirable to avoid the obvious penalties of reducing or notching bandpasses to "eliminate" interference intrusions.

Consequently, you always pay some penalty for their use, but many times such a consequence is unavoidable. As we learn more about C-band characteristics and their co-located interferences, Ku-band problems are beginning to emerge also, and so we're now looking at double trouble as more systems and satellites assume their alotted positions. Now we have some 30-odd frequency translators operating in the sky, but as soon as the Ku spectrum becomes filled you'll be dealing with 60. So "double trouble" may have even more meaning later than it does just now—we'll all have to wait and see; and these don't even include the hundreds and even thousands of mobile uplinks that could be touring the countryside during the next few years of the 1980s and 1990s, working both bands with full FCC approval. Therefore "be prepared" is considerably more that some proud Boy Scout motto; it's also very much a banner slogan for all those involved in microwaves!

TYPICAL FILTERS

In bygone days when electronics was young, simple capacitances, inductances, and a few resistors combined to do all the filtering necessary to either block or swallow some undesirable frequencies (Fig. 10-8). But even then one could beg or buy such filter items as band pass, low pass, high pass, and chokes. As frequencies increased, however, these simple passive networks become complex, and even now have developed into active filters for such applications as power-supply ripple reduction.

Then, as now, low frequencies were usually capacitively filtered and higher frequencies choke filtered, especially when radio frequencies (rf) threatened to upset direct-current power supplies. After that, chokes were used (and still are) to buck alternating current at low frequencies and either peak or impedance-limit signals, especially video, at the higher frequencies. Large capacitors, then, shunt

197

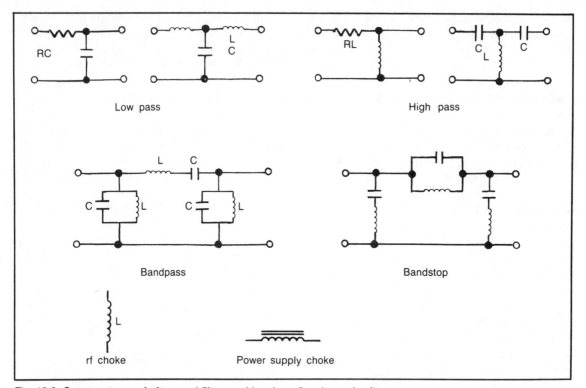

Fig. 10-8. Common types of often-used filters and bandpass/bandstop circuits.

undesirable dc ripple to ground or, conversely, pass ac in series configuration, blocking dc. So when you hear of a dc block at microwave frequencies, you'll know it's some capacitance that will stop dc but is seen as a short circuit to ac *above* a certain impedance and frequency.

Impedance, then becomes the reactance of various components to different frequencies as they interact with other involved impedances. Because small signal microwave power often hasn't many decibels (dB) to spare in the way of loss, you'll have to remember that even conjugate *matched* impedances in connecting circuits only deliver *half power*. Therefore, losses due to filtering and passbanding in small signal designs are *always* critical! Especially is this true where standing-wave ratios (SWR), leakage and mismatches are involved, because 50 ohms is the microwave characteristic. A coupling between 50 and 75 ohms impedance usually means a *loss* of 5.72 dB every time—almost *doubling* the half power 3 dB characteristic *matched*

drop we just described. This is why insertion, passive, and cabling losses are so very important in the satellite earth station industry.

Resistance/capacitance filters always have finite time constants and usually slow rolloffs and should have cutoff frequencies equivalent to 3 dB (voltage and current) which is 0.707, or 71% of the input. As an example, with no input and output resistances, the ratio of input and output voltages in this type of RC filter would amount to:

$$E_o/E_i = R/\sqrt{R^2 + X^2} \text{ or } 1/\sqrt{1 + (X/R)^2}$$

and its cutoff frequency f = $1/(2\pi RC)$ cps. R, of course, stands for resistance in ohms, and C for capacity in microfarads. RC, then, multiplied together becomes the time constant.

Here, if C = 100 μF and R = 1,000 ohms

$$f = 1/(6.28 \times 100 \times 10^{-6} \times 1 \times 10^3)$$
$$= 159 \text{ Hz (cps)}$$

As you can see, when these RC numbers become smaller, time constants become faster. Remember, too, that the X^2 in the first equation is not simply a capacitance, but must be treated as capacitative *reactance* of the frequency being filtered.

Therefore,

$$X_c = 1/2\pi fc$$

and is represented in terms of ohms, the same as resistance. So once again we tangle with the term reactive impedance.

An inductor/resistor combination is handled the same way, except that its reactance is derived directly and not inverted and divided:

$$X_L = 2\pi fL$$

but it charges and discharges the same way as a capacitor.

Now with both inductors and capacitors available, you have all the components for both high-pass and low-pass filters. High-pass filters permit frequencies *above* a certain reference to flow freely, while low-pass filters only permit information flow *below* a specified level. The more sections of each the better filtering that is obtained. Inductive chokes, on the other hand, are usually used singly and have reactances to stop specific rippling electron flow from passing into critical circuits. Symbolic basic filters and chokes are shown in Fig. 10-8 for low- and medium-frequency applications. Having said that, we are now ready to proceed with microwave filter techniques, which are substantially different and considerably more complex. However, LC components are still in heavy use up to about 500 MHz.

MICROWAVE FILTERS

Above 0.5 GHz, however, distributed line cavities and waveguide cavities take over. This is especially true for both TVRO bandpass and first converter-to-receiver notch filters that Microwave Filter is currently marketing. Nominally, square waveguide-like tubes are used for the outer conductor and round tubes for the inner conductor. Often there are coaxial centers coupled to striplines and tuned with capacitors. Any schematic would show the usual LC components, but hardware diagrams would only exhibit pieces of pipe with an occasional and very small capacitance tuning element. Therefore there's no point in attempting to illustrate pieces of pipe, while tiny trimmer capacitors simply have a slot cut in the top for tuning away from some prescribed frequency.

Applications of these filters, however, is something else again, and this we intend to fully explore with available information and personal experience (Figs. 10-9 and 10-10).

In all the newer receivers the 70 MHz final i-f is being rapidly supplanted by 950 to 1450 MHz blocks that serve up-frequency i-fs from 140 MHz to almost 700 MHz, depending on the manufacturer. You might also like to know that most filter manufacturers presuppose there is an i-f loop through at the rear of each receiver—a supposition that isn't always true. Consequently, in some instances you may be required to go *inside* certain receivers to make desirable filter connections, and that, sometimes, could be very messy and even harm operation of the receiver itself, especially if your soldering techniques are suspect or if your 40-watt iron destroys a perfectly good printed circuit board.

At the moment, probably 80 percent of the receiver i-fs now belonging to consumers have 70 MHz i-fs. But in several years, commercial and consumer i-f frequencies will have changed considerably due to personal manufacturing preferences, less subject to outside interference, and standardization for both Ku- and C-band operation.

Even now, Microwave Filter Co. has developed a terrestrial interference notch filter, Model 5020-1, that tunes the entire 950-1450 MHz LNB/C band, and is also available for the lower frequency blocks at 270-770 and 450-950 MHz. So here there is no special worry about whether the final i-f has a receiver outlet or not, the 5020-1 covers the entire block down band *before* the receiver even sees the interference with a minimum 15 dB notch at a bandwidth of 4 MHz, matching the dispersion of most interfering carriers (Fig. 10-11).

With this piece of equipment, which sells for $375, coupling it into a power splitter, along with a spectrum analyzer for positive T.I. identification should take care of most types of in-band interference provided the problem was single and not multiple. If there's more than one interferer, the other problem points may also be located and then permanent filters installed in the 5020-1's place. Resonant frequency notches should absorb the rest. A pair of Model 3217LS-60/80 traps would be satisfactory in 70 MHz systems *between* the downconverter and receiver. Other models *may* be available for *different* i-fs by the time you read this. Such traps, however, will not cure "wipeouts" and other measures should be instituted when interfering signals are this strong. The same specifications or directions apply to the 4612-(15) dual filter with narrow passband for snowy pictures, and a built-in trap for sparklies, including an in/out switch to turn it off when not needed—all by Microwave Filter, of course (Fig. 10-12).

Microwave filter has also developed another tunable block downconverter trap that's installed *between* the block converter and the receiver, and identified as Model 5111 (Fig. 10-13). This one not only blocks mild or heavy T.I., but may also "cure"

Coaxial Microwave Filters For 1-4 GHz

Filters from about 1–4 GHz are most conveniently executed in coaxial elements or cavities. An exception is made for very narrow band, low loss bandpass filters where connectorized waveguide cavity filters are more efficient.

Lowpass Filters

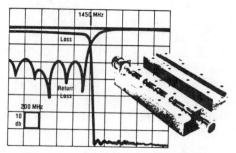

This cascade of low and high impedance sections in this lowpass L-band filter is typical of high power design practice.

Highpass Filters

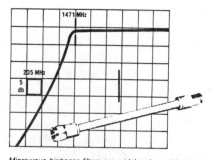

Microwave highpass filters are wideband quasi bandpass filters utilizing tandem transmission line sections.

Bandstop Filters

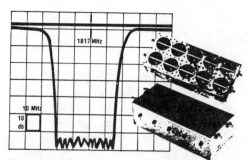

This 110 db, L-band frequency rejection filter features periodic line loading by decoupled resonators.

Fig. 10-9. Waveforms of various filters effective between 1 and 4 GHz (courtesy of Microwave Filter Co.).

(suppress) channel wipeouts when this results from second converter overload (too much signal into the receiver). New, too, are the 4616 switchable i-f traps with two independently switchable traps for use on one or more channels—but it may not help wipeout. There's also a switchable *bandpass* filter for weak channels, which may be made inoperable for strong channels, and will suppress mild to heavy T.I.. Weak signal snowy or grainy pictures use this filter, which has already been identified as the 4612-15. Among the traps, watch for shading of certain positive or negative polarity channels in series—this decidedly denotes 4 GHz terrestrial interference.

Microwave Filter Co. has also provided a remarkably complete listing of existing TVRO receivers showing their various final intermediate frequency amplifiers, as well as those receivers with block downconverters. This listing, courtesy of Microwave Filter Co. Inc., will certainly aid you in selecting any necessary filter. Use it with confidence. See Table 10-1.

Bandpass Filters

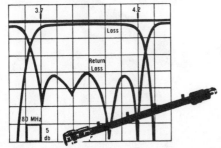
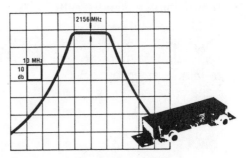

Wide bandpass filters can be realized as tandem, distributed resonators to give a compact DC-passing design, while those requiring greater selectivity are realized in comb-line or quarter-wave digital resonators.

Diplexers

L-Band diplexer illustrates design technique to combine several functions: transmit and receive path separation, transmitter second and third harmonic suppression and forward and reverse power monitoring.

Preselectors

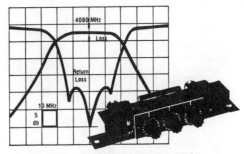

This three section preselector tunes the 3.7-4.2 GHz band with 30 MHz tuned bandwidth. The proper placement or coupling rises results in constant tuned bandwidth.

Obviously there are other manufacturers who make representative filters some, perhaps, larger than Microwave Filter Co. But for both TVRO and CATV (cable TV), this company supplies a multitude of attractive designs and produces highly reliable merchandise.

PHANTOM ENGINEERING

Another company that's being noticed is Phanton Engineering, Inc., which is not only making selective filters but also an inexpensive spectrum display to go with them. This becomes very handy for those who haven't the real thing. Connected be-

---

Waveguide Microwave Filters For 2-18 GHz

Filters and networks having narrow to moderate bandwidths are more efficiently realized as an arrangement of waveguide resonators. Where coaxial terminals are required, transitions are incorporated into the design.

Lowpass Filters Very High Power

Waveguide transmission line is essentially a highpass device. Because of the dispersive nature of waveguide, bandpass filters have a second resonance at approximately 1.5 center frequency. Where the filter must combine substantial suppression of near-upper frequencies and high power handling. the "waffle-iron" design technique is suitable.

Lowpass Filters Medium Power

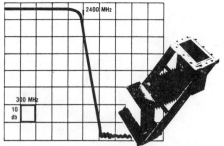

For medium power handling and high upper rejection, a coaxial lowpass filter may be inserted between two waveguide-to-coaxial transitions.

Bandstop Filters

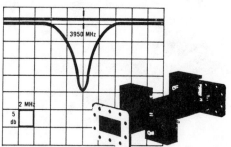

Broadwall coupling of separately tuned resonators allows rejection of several separate undesired frequencies, while synchronous tuning and proper spacing produces very deep notches at a single frequency.

Fig. 10-10. More filter examples, but used here in the 2-18 GHz band, in addition to a quadraplexer that will multiplex several narrow-band signals simultaneously (courtesy of Microwave Filter Co.).

tween converter and receiver, this unit displays relative amplitudes of the various channels in 10 dB steps, and is also calibrated in megahertz (MHz) across its horizontal span. It does not have a cathode-ray tube, however, since all amplitudes are shown in light emitting diodes (LEDs), spaced at 3 dB intervals. Battery operated, or dc driven via a separate transformer/rectifier/filter plug-in source, the unit is small (about the size of a book) and can be carried anywhere (Fig. 10-14).

Unfortunately, we have not yet been able to test or observe this unit first-hand and cannot, at this

Bandpass Filters

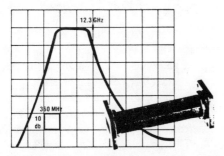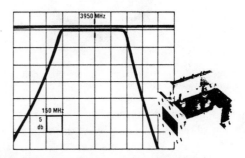

Because of the higher Q of waveguide line (relative to coaxial), waveguide bandpass filters realize passband losses only a fraction of coaxial filter losses. Alternate coupling structures are posts, center circular openings or septums, depending on specific, final filter requirements. Where the second passband of waveguide filters must be avoided, coaxial (digital) bandpass filters are inserted between adapters. The adapters and filter must be co-designed to produce the best passband characteristics.

Quadraplexer

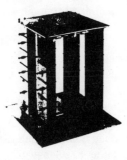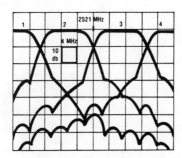

For low loss multiplexing of several narrow passbands, waveguide channel filters are combined to a single output through a coaxial network.

Tunable Notch Filter for Block Downconverters

Clearer Pictures

Fig. 10-11. An LNB/C filter that notches before the receiver (courtesy of Microwave Filter Co.).

time vouch for either its applications or accuracy. However, of all the various devices of this type on the market, the unit has obvious merits.

Phantom Engineering, Inc. correctly observes that better than 70 percent of all TVRO systems are of the 70 MHz final conversion i-f variety. Their immediate concern is with these rather than the block down units to come. Engineers, are now designing additionally effective passband and notch filters to be used in such systems as well as a handy and relatively inexpensive but calibrated spectrum display. It is fully field compatible because it operates on internal NiCad batteries at 15 Vdc, or on 120 Vac.

As an indication of how Phantom is approaching the T.I. problem, their design people have offered a figure showing some of the characteristics of their own and competing brands. See Fig. 10-15.

The top 38 dB example begins with an input of - 7 dB and an output of + 20 dB, with a noise figure of 3 dB. Phantom points out there's no signal amplification prior to the input attenuator and filter. It can, says Phantom, accommodate high level signals, but produces a high noise figure. You could see "grainy" pictures.

The second 19.7 dB has an input amplifier before the -28 dB SAW element, and does offer a superior noise figure, but the input stage can overload

very easily with even moderate levels of T.I. and interfering products will be generated within the amplifier. Ghosting and blackouts are possible.

The bottom illustration is the one advanced by Phantom. It is said to offer good stage gain distribution, with high overload margin plus a low noise figure, which, produces good pictures with a more than adequate noise figure.

A new double SAW (surface acoustical wave) filter is built with the idea of solving *severe* T.I. in 70 MHz systems. Being flexible, it permits mild, severe, and even bypass filtering, with all adjustments customer-operated by the simple push of a button. It is tolerant of frequency drift, producing best video quality with varying conditions, and is said to operate at all levels of T.I., even up to 50 dB of T.I. rejection. A block diagram of this new filter supplied by Phantom, shows signal/dc splitter and overpass followed by an attenuator, an amplifier, and then the electronic switch consisting of diodes (Fig. 10-16).

This switch is also mechanically controlled by the customer via the Switch Control, and can bypass the two SAW filters, if required, for an additional attenuator and matching network above, and the final amplifier output.

If the two SAW filters are engaged, moderate or severe T.I. is then controlled by additional attenuation and matching networks, in addition to amplification, compensating for traditional SAW losses. These outputs then continue on to one or both electronic diode switches, and finally to the amplified output and the signal/dc combiner output. A gain control (probably dc in nature) controls the gain of both input and final output amplifiers. Model No. for this amplifier is TM-70.

Another innovative filter for 70, 134, and 140 MHz final i-f frequencies is the IFP-70 with a dual-reactive tuned notch arrangement and a three-pole bandpass filter. Previously discretely adjustable for bandwidths of 32, 26, 22, 18, and 12 MHz, it is now continuously tuned between these extremes for maximum flexibility. Its nominal maximum attenuation is 9 dB, and it has a gain of 12 dB. A power button, gain control, and bandwidth adjustment are visible on the front panel.

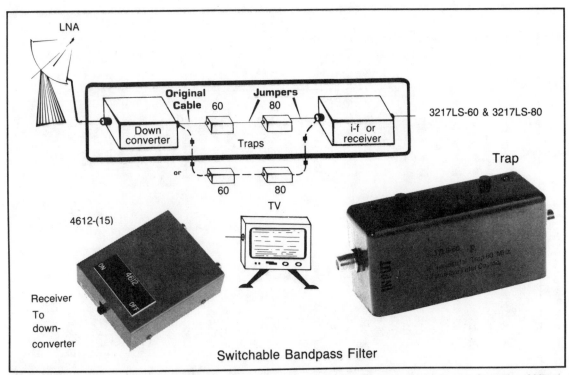

Fig. 10-12. For 70 MHz i-f systems that also remove interference following the block downconverter (courtesy of Microwave Filter Co.).

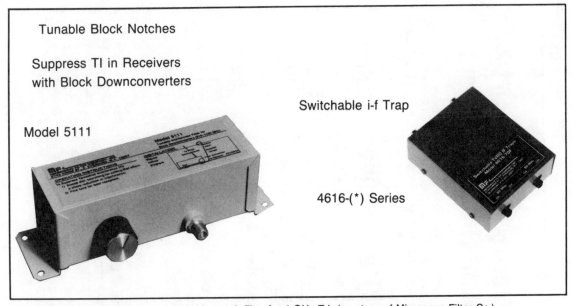

Fig. 10-13. Newest tunable and switchable notch filter for 4 GHz T.I. (courtesy of Microwave Filter Co.).

Table 10.1. Filters for TVRO Receivers (courtesy of Microwave Filter Co. Inc.).

Use 4616-( ) or 4612-( ) With These Receivers

They are standard downconverters or block downconverters with a "loop-out" for filter connection. If you can't find your receiver on this or the following pages, please call our technicians for assistance.

TVRO Receiver Listing

REVISION E, March 17, 1986

Receivers with 44 MHz IF:

Radio Shack (Regency Electronics)
2010

Regency Electronics
SR-2010
SR-900

T.D.P. Electronics
TDP-500
TDP-900

Receivers with 70 MHz IF:

Advanced Electronics
STAR TECH-1000
STAR TECH-2000

Amplica
R-10 (Rec only)
R-20

GLR-514
GLR-520
GLR-530BD
GLR-550
GLR-560
GLR-561
GLR-750
DSR-900

Avcom of Virginia, Inc.
Com-2
Com-2A
Com-2B
Com-11
Com-12
Com-20 Std.
Com-20T Std.

Basic Systems
3250

Beddingfield
Falcon

Draco
Aimer
SBR 6100

R.L. "Drake" Company
ESR-24
ESR-24 (Dual)
ESR-224
ESR-240
ESR-240A
ESR-2220
ESR-2240
ESR-324
324S
2204
ESR-324B
ESR-424
ESR-424B
ESR-524
ESR-2225

Electron Consultant Association
Video Four

El-Tech
DSV-804D

Equincx

Curtis Mathis
MSR330

Dexcel
DXP-1000
DXR-1000
DXP-1100
DXR-1200
DXP-2100
DXR-1300
SCP-900

DXP-900

Heytronics
STR-120

Houston Traker System
Tracker 5

I.C.M. Video
ICM-440
SR-4620P
SR-4600P/DC-66
SR-4650P

"I.S.S." International Satellite Systems
GL-5000

"Intersat"
IQ-160
SRDC-20
SR-20
SR-30
SR-40

Kem-Tron Industries
Interceptor-2400
Interceptor-24

Key Satellite
ST-120
ST-550
ST-560

KLM Electronics Inc.
Sky Eye IV
Sky Eye V
Sky Eye VI
KLM VII
KLM VIIIX
Olympiad I
KLM-X Pioneer

RDL-10
CSR-100
CSR-100A
CSR-200
CSR-300
CSR-300A
CSR-300B

Amway
ASR-500

Anderson-Scientific Inc.
ST-910LO
ST-1010LO
ST-2010LO
ST-910HI
ST-1010HI
ST-2010HI
ST-4010LO
ST-4010HI
ST-4010 Dual LNB

Arunta Satellite Telecommunications
DD-3000
DD-3300
Interceptor II (418 old model)
Interceptor II (418B new block model)
Interceptor III (419 model)
Interceptor 416
Challanger 421
Invader 425

Austron Inc.
AR-110

Automation Techniques
GLR-500
GLR-500R
GLR-500BD
GLR-511
GLR-512

Boman Industries
SR-800
SR-1200
SR-1500
SR-2500

"C.S.S." Consumer Satellite Systems
Ranger-I

Camden Marketing Inc.
WS-1000

Channel Master
6127
6128
6128A
6129
6130
6131
6134
6138

Chaparral Communications
Cheyenne
Sierra

Collin-Rockwell
SVR-4F-1

Columbia Satellite Systems
MCE

Comet
HSR-200H

Conifer Corporation
RC-2201

Cook Communications
The Series III

Cosima (S.T.S. Manufacturing)
Cosima

102

Fannon
Fansat 500
Fansat 1500
Fansat 3500

Farrall Instruments
SR-100

Freedom Systems
Freedom X

Fujitech
SD-2200

Futurex System
JFX-1000A

"G.C.I." Gillaspie Communications
7500
7600
7600A
5500
9600
GCI-8300

Gamma-F Corporation
Series 412

General Instrument
C4R
CRHF-IQ
Baby Q
CR-70 (brown)

Gould
DXP-1000
DXR-1000
DXP-1100
DXR-1200
DXP-1200
DXR-1300

Sky Eye VIII
SBR-6100

Lowrance Electronics Inc.
System 7
System 70S
System 70X

Luxor Corporation
190-9530
190-9533
190-9540
190-9550
Mark-One
9539

McCullough Satellite Systems
ELC-24
ELX-24
KT-24

McKinley Enterprises
McStar 700

M/A Comm Microwave Association
MA-1003
CR-1000
CR-2
M1

Maspro—U.S.S. (United Satellite System)
SR-1
SR-2J
SR-2

Maxum
007
FMVR-70

M C E
MCE

Table 10-1. Filters for TVRO Receivers (courtesy of Microwave Filter Co., Inc.) (Continued From Page 207.)

Receivers with 70 MHz IF:

Micro-Dynamics
Zeus-30
Zeus-40
Zeus-50
Baby Zeus

National Microtech
Z-1 Apollo
Z-70 Apollo
XA
XK
Executive

N.E.C. Broacast
NEC-24
NEC-204

Nexus Engineering Corporation
SR-5

Norsat International
2040
NFR-300R
NRF-300S

Northwest Satlabs
Cosmos II

Outrast
2000

Peace Electronics Inc.
Micro TV GH-2200

Pico Products Inc.
HR-1000

"S.V.S." Satellite Visual Systems
SVS-77
SVS-1800
SVS-2000
SVS-2400

"Sales Inc." Satellite Antenna Systems Inc.
Astro-20

Satellite America
SA-1000
SA-2000

Satellite Systems Unlimited
Infra Tek 1800
2000
2400

Sat Star
ELAN

Sat Tec (Division of Ramsey)
R-5000SP
R-5000XL
R-7000 Prostar

Satfinder Systems
Freedom I
Freedom II

Scientific-Atlanta
9530

Sensini (also see S.T.S.)
Sensini

Sigma Communications Inc.
Mark II
Mark II A

Uniden Satellite Technology
UST-1000
UST-2000
UST-3000
UST-5000
UST-6000
UST-7000

United Satellite Systems (Also see Maspro)
SR-1
SR-2

Universal Communications
DL-2000

Vista Electronics
XR-500
XR-750
XR-1000

Wilson
YM-400
YM-450
YM-1000

Winegard Company
RF-1000
RF-800
RF-600
RF-102
SC-70375
SC-7032
SC-7035

World Tech
WSR-8401
WSR-8402

Receivers with 300 MHz IF:

Hughes Aerospace Corporation
SVR-463

Phasecom
3900

Receivers with 400 MHz IF:

Luxor
9995

Maspro—U.S.S.
SR-3

Skantic
9995

United States Satellite Systems
SR-3

Receivers with 510 MHz IF:

Scientific Atlanta
9630
800 Home Sat
HS-900

Receivers with 520 MHz IF:

Harris Corporation
6529

Receivers with 612 MHz IF:

Standard Communications
Agile/Omni

Receivers with 130 MHz IF:

Blonder-Tongue Laboratories
DSA-643A

D.X. Communications
DSA-643A
DSA-654
DSA-654TM
DSA-654T

Viewstar
VSS-1450

Receivers with 134 MHz IF:

Channel Master
6136
6121

Electrohome Electronics
S-3133
E-1
SRM-36
SR-24

Receivers with 140 MHz IF:

R.L. "Drake" Company
EST-924

Receivers with 230 MHz IF:

Scientific Atlanta
6680
SR-5

Pinzonne Communications
8200
8200-IR

Precise Parabolics
1300

Proline
Stereo RCVR

Rainbow Electronics
Rainbow Kit

Recency Electronics
SR-3000
SR-1000

Rock Dale Inc.
SM-09
CT-12
CM-1100

Ross Electronics
RMR-1000

Royal Sat
SR-120

"S.C.I." Satellite Consultants Inc.
BR-200

"S.E.D." Systems Inc.
RS-04-44

"S.R.I." Satellite Receivers Inc.
SR-400
SR-500
SR-600
SR-40

S.T.S. (Satellite Technology Service)
S.T.S.
STS-MBS-SR
Sensini
Consima

Skantic (See Luxor Corporation)
Mark I

Standard Communications
AGile 24 M
24 S
24 SC
24 AGile SK

Startrak
ST-4 Kit

Starview
Omega-I 3742-C
3742-D
S-70

Coleman, Craig, Texas (See Starview)

T.L. Systems
SR-1
7682

Tee Comm Electronics Inc.
TCR-4520R
TCR-6520R

Telcom Industries
TX-4000

Toki
TR-99
TR-110
TR-110 S
TR-220
TR-330
TR-747 B

Tripple Crown Electronics
TSR-4000
CVR-B

Ultrasat
2000

Use 5111 or 5234 With These Block Downconverter Receivers

Use Model 5111 tunable trap (900–1450 MHz)

Amplica
CSR-300B
CSR-1000

Anderson-Scientific
ST-910HI
ST-1010HI
ST-2010HI
ST-4010HI
ST-4010 Dual LNB

Arc Finder Mfg. Inc.
2000
4500

Arunta Satellite Telecom
Interceptor III
418B
419

Avantek (Simulchannel)
AR-1000
AR-2000

Blonder-Tongue
DSA-643A

B.E.L. Electronics
SBR-1400

Channel Master
6135
6136
6121
6156
6144

DSB-700
DSB-700A
DSB-700S
DSB-800
DSA-644
DSA-654
DSA-654TM
DSA-654T

R.L. "Drake" Company
ESR-324B
ESR-424B
ESR-924

Electrohome Electronics
S-3133
E-1
SR-24

Gardiner Communications
4350

General Instrument
960
1000
C4R
CR-24 (Black)
GI-950
MRS-1
MRS-2
S412R
SRX-102
SRX-103
SRX201AA
SRX-205AA

I.C.M. Video
SR-4600P/DC-66
SR-4620P
SR-4650P

Kenwood
KSR-1000

KLM
SBR-6100

L.S.I. (Lindsley Seay Intl.)
DL-145 A

Luxor
9570
9900
9995
Mark 2

McCullough Satellite Systems
KB-24

M/A Comm Micro. Assoc.
CR-2
CR-1000
CRST-1001
H-1
T-1
T-2

Maspro — U.S.S.
SR-3
SR-4

Nexus Engineering

Pico Products Inc.
HR-1000

Royal Sat
BR-200
BR-300

S.T.S. (Satellite Tech. Service)
MBS-SR Block
STS-LSR
STS-MBS-SRB

Scientific Atlanta
800 Home Sat
9570
9630
HS-900

Skantic
9900
9900
9995

Standard Communications
24 PC
24 SC
24 Agile SK
Agile Omni

Tee Comm Electronics Inc.
TCR-4520R
TCR-6520R

Tripple Crown Electronic
CVR-B

Chaparral
Cheyenne
Sierra

Conifer Corporation
XT-200

D.X. Communications
DSA-642
DSA-643A
DSA-606
DSB-600
DSB-600A
DSB-500

Use model 5234 tunable trap (430–950 MHz)

Anderson-Scientific
ST-900
ST-910
ST-910LO
ST-1000
ST-1010
ST-1010LO
ST-2000
ST-2010
ST-2010LO

Bowman Industries
SR-1600

"I.S.S." (Intl. Satellite System)
GL-5000

Janiel
BCR-100
BCR-200

Gensat Comm. Corp.
BSR-1200
CSR-1200

Goldstar Electric Company
GSR-420M
GSR-420R
GSR-420S

Houston Traker System
Tracker 5

Hughes
SVR-463

BCR-250
BCR-280
BCR-300
BCR-2000

Key Satellite
BP-550
BP-560
ST-550
ST-560

Locom
BR-220

L.S.I. (Lindsley Seay Intl.)
DL-125
DL-145

Pro Star
XR-1

Norsat
JR-100
JR-200
NRF-300R
NRF-300S

Panasonic
2000
KU-6000

Phasecom
3900

Radio Shack
2010

Regency
R-5000
SR-900
SR-2010
SR-3500
SR-5000

Royal Sat
BR-100

Sat Tec (Div/Ramsey)
R-5100
XR-1 Ramsey
SR-3240 Prostar

Sigma-Vu
Mark III

Mark V

T.D.P. Electronics
TDP-500
TDP-900

T.L. Systems
7682

Tee Comm Electronics Inc.
TCR-1520D
TCR-2520D

Toki
TR-150 B

World Tech
WSR-8403

Uniden Corporation
UST-5000
UST-6000
UST-7000

Viewstar
VSS-1450

Winegard
RF-90
RF-102
RX-1020

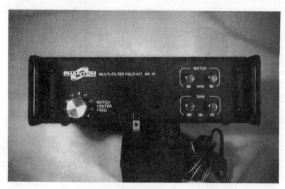

Fig. 10-14. A Phantom bandpass and notch filter unit that is customer-operated and may be switched on or off.

We have also received word of an MF-70 combined switchable notch and bandpass filter that Phantom now has on the market. Also customer controlled, and for various values of final i-f, this filter will not only control 10 MHz offset (from the carrier) T.I., but will also handle many of the out-of-band problems in two bandwidths that are easily controlled by the operator. This equipment is based on the premise that not all T.I. is received continually, and sometimes it may be advantageous to have or not have these filters engaged.

AN INEXPENSIVE SPECTRUM DISPLAY

While some would call this a "spectrum analyzer," it's really a spectrum display, with nine rows of ten light-emitting diodes (LEDS) representing values of 3 dB each, and each row separated by three or four MHz and calibrated between 57 and 83 MHz on the horizontal scale (Fig. 10-17).

Designed for 70-MHz system operation, this receiver, Model TD-1, has a spectrum width of 26 MHz, an accuracy of ± 1.5 dB, and a dynamic range of 30 dB. Its sensitivity is spec'd at -50 dB, but is said to be adjustable. If block down frequencies between 900 and 1500 MHz are necessary, a BT-70 tuning module can be made available.

On the front panel you will find the nine rows of LEDs, a sweep control, 70 MHz in and out jacks, a battery indicator and a sensitivity control. Uses include preliminary site surveys, interference locator, and signal strength meter and may be attached to the block downconverter or looped through the

70 MHz final i-f line. Power is derived either from nickel-cadmium batteries or line voltage. A new version just appearing will have brighter LEDs and one or two other innovations.

IN SUMMARY

The filter story could go on forever. As Microwave Filter Co. so correctly observes, "all problems have more than one solution, each of which comes with its own price tag." This alludes to both the problem and how you go about solving it. Bandpass filters or traps offer the usual solutions and are effective closer to the LNA and/or block downconverter because phase shifting due to polarization tends to *reduce* some of their effectiveness when restricted to receiver applications. This is especially true for bandpass filters, which actually remove dual (right and left) portions of the receive signal, narrowing the incoming spectrum so that interference is *excluded.*

Traps, on the other hand, deal with individual portions of interference and block only a finite portion of the signal, usually not more than 3-4 MHz with notches that usually vary from 15 to 40 dB down. There are both single and double traps or notch filters that are fixed frequencies or may be tuned collectively or independently, depending on the specific use. For Ma Bell's 10 MHz problems on either side of the carrier, a single-tuned or switched dual filter will probably solve the difficulty, but it will narrow the bandwidth somewhat because of the 8-10 MHz removed. Consequently, if a receiver has a nominal bandwidth of 25 MHz (too narrow for superior overall reception) then an additional 10 MHz remoted will leave only 15 MHz of bandpass signal, and that's not nearly enough. We would recommend receivers with *not less* than 27 MHz bandspread for best reception and better trap-accommodating spectrums. Although you won't normally be using traps in the 12 GHz Ku and DBS (to come) donwlinks, their 40-60 MHz transponder passbands do require broadband receivers for top quality pictures.

The foregoing has dealt exclusively with C band except for the bandwidth reference. In filtering, there have been few reports of 12 GHz *terrestrial*

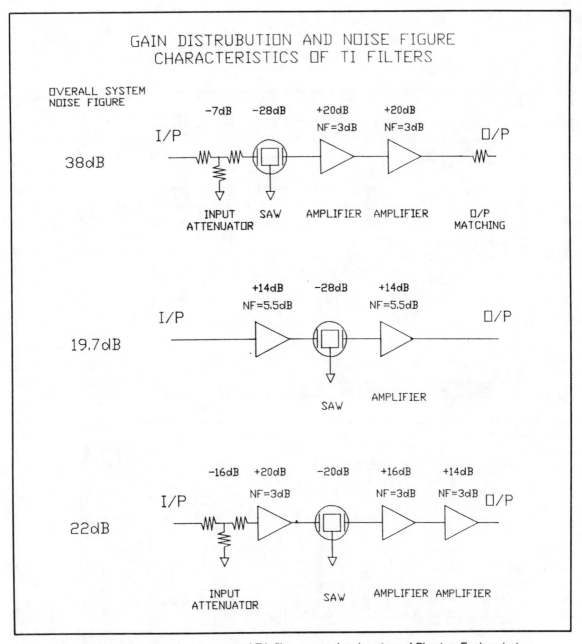

GAIN DISTRUBUTION AND NOISE FIGURE
CHARACTERISTICS OF TI FILTERS

OVERALL SYSTEM
NOISE FIGURE

38dB

19.7dB

22dB

Fig. 10-15. Phantom engineering observes several T.I. filter approaches (courtesy of Phantom Engineering).

interference at Ku but there is filtering at and for baseband. Subcarriers, for one purpose or another on the baseband signal, are something of a plague now and then, so that they have to be limited or trapped out to ensure reception of a ''pure'' or desirable signal. Once again, some of the older 10 MHz units (70 MHz center frequency) are being trotted out and modified for these new problem solutions as well as new designs applicable to lower frequencies.

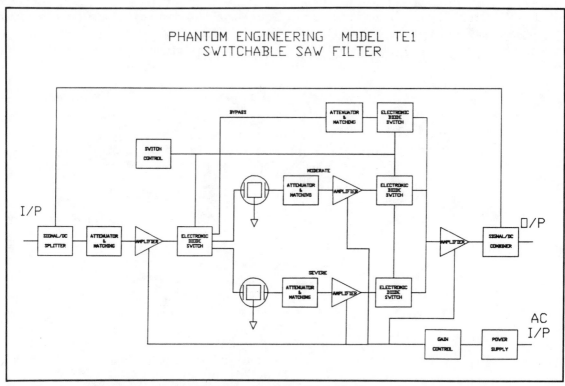

Fig. 10-16. A new Model TE1 switchable SAW filter (courtesy of Phantom Engineering).

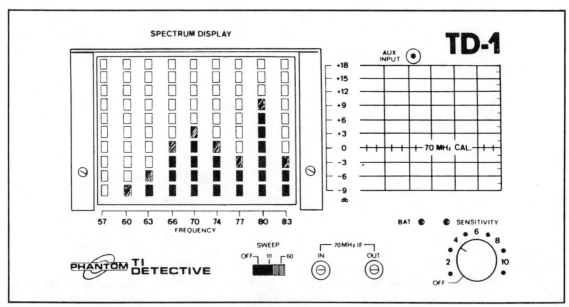

Fig. 10-17. A low-cost spectrum display device especially designed for field use. Each LED represents a gain or loss of 3 dB (courtesy of Phantom Engineering).

For TVRO at Ku this may not be a problem initially, but as 12 GHz services increase, what's happening commercially now may well translate to consumer interference later, especially since Ku has bandwidths somewhere between 36 MHz and 120 MHz, several of which are already at 54 MHz on the K-birds of RCA. The subcarrier traps, however, are not 3-4 MHz in notch width, but measure only kilohertz to accommodate subcarrier emissions. This may prove especially true for multichannel stereo/SAP/professional carrier sound because this would automatically add more subcarriers to satellite video/audio transmissions if combined with those already on the air. This may or may not occur but, nonetheless it's a logical assumption and a factor that bears watching for both picture and sound. In our business, you never know until you're faced with a new dilemma that demands a reasonable solution, and something like this could almost appear out of nowhere at any time.

Without belaboring the subject unnecessarily, that's about the story of filters as they apply to TVRO. If you want a *thorough* treatment of the subject and many more of its aspects than given here, subscribe to Microwave Filter's ASTI Handbook and investigate the subject in intensive detail. Glyn Bostick, Bill Johnson, and John Fannetti have done a remarkable job!

T.I. SYMPTOMS REVIEW

For *light*, inband T.I., you will find sparklies on several transponder generated channels. Tune away from these if you can, adjust the mount and reflector north-south heading, and check the feed elevation for this particular satellite. If all else fails, use a tunable notch filter, or one that's built into your receiver. I-f bandwidth reduction *will* affect picture.

For *moderate* T.I. you will have many sparklies. For *heavy* T.I. there may be no picture at all. The nature of your interference is *always* highly important! You must determine whether it is inband or out-of-band, and be prepared to apply whatever filtering is needed. There are actually two basic solutions for T.I.:

1. Increase the incoming signal.
2. Decrease the level of interference.

One of the surest ways to minimize problems is the installation of *matching* equipment. You can't randomly put together any old LNA/LNB, cheap feed, and "special sale" receiver. Nor can you expect worthwhile results from ordinary RG59/U cable. Double-shielded RG6/U with AWG 18 center conductor (we *continue* recommending) is the prime means of signal transfer between block downconverters and receivers. The days of 1981 single conversion and 70 MHz i-fs with attendant drift and possible radiation should be equipment of the past. By all means *upgrade* any and all installations with antiquated LNAs. At the same time, check feed specifications for adequate f/D ratios. One designed for a 0.3 reflector absolutely operates poorly with one that has a 0.4 ratio. With 2° spacing at C band approaching rapidly and possibly tighter requirements for Ku, you should become considerably more conscious of all desirable characteristics.

And once more emphasis must be placed on shielding such as tight screens and buildings rather than traps and filters. Talk to the phone company and see if they won't help in identifying microwave paths. Ask for frequency, power, and direction, then obtain a metro-county map and plot the paths of interference, allowing about five extra miles for additional radiation. Then, if you're erecting any screening, remember that its supports must be very strong or the wind will make short work of your efforts. Furthermore, *never* place a screen at right angles to the reflector—bounce signals will ruin your efforts.

Index

A

A-MAC, 124
absorbent areas, 8, 9
ac power, 138
    conversion to, 159
ACG, 70
actuator tuning charts, 78
address processor, 127, 129
adjustable scalar ring feed, 30, 31
adjustments, 143
AFT, 70
AGC, 69
analyzing reflectors and mounts,
    1-21
    mounting reflector in, 2
    sidelobes in, 11
    tolerance factors in, 1
    TVRO site surveys in, 11
    Y2 = 4PX rms curvature in, 2
ANIK B, 93
ANIK C, 106
antenna gain, 40
antenna positioner, 66, 74, 76
antennas
    construction of, 14
    gain in, 40
    mounting of, 19
    positioner for, 66, 74, 76
APS-424, troubleshooting, 177
Astro Electronics, 99
asymmetric patterns, 45
attenuation
    feeds for, 33
    space, 39
attenuation feed, 33
audio demodulation, 63
audio detection process, 71
audio response, 87
audio testing, 86
audio transmission, 42
Aurora, 93
AUSSAT, 106

azimuth, 13, 20
    Ku-band, 111
    universal, 111

B

B-MAC, 124
bandpass filter, 201, 203
bandstop filter, 200, 202
bandwidth, 84
baseband FDM/FM, 51
baseband video, 88
Belden, 35
Bessel function charts, 84, 85
binary phase-shift keying (BPSK), 56
bit error rate, 54
Boltzmann's constant, 41
Boman, 30, 31, 118
boxing, 3, 4
buried cable, 36

C

C bands
    feeds and cabling for, 21-37
    propagation at, 44
C-MAC, 124, 126
Cable News Network (CNN),
    deciphering for, 120
cable TV, scrambling signals from,
    119
cables, 21-37
    buried, 36
    considerations for, 33
    F connectors and, 36
    facts and fiction about, 35
    foamed, 36
    grounding, 37
    home-entrance, 37
    impedance in, 36
    length of, 36
    measurement of, 33
    multi-, 35
    multi-leg, 34

propagation velocity, 35
RG59U vs. RG6, 35
rooftop, 37
sizes of, 37
swept, 36
TV/satellite mix, 37
webbed, 36
capacitive reactance, 137, 199
carrier-to-interference, 1, 31, 41, 80
carrier-to-noise, 1, 31, 62, 80
    receivers, 41
Cassegrain feeds, 18, 23, 24
Chaparral Communications, 28
    prime focus feeds from, 25-27
chroma, 83
Ciclops, 55
Cinemax, deciphering for, 120
circuit design, 143
clamping amplifier, 129
Clarke Orbital Belt, 93
clock and timing generator, 129
CMS, 55
coaxial conductor feeds, 27, 28
code division multiplexing, 55
codec, 54
color bars, 86, 147
combiner, 128
compass, 5
    boxing, 4
compass variation, 3, 4, 112
COMSTAR, 93
configurations, 91
confocal coaxial feeds, 108, 118
control circuits, 54
control voltage, 69, 70
controllers, 54
controls, 143
CONUS, 53, 96, 97, 98, 102
conversions, 159
copper flashed center conductors,
    36
corrugated feeds, 23

Crimson Satellite Associates, 97
crosshatch, 86
CW signals, 88, 89

D

D-MAC, 126
Data Encryption Standard (DES),
    120
dc power, 139-143
    conversion to, 159
declination, 3, 4
decoders, 128
demodulation, audio, 63
demonstrator mounting, 5, 7
    trailer-bed, 6
descramblers, 14
    troubleshooting, 132
detection processes, 61-62
    phase-lock detector in, 61
deviation, 4, 5, 84, 157
diamond-mesh reflectors, Ku-band
    unsuitablity for, 15
digital multimeters, 160
    applications for, 161
digital processors, 128
digital transmission, 52
digital voltmeters, 159
diplexer, 201
Direct Broadcast Service (DBS), 96
discrete voltage channel tuning, 58
Disney Channel, deciphering for,
    120
dispersal wobbulator, 88
displays, 143
domestic satellite system (US), 95
DOMSAT, 53, 93, 99, 102
downconverters and receivers,
    79-92
    configurations for, 91
    deluxe testing of, 81
    local testing for, 80
    single and dual conversions, 92

typical installation of, 90
drift, 112
dual conversions, 92
dynamic noise reduction, 63

E

Earth stations
  C-band receiver-transmitter for, 54
  Equatorial, 53
  master, 54
Echos, 55
EIRP contours, 53, 97, 98, 99
electrically programmable read only
  memory (EPROM), 76
electricity, introduction to, 136
electromagnetic interference, 192
Electronic Industries Association,
  112
elevation, 20
  Ku-band, 111
  universal, 111
encoding and encyphering, 129
Equatorial Earth stations, 53-56
  data transmission of, 56
  equipment for, 54
ESR-224, troubleshooting, 174
ESR-24, troubleshooting, 172
ESR-240, troubleshooting, 174
ESR-324, troubleshooting, 176
ESR-424, troubleshooting, 176

F

F connectors, 36
f/D ratios, 32
f/ratios, 31
far-field reflector analysis, 8, 10
Federal Communications Commission (FCC), 57
feeds, 21-37
  adjustable scalar ring, 30, 31
  Cassegrain, 23, 24
  coaxial conductor, 27, 28
  confocal coaxial, 108, 118
  corrugated, 28
  Gregorian, 23, 24
  heater equipped, 30
  hybrid, 29
  interference entrance to, 12
  John Seavey, 27
  offset, 17
  piggy back, 108, 109
  prime focus, 24
  typical and special, 22
fiberglass reflectors, 16
filters, 212
  bandpass, 201
  bandstop, 200
  highpass, 200
  Ku-band, 213
  lowpass, 200
  microwave, 197, 199
  Model 5111, 14
  notched, 205
  Phantom Engineering, 202
  RC, 198
  specific, 14
  TVRO receiver, 206-211
  typical, 197
  waveforms for, 200
  waveguide microwave, 202
FM audio selection and detection,
  62
FM video detection, 60
foamed cable, 36
focus offset, 18
frequency, 10
frequency division multiple access
  (FDMA), 55
frequency shift, 84
front end, 68

G

gain
  antenna, 40
  over temperature (G/T), 40
GALAXY, 46, 53, 106
graphite lubricants, 5
Gregorian feeds, 18, 23, 24

gross positioning, 2
grounding, 37
GSTARs, 99
  footprints in different configura-
    tions for, 101
  uplink/downlink plan for, 100

H

half power, 198
HBO, deciphering for, 120
heater-equipped feeds, 30
highpass filter, 200
home-entering cables, 37
Hughes Aircraft Company, 102
hybrid channel frequencies, 59
hybrid feeds, 29

I

I-F, 69
ICA01 microprocessor, 75
ICX01 microprocessor, 77
impedance, 137
  cable, 36
in-band interference, 193
  solutions for, 195
input audio processor, 127
input video processor, 128
installation, 19-20, 90
  hints and suggestions for, 20
  Ku-band, 106
  problems with small reflectors in,
    20
INTELSAT, 106
interference
  feed entrance of, 12
  in-band vs. out-of-band, 193
  resistant transmissions to, 54

K

king post, 2
Ku-band, 93-118
  azimuth and elevation at, 111
  confocal feed for, 118
  feeds and cabling for, 21-37
  filters for, 213
  installations of, 106
  late developments in, 113
  low side injection in, 112
  oscilloscopes for, 113
  propagation at, 44
  PSN B-Mac receiver, 115
  RCA development and use of,
    96-98, 96
  reasoning behind, 93
  reflectors and mounts for, 1
  spectrum analyzer for, 113
  terrestrial interference with, 212
  troubleshooting in, 112

L

lambda, 10
latitude, 2, 3, 111
leakthrough, 40
LEASAT, 106
light-emitting diodes (LEDs), 212
linear displays, 165
linear staircase waveform, 147
LNA, tuning systems for, 57
LNA/LNB, testing basics for, 80
local oscillators, tuning with, 59
longitude, 3, 111
low side injection, 112
lowpass filter, 200, 202
LSR receivers, troubleshooting, 178
lubrication, 5

M

M/A-COM, 28, 64, 120
  T1, troubleshooting of, 180
  VCIIC descrambler, 132
magnetic deviation, 5
magnetic north, 3
master Earth stations, 54
matching impedances, 198
MBS-AA receivers, troubleshooting,
  178
MBS-SR block, troubleshooting, 180
mesh reflectors, 16

meters, 137
microwave filters, 197, 199
microwave intrusion, 11
Model 5111 filter, 14
Model 77 DMM, 160
modems, 54
modulation, 85, 157
modulation index, 84, 157
modulators/demodulators, 54
monitor circuits, 128
MORELOS, 106
mounting
  demonstrator, 5
  gross positioning and adjustment,
    2
mounts
  analyzing of, 1-21
  changing of, 8
multi-cable, 35
multi-leg cable, 34
multiburst waveform, 146
multimeters, 160
  Model 77 DMM, 160
multiplexed analog component
  (MAC) signals, 124, 125
multiplexing, code division, 55

N

NADL, 28
near-field, 10
noise figures, 40
north/south pointing, 3
notched filter, 205

O

Oak Industries, Inc., 126
Oak's cable system, 129-130
Oak's Orion, 126-129
offset feed, 17
  Cassegrain, 18
  Gregorian, 18
Omni-Rotor, 28
orbital assignments, satellites, 94
orthogonal down conversions, 20,
  45
oscilloscopes, 113
  troubleshooting with, 164
out-of-band interference, 193
  solutions for, 196
output audio processor, 127
output buffers, 129
output video processor, 127, 128

P

packet-switching, 54
PALAPA, 106
parabolic reflector, 10
peak, 137
peak deviation, 42
peak-to-peak, 137
perforated reflectors, 15
Phantom Engineering, 202
phase detector, 62
phase errors, 61
phase-lock detector (PLD), 60
phase-locked loop (PLL)
  tuning with, 59, 60
piggy back feeds, 108, 109
point-to-multipoint networks, 54
Polaroid satellite spectrum display,
  48
polarization excitations, 163
polarizer, 78
Polorotor, 25, 28
post encoder, 128
power equations, 136, 137
power supplies, 71, 72, 138
  ac, 138
  dc, 139-143
preselectors, 201
prime focus feeds, 24
  Chaparral Communications, 25
Private Satellite Network (PSN), 113,
  115
probe heater, 30
propagation
  C band, 44
  Ku band, 44

protocol, 54
PSN B-Mac receiver, 115
  block diagram for, 116-117
pulses, 164
push-pull configuration, 70

Q

quadraplexer, 202

R

range, 8, 10
RC filters, 198
RCA, 95
  Ku-band and, 96
receiver systems and circuit analysis, 57-78
receiver threshold, 43
receivers, 38-56
  actual measurements for, 43
  audio transmissions and, 42
  carrier-to-interference, 41
  carrier-to-noise, 41
  direct satellite signals, 45
  direct testing of, 84
  filters for, 206-211
  G/T, 40
  Ku-band, PSN B-Mac, 115
  mathematical parameters for, 38
  popular satellite spectrum dis-
    plays for, 45-48
  propagation at C and Ku bands,
    44
  signal-to-noise, 41
  signals to, 38
  slant range for, 38
  space attenuation, 39
  space loss in, 43
  system noise temperature in, 40
  testing basics for, 79-92
  testing equipment checkout for,
    88
reflectors
  analyzing of, 1-21
  diamond-mesh, 15
  far-field analysis of, 8
  fiberglass, 16
  Ku-band, 18
  mesh, 16
  perforated, 15
  problems with small sized, 20
  solid, 44
Regional Administrative Radio Conference (RARC), 57
resistance/capacitance filters (RC),
  198
resonance, 137
RFI, 192
RG59U cable, 35
RG6 cable, 35
rooftop cable, 37
rotor polarizer drive, 66

S

SATCOM, 25, 46, 47, 93, 96
Satellite Business Systems (SBS),
  95, 102
satellite spectrum displays, 45-48
  GALAXY, 3, 46
  Polaroid, 48
  SATCOM F1-R, 47
  SATCOM F3-R, 47
  SATCOM F4, 46
  SPACENET I, 46
  TELSTAR T301, 46
  TELSTAR T302, 46
  TELSTAR T303, 47
  WESTAR V, 46
satellite technology services,
  troubleshooting, 178
satellites, 45
  FCC orbital assignments for, 94
  GSTARs, 99
  Ku-band, 93
  scrambling signals from, 119
  solar paddles on, 96
  space shuttle launch of, 96
  US domestic system of, 95
SATMON, 55

SBS, 93, 102
  general configurations for, 107
SCPC transmission, 49
SCPC/PSK, 99
scramblers, 12, 13, 14, 45, 119-134
scrambling enhancer, 128
Seavey Engineering Associates, Inc., 27
Seavey, John, 27
SECAM, 124
Showtime, deciphering for, 120
sidelobes, 11
Sidewinder, 26
Sigma system, 129
signal generator, 86, 88
signal-to-noise, 1
  receiver, 41
single conversions, 92
sky darkening, 45
slant range, 38, 39
solid reflectors, 44
Sony Corporation, 113
space attenuation, 39
space loss, 43
space shuttle, 96
SPACENET, 46, 99, 110
  block diagrams for, 104
  EIRP performance of, 105
  frequency plan and exploded view of, 103
special feeds, 22
spectral signals, quality of, 167
spectrum analyzers, 113, 149-152
  controls for, 153-157, 153
  example of, 157-159, 157
  receiver testing with, 43
  troubleshooting with, 167

spectrum display, 212
square wave, 158
SR block, troubleshooting, 180
standing wave ratio (SWR), 198
stereo tones, 83
surface wave acoustical (SAW) filters, 69
swept cable, 36
switcher, 115
system noise temperature, 40

T

T6 receiver/positioner, 64-68
  audio detection process, 71
  block diagram for, 66
  front end for, 68
  I-F, AGC, and detection in, 69
  operational theory of, 66
  power supplies for, 71, 72
tangents, 8
TDMA, 99
Tektronix, 113
TELSTAR, 46, 47, 106
terrestrial EMI/RFI interference, 192-215
  symptoms review of, 215
test equipment and applications, 135-169
  checking for accuracy of, 88
threshold, receiver, 43
time division multiple access (TDMA), 55
timing generator, 127, 128
tolerance factors, 1
transmit radiators, 23
transponders, 12, 13

trapping, 195, 212
trigonometry, 8, 9
troubleshooting, 170-215
  APS-424, 177
  descramblers, 132
  ESR-224, 174
  ESR-24, 172
  ESR-240, 174
  ESR-324, 176
  ESR-424, 176
  Ku-band, 112
  LSR receivers, 178
  MA-COM T1, 180
  MBS-AA receivers, 178
  MBS-SR block, 180
  procedures for, 171
  satellite technology services and, 178
  spectrum analyzers for, 167
  SR block, 180
  using oscilloscopes in, 164
true north and south, 4
tuning systems, 57-59
  discrete voltage channel, 58
  hybrid channel frequencies, 59
  local oscillator, 59
  PLL, 59, 60
TV/satellite mix cables, 37
TVRO site surveys, 11
Twister, 25, 26

U

universal azimuth and elevation diagram, 111

V

VARIAC, 136

VCIIC descrambler, 132-133
vertical color reference signal, 147
vertical interval test signal, 147
video FM baseband transmission, 50
video, digital, and audio transmission, 50
video/audio outputs, 88
Videocipher, 120-124
  descrambling checks for, 133-134
VIRS, 147
VITS, 147
voltage-controlled oscillator (VCO), 61
voltmeters, digital, 159
VSAT, 53

W

waveforms, 137, 146
  filter, 200
  linear staircase, 147
  multiburst, 146
  square, 158
waveguide microwave filters, 202
webbed cable, 36
WESTAR, 25, 46, 93
wideband digital transmission, 52
wobbulator, 88
World Administrative Radio Conference (WARC), 57

Z

Z-TAC, 130-132
Z-VIEW, 132
ZS-4000 receiver/positioner, 73
  PLL tuner unit in, 73

Edited by Roland S. Phelps